VARI___ . .
IS
THE SPICE OF
LIFE

THE WORLDS
OF
ERIC MIDWINTER

Dr Eric Midwinter OBE, DPhil, MA
Speaking at the Nottingham U3A AGM, 2011
Photo by Peter Alvey

VARIETY
IS
THE SPICE
OF LIFE

THE WORLDS
OF
ERIC MIDWINTER

JEREMY HARDIE

WITH A FOREWORD BY
JOHN WADE

Third Age Press

ISBN 978-1-898576-45-7
First edition

Third Age Press Ltd, 2015
Third Age Press, 6 Parkside Gardens
London SW19 5EY
Managing Editor Dianne Norton

Cover illustration and cartoon on page 12
by Robin Mackervoy
Layout design by Dianne Norton
Printed by IntypeLibra London

CONTENTS

ACKNOWLEDGEMENTS

First and foremost, I am sincerely grateful to the subject of this book, Eric Midwinter, for allowing me to embark upon such a biographical study in the first place, and for his unstinting generosity in providing copious amounts of material, wise counsel and helpful guidance at every stage. In response to my frequent requests for information, he has often written short essays, and sometimes even lengthy ones, on particular topics and many of these have been incorporated into the text.

Particular thanks are due to John Wade, that extraordinarily gifted magician, entertainer and fellow Brother Savage, who so willingly agreed to write the revealing and insightful Foreword to this book, and to the artist Robin Mackervoy for his excellent book cover design and cartoon, as well as for some of the Savage Club menu cards that have been featured as illustrations.

A significant proportion of this book consists of testimonies and quotations from many of Eric's friends and colleagues, some of whom have known him since early childhood days in the 1930s and 40s. For editorial reasons, it has sometimes been necessary to abridge these excellent and revealing contributions; I do hope the individuals who have so kindly provided these will not be offended if any parts of their recollections have been shortened or omitted in order to avoid unnecessary repetition.

THE WORLDS OF ERIC MIDWINTER

Poignant memories about Eric's schooldays in Sale and some of the activities of the Old Salians have kindly been provided by Peter Day, John Hough, Brian Eldred and, although of a slightly later vintage, Dave Walmsley. The latter Old Salian has created an extensive Sale Boys' Grammar School Archive, available on-line, which contains many photographs from the time when Eric was a pupil there, and is a useful source of additional material. Thank are also due to Penny Dynan, the daughter of Roy Hope, Eric's history teacher at school, for her charming recollections.

From Eric's time as an undergraduate at Cambridge, sincere thanks are due to fellow students Tony Pearce, Mike Brookbank and Doug Bowler for their reminiscences of those days. I am also extremely grateful to the Archivist at St Catharine's College, Elizabeth Ennion-Smith, and to the Librarian, Colin Higgins, for their help in providing additional information from the official records. Whilst on an academic theme, it was delightful to receive an encouraging letter from Lord Asa Briggs, the distinguished historian, who was the external examiner for Eric's DPhil thesis and, some years later, also presented Eric with his honorary doctorate from the Open University.

From the world of teaching and education, very helpful comments and recollections have been gathered from Bob Osbourn, Maurice Craft, Tony McGrath, John Martlew (and his interviewer, Tim Jones, who provided a DVD of John's reminiscences), Louis Cohen and Eric's great friend Brian Walsh, all of whose contributions are greatly appreciated.

The late Professor A.H. (Chelly) Halsey, Keith Pulham, Keith Williams, Phil Street, Harry Pepp and the late John Rennie have all generously responded to requests for feedback about Eric's time working in the Liverpool Educational Priority Area and his many contributions to community education, particularly with CEDC. Sincere thanks also to Cynthia Rennie for her kind hospitality when I visited John at their home and for providing a photograph of him.

My thanks to Wendy Toms of the National Consumer Council for her contribution about Eric's tour of duty there, and to Rufus Barnes and Sir Alan Greengross who have helpfully recalled his lengthy term as Chairman of the London Regional Passengers Committee. Thanks also to Richard Freeston-Clough, Communications Officer at London Travel Watch, for generously proving copies of some of Eric's LRPC publications.

From Eric's time as Director of the Centre for Policy on Ageing, most useful comments have been received from Gilly Crosby, Miriam Bernard, Robin Webster, Stephen Shaw, and Baroness Sally Greengross, former director of Age Concern England (ACE) (now Age UK). His extensive and continuing involvement with the University of the Third Age (U3A), from its foundation in the UK to the present, has been recalled vividly by Dianne Norton, Lin Jonas, Barbara Lewis, Audrey Cloet, Roy Evans, Ian Searle, Keith Richards, Norman Richards, Brian Groombridge and Francis Beckett, editor of Third Age Matters. Julie Travers of the Third Age Trust kindly sent the author a copy of the DVD of Eric's U3A Founder's Lecture, so skilfully filmed by Winstan Whitter, who has also, with Francis Beckett, recorded Eric's recollections of his father's time as a fire officer. Fran Walton, also of Third Age Trust, very helpfully sent a number of photographs taken during and after the U3A Founder's Lecture by Peter Arkell. Pat Taylor, producer of the original BBC 'You and Yours' broadcast in 1981 when Eric first spoke publicly about the U3A has recently been in touch. She herself evidently answered Eric's call and later became an active member of the North London U3A.

Many of Eric's friends from the world of cricket literature and history have kindly responded to requests for comments about his numerous contributions to this field. My warm thanks to

Dave Allsop, Richard Hill, Peter Hartland, Stephen Eley, Stephen de Winton, Nigel Hancock, Clive Porter, Keith Hayhurst, and three distinguished Australian authors, Bernard Whimpress, Gideon Haigh and J. Neville Turner, for their considered and heart-warming responses. Considerable help was also received from Zoe English, from the MCC library, who tracked down a number of reviews of Eric's books about cricket.

Whilst seeking feedback on Eric's writings about comedians and other popular entertainers, I was most grateful to receive some helpful comments from the veteran performer Ken Dodd, as well as thoughtful and constructive pieces from the actor David Howe (Gerard Hayling), Michael Pointon and Geoff Bowden, editor of the theatrical journal *Call Boy*.

Several members of the Savage Club have sent much appreciated comments about Eric's involvement with club affairs and have remarked on the high esteem in which he is held there. My particular thanks go to The Venerable Brian Lucas, Kin Wang, Stephen Henderson, John Carpenter, Max Brittain, Melvin Crabb, and, once again, to Dave Allsop and David Howe for these. Gathorne Butler generously sent some splendid examples of Savage Lunch menu cards he had drawn, featuring Eric. Delightful responses were also received from Susan Bradbury and Jean Jaffa, two of the club's much-loved Rosemarys, and from a visitor to the club, Tony Ring, who kindly sent his reactions to one particular event about P.G. Wodehouse in which Eric was heavily involved, along with Max Brittain.

Eric's neighbours David and Wendy Rankin, Chris Marsden and Richard Thomas have provided some interesting comments about Eric as a friend and local activist, highlighting some characteristics not revealed by other correspondents, for which I am most grateful. For recent photographs of Eric, sincere thanks are due to Alison Smith, editor of *Age Matters*, and to reporter Philippa Le Marquand, Palm PR, and also to Kim Rule of *Choice* magazine.

Additional information about Eric's Honorary Degree Ceremony for the Open University was gratefully received from Cheryl Brookman, OU Senior Secretary, and from the Orator on that occasion, Professor Malcolm Johnson. Tracing details of the dance, Midwinter's Jig, involved several people who have been extremely helpful, notably Laura Smyth, Librarian of the Vaughan Williams Memorial Library at the English Folk Dance and Song Society, Ann and Derek Appleing of Folksales, Chris Turner, Richard Thom and Chris Shea, son of the late Peter Shea, creator of the Jig. Pam Evans, leader of the Malvern U3A Country Dancing Group, most kindly helped to interpret the steps of the dance, and Laura Smyth managed to track down the recommended tune to which it may be danced, *Silver Celebration*.

My friend, colleague and fellow Brother Savage, Bo Drašar, read through the completed manuscript and has made some most helpful and constructive suggestions, but any remaining errors, omissions or other infelicities are, of course, the responsibility of the author, whose photograph was kindly taken by Richard Clifford.

Finally, sincere thanks to publishers Third Age Press, and, in particular, to Dianne Norton, for her skilled editing and her constant encouragement from the start of this project.

Jeremy Hardie

Foreword
by John Wade

Eric Midwinter has himself written five biographies. His subjects have been, W.G.Grace; W.E.Forster, Gladstone's influential education minister; Lord Salisbury, the Conservative premier; George Duckworth, the celebrated Lancashire and England wicket-keeper, and John Wade, Brother Savage and masterful magician. As John was the only survivor of this gifted quintet, he was invited to write the following foreword to Eric's life-story.

This is an unusual book about an unusual man. Author Jeremy Hardie has interviewed or corresponded with dozens of the people whose paths have crossed with Eric Midwinter's over the decades, and the quotations give the book the feel of an extended version of 'This is Your Life'. There is even an illustrated description of a sort of Square Dance named after him, which should give amusement to those reading the book on a train going home who might want to ty it out to pass the journey.

The Eric Midwinter I have known over thirty years is a man who has taken on many different roles in his life, many of them social, and has always given any new project momentum, dedication and enthusiasm. Eric's presence in a room, be it a drinks gathering or administrative occasion, lends an air of assurance that all will be well. As a speaker he is witty and authoritative and his hands-on experience in so many different fields (and quite a few offices), is invaluable.

Over our encounters together I have learned many things, but to me the most important is that whenever I want to get a name or a place from the past he will advise adding ten years back to the date I am aiming for. If I suggest 20 years ago he will say 30, and he is always right, as time passes so quickly.

Eric would be the best travelling companion, although we have never done it, or the best man with whom to occupy a prison cell, which we have not yet done either. Just don't hope for any help in the practical area. He doesn't drive and might just be able to sharpen a pencil. And don't hang around if some Southerner labels him a Yorkshireman.

THE WORLDS OF ERIC MIDWINTER

INTRODUCTION:
Discovering the Worlds of Eric Midwinter

This book is about a remarkable man who has achieved great success in a number of areas during his long and highly productive life. When trying to decide on a suitable title, one of the possibilities, eventually rejected, was *Eric Midwinter: You Name It, He's Done It.* Although this might reasonably be considered a little too jokey for the purpose, it has the merit of conveying succinctly the point that here is a man of many parts, a true example of a modern-day polymath. In the end, however, the chosen title *Variety is the Spice of Life: The Worlds of Eric Midwinter* seemed to fit the bill more appropriately, since it emphasises the great variety of fields in which he has excelled. As many will recognize, the first part of the title is a slight misquotation from a poem by William Cowper.

It should be made clear at the outset that this book is not strictly a biography, in the full sense of the word, but rather it is a study of Eric's professional and creative life, each phase of which is treated as a different world. Thus the approach will be broadly chronological, starting with Eric's early days in Sale, near Manchester, following his progress through

School, National Service, University, then into the world of paid employment. Attention will be concentrated largely on academic and professional aspects of his adult life, rather than personal and family matters, and important social, theatrical and sporting influences will be featured as part of the story. Three of Eric's books, *The Rhubarb People*, *Red Shirts and Roses*, and *Make 'em Laugh*, contain significant amounts of autobiographical material, which have been drawn on heavily whilst researching this account of Eric's life.

The author has known Eric Midwinter since joining the Savage Club in London in 1998. Whilst still in full-time employment as a busy university academic, there were few opportunities to enjoy the delights of the club, but on reaching retirement in 2000 it became possible to spend more time with other members there and to attend more of the many highly enjoyable social events put on by the club.

Amongst these Savage Club functions are the monthly Club Lunches, at which diners are treated to a post-lunch talk, given either by one of the members or by an invited guest. It was during one of these lunches in 2003 that I found myself congenially seated between Eric Midwinter on one side and the amiable Dave Allsop on the other, the latter being at the time Chairman of the Cricket Society. Eric had just been appointed as Chairman of the Cricket Society's Book of the Year Committee and he was looking for someone to take on the administration of this prestigious literary award. The outcome of this situation, at the end of such a convivial lunch, was that the two of them ganged-up mercilessly on this poor, defenceless scribe, making him an offer that he was unable to refuse. Apparently these two rogues had looked up, looked at me and looked at one another and nodded significantly at exactly the same time during the meal. This proved to be the start of a thoroughly enjoyable and entirely amicable four years of working closely with Eric, as administrator, on the Cricket Book of the Year Awards.

More recently (in April, 2012) the author published a book entitled *Troyte Griffith: Malvern Architect and Friend of Elgar*, which took about four years to research and write. Eric was always most encouraging at every stage of this venture, very kindly reading drafts of the manuscript and making most helpful and constructive editorial suggestions in his characteristically thoughtful and sensitive way. There is no doubt that this generous and erudite input greatly enhanced the final product. This had been my first foray into any form of biographical writing, after an academic career spent producing scientific papers, book chapters and reviews, and it made for a refreshing change in style and subject matter. After the dust had settled following the publication of the Troyte Griffith book, it occurred to me that it might be a good idea to attempt another biographical study, this time of a living subject. The person who sprang immediately to mind was Eric Midwinter, and, to my great delight, he kindly agreed to allow me to undertake this task.

Eric's view, with which I concurred, was that, whilst his eminence might be considered insufficient to warrant a full-scale biography involving domestic, allied events and all the trimmings, the unorthodox trajectory of his career and concerns could be of interest, especially to his friends and colleagues in one 'world' who might be intrigued to find he had been active in several others. The tracing of his vocational journey became, then, the specific thrust and purpose of this study.

As will become increasingly apparent, Eric Midwinter has held a wide variety of jobs that cover the fields of Teaching and Education, Educational Priority Areas, Consumer Affairs (including the concerns of public transport passengers), and Policies on Ageing. He has applied his considerable skills as a social historian and social analyst to all his writings, resulting in the publication of a large number of books, papers, and articles on an extraordinarily wide range of subjects, always presented with a strong dose of common sense and laced with characteristic wit. Importantly, Eric was also one of the three founding fathers of the University of the Third Age, an organization that continues to grow and provide opportunities for older people.

At an early stage in planning this book, Eric provided an extensive list of living friends and colleagues he had known or worked with at different stages throughout his life, from his early school days in the 1930s until the present. Almost all of these fifty or so people kindly responded to my request for information and comments about Eric, either in writing or verbally, thus allowing me to build up a rounded picture of the man and his career from many different viewpoints, and they also provided a number of illuminating anecdotes, many of which I have quoted. As previously acknowledged, Eric himself has made available many personal documents and other material. These abundant sources have been further augmented by Eric's many published works, as well as assorted audio-tapes, videos, DVDs and scripts of various interviews, radio and TV programmes, lectures, informal talks, entertainments, and other occasions. All-in-all, the author has been almost overwhelmed with an embarrassment of riches from which to select whilst writing this biographical study; I sincerely hope that what emerges from all this is an accurate, interesting and affectionate portrait of a truly singular man.

Although Eric's career has been unorthodox and varied, what is immediately apparent is that his approach has been a consistent one. It is driven by a deep concern for the well being of his fellow citizens, and for the various institutions, local and national, responsible for their welfare, together with a genuine wish that everybody should be having a good time. This highly developed and vigorously held 'communitarian' belief, fed by his extensive knowledge of and thoughtful grasp of 19th and early 20th century social history, is the force behind all his endeavours. He came to such views in embryonic fashion as a teenager but obviously, they have been refined, yet never basically shaken, over the years.

Eric was reared by a God-fearing grandmother who was, in a term coined by Chelly Halsey, with whom Eric was closely connected in his educational work, Eric's primary 'Aspirer'. He was brought up in the low Anglican tradition with regular attendance at Sunday school and church services. However, when he was about sixteen, and with a substantial weight of biblical and allied study behind him, he shifted radically to an agnostic position.

But it was not a limp, negative, sitting on the fence, 'don't know' vote of someone either not interested or who couldn't make up his mind. He still considers that the general religious question is, for fairly obvious reasons, the most solemn one facing humans and he continues to be concerned by it. In a curious sense, he feels he has more in common with, say, the committed Christian, the committed anything, than with the Christian who takes his faith for granted and never gives religion a thought, except at occasional baptisms, weddings and funerals. Eric is a committed, indeed, militant agnostic. True to his consistent devotion to Victorian thought and action, his hero is 'Darwin's bulldog', T.H.Huxley, that stout defender of the theory of evolution, credited with coining the term agnostic.

Huxley's 'A-gnostic' proposition states that not only is it impossible to know if there is an overriding supernatural 'agency' but, if there is, you can't do anything about it – for such an 'agency' must be an omniscient, omnipotent being, cognisant of all human and other activity over all time. Such omnipotence, in this view, does not allow for random deviation from the eternal pattern. Therefore, there can be no free will, not least because the free action of one individual effects and inhibits that of others, inadvertently upsetting the omniscient apple cart. Eric exemplifies this in his approach when faced with door-knocking Jehovah's Witnesses, 'God has known for all time', he might say, 'that you two chancers would turn up on my door step this morning, ring the door bell and that I would delay your mission with a twenty minutes harangue on agnosticism. You cannot surprise God. As I used to tell students when discussing this with them, "God knows what you are going to write in your exam papers next month, and if that doesn't surprise him, nothing will".'

In that this is true – and he is acutely aware of the towering defence that might be mounted by theological philosophers of huge stature – then the route-way is clear. You accept the human condition and work as hard as you can, whenever possible with others, to make the best of it for yourself and everyone else, and live life as fully as possible by a secular, humanist rather than a religious code.

This chimes with Eric's political views. Most people who know Eric, even slightly, are aware of his egalitarian left-wing political views and respect the way he has put these into effect in practical and constructive ways during his life, including his active participation in local affairs in his home town. Indeed, some friends have expressed the view that he might easily have taken up politics as a career.

As a teenager he became and remained a Socialist. Aged thirteen, the 1945 Labour victory also made a huge impression on him. He later recalls how pleased his mentor Michael Young was when told he had a copy of the Labour manifesto *Let Us Face the Future* which Michael Young had drafted. He saw 'the silent revolution' wrought by Clement Attlee amid a time of dire austerity, producing a Welfare State with the NHS at its heart, as a warming triumph.

In the army, where his job included running the unit library, he continued to read and to write for his own interest about politics, while at university he was active in the Labour Club, along with his friend Doug Bowler, even if both of them came a trifle disillusioned with the excessive talk and little action. He had a summer vacation job with the Labour Party on membership drives in northern towns like Oldham, Accrington, Hyde and the West Derby constituency of Liverpool, where the team was met with cups of tea by Bessie Braddock. He was, however, naturally edging away from any prospect of a political career. Years later Michael Young told him how, when working with William Beveridge on plans for the National Health Service, Beveridge advised that one had to make one's mind up early in one's career whether to opt for 'influence or power'. 'Michael patently opted for the former,' Eric says. 'I suggested to him that most people are lucky to get the option of either, but, not quite as consciously as all that, I suppose I had opted for 'influence' as far as my tiny sphere allowed.'

Another consideration was the beginnings of a swerve he made from Labour orthodoxy towards a more communitarian stance that cut across some of the purported chasm between right and left. That definitely affected his thinking about education and the community school, and was very much firmed up, as will become apparent, in his 30 years association with Michael Young. R.H.Tawney, who was Michael Young's mentor, was also an influence. Tawney believed in equality and in local popular democracy, stating that the argument was not between central public ownership and private enterprise; the other option was decentralised public ownership. Thus it all came together for Eric, again with the Victorian heritage uppermost – the co-operative movement, mutualism, the Utopian Socialists like Robert Owen, Charles Fourier, Saint-Simon and Peter Kropotkin, and English Ethical Socialism.

It was to an extent cross-party; Michael Young used to tell Eric, when sent out to do his bidding with this or that project, 'if it is a Labour authority call it mutual aid, if Conservative then self-help' – and it was only half a joke. Michael made a constant attack on 'Giantism' in all institutional shapes, public or commercial, as the foe of the ordinary person. Like Michael, Eric has retained a resilient and lifelong faith in the idea that every human being has something of value to offer. He is not too puritanical or solemn about this, often citing the definition used by his erstwhile colleague Brian Jackson that Socialism is 'equality plus fun.' But, in simple terms, without some rough and ready equality of conditions – and this particularly appertains to children – Eric believes it is impossible to avoid that social divisiveness that denies many ordinary people the chance to reveal their best self.

With these preliminary insights into Eric Midwinter's mindset and values as guides, it is time to explore the worlds which have formed him and in which he has worked. Hopefully, his constant desire for life to be fun as well as hard work, and his appreciation of the power and value of laughter will also shine through this account.

THE WORLD OF CHILDHOOD:
THE PROMISING SCHOOLBOY

Eric Midwinter has led a long and distinguished life, during which he has achieved so much in different fields that it is a little daunting to know quite where to begin when attempting to tell his intriguing life story. However, the obvious thing to do when embarking on any new project is to start at the beginning, hence this chapter is about Eric's childhood and schooldays. The variety of other 'worlds' that make up this story, as will be revealed in subsequent chapters, cover many different areas of activity, but the basis of his interest in each of these can be traced, in one way or another, to the vital influences of his family and his early upbringing at home and at school.

The story starts in Sale, part of the Metropolitan Borough of Trafford in Greater Manchester. First the Bridgewater Canal and then the Manchester to Altrincham railway helped convert an agricultural settlement, historically part of Cheshire, into a busy commuter suburb of the great northern city. Noted for its rugby club, which Eric first saw play in 1938, Sale's population was about 28,000 in his childhood.

Eric Clare Midwinter was born on Thursday, 11th February, 1932 in Sale Cottage Hospital. He was the younger son of Harold and Edna (née Ashworth) Midwinter, his brother Bryan

*Left: Bryan and
baby Eric with
grandfather
Harry
Midwinter*

*Below:
Eric in 1933,
aged one
year and nine
months*

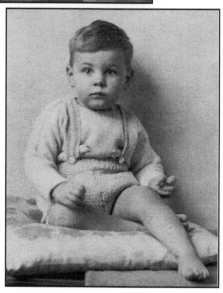

Ashworth Midwinter having been born in the same hospital almost five years earlier on 1ˢᵗ April, 1927. The family lived in the house of the paternal grandparents, Harold (Harry) and Ada (née Clare) Midwinter, at 16 Lynwood Grove, Sale. Fortuitously, and rather unusually, this house and all its contents had been given to Ada Margaret Midwinter in December, 1923 by Mr Algernon Preston. The property had previously belonged to his late son, Dr Charles Henry Preston, a distinguished dentist for whom Ada had worked as housekeeper and who, tragically, committed suicide earlier that year. So, although the family was by no means prosperous, and could legitimately be described as working-class, they did enjoy the considerable security of owning their own home.

As is described in Eric's amusing autobiographical voyage of rediscovery, *The Rhubarb People*, he first referred to his elder brother as 'Brum Bry' and himself as 'Lectric Me', much to the amusement of some of the neighbours, as recalled by Eric at his brother's funeral in January, 2013: 'My very earliest memory is of sitting in my pram and our next door but two neighbour, Mrs Blinkcorn, sticking her face in mine and saying 'where's yer Brum Bry then?' 'Brum Bry' because my infant lips could not cope with the complexity of Brother Bryan, but I soon learned the answer to the question – Brum Bry was always there when he was needed.'

In *The Rhubarb People*, several of his relatives are affectionately described, and a fascinating picture is painted of their family life in Sale from the early 1930s up to and including the Second World War. Whilst growing up, Eric acquired the nickname 'Urd', apparently invented by his brother after they had seen the short Walt Disney film *Ferdinand the Bull* which was released in 1938 (Ferdinand -> Ferd -> Urd). He is still known as 'Uncle Urd' to his nephews 75 years later.

So the main characters in Eric's home life in the early days were Ada (grandmother, affectionately know as Grank), Harry (grandfather), Edna (mother), Harold (father, commonly referred to as Ack), and Bryan (brother), augmented from time to time by a large cast of other aunts, uncles and cousins, including especially Great Aunts Doris and Clara, who played occasional but significant walk-on parts. Of this list of family runners and riders, undoubtedly the most significant influences on Eric were Ada and Ack.

ADA MIDWINTER (1876-1956)

Eric's grandmother was very much the dominant, matriarchal figure in the family that lived with her at 16 Lynwood Grove, and she evidently had a profound influence on her young grandson. As he has written, Ada was 'by far the most important and influential' of the older relatives, and she 'ruled the house with pleasant sensitivity and a not-overwhelming inflexibility'.

She was born Ada Margaret Clare in 1876, one of the fourteen children of Joseph and Margaret Clare, in Lymn, Cheshire (about ten miles from Sale). Joseph was chief ostler on the Bridgewater Canal, which ran through Lymn, looking after the horses that were used to pull the barges transporting coal and other goods between Manchester and Liverpool. This position as a respectable artisan meant that he had a house, free coals and was paid two guineas a week in the 1870s. As Eric has commented, this is about the same as his father earned in the 1930s, minus the house and the coals. He goes on to describe Joseph Clare as ' a member of the Conservative-inspired Primrose League, a devoted low Anglican and one of the first of a never-ending queue of working-class Tory voters, deluded by the snare of confining respectability.'

Ada met Harry Midwinter in 1895 and they were eventually married in Manchester in 1899, when she was 23. She was a milliner, later becoming mistress milliner in charge of the other hat-making girls at her place of work. By the time she and Harry were married, Harry had already started his own business as a newsagent, selling newspapers at or near the local railway station.

Ada was, like her father, conservative, a religious low Anglican, a strict observer of the Sabbath and a monarchist, all beliefs from which Eric was later to turn away as he grew up. However, he freely acknowledges that she taught him two important things about personal beliefs. One was that commitments, whether political or religious, must be held strongly and not in any namby-pamby fashion. The other was her deep sense of civic duty, which proved to be a perfect example for one who chose to spend his whole career in the public and voluntary service.

Ada, at the age of seventeen and working at the time as an apprentice milliner, was present at the grand opening of the Manchester Ship Canal by Queen Victoria on 21st May, 1894. Despite being a devout monarchist, Ada's chief memory of the great event was evidently of the dreadful hat worn by her beloved Queen.

Grank was extremely civic-minded, taking to heart any official instructions from government or other authorities, particularly during wartime. One example of this tendency, amusingly detailed in some of Eric's writings, includes turning the front room into a well-appointed gas shelter, complete with beautifully upholstered plugs and screens that were fitted over the door and fireplace, complementing the previously hung blackout curtains that were reinforced against blast damage with criss-crossed sticky paper. Another instance occurred when street fire guards were appointed and the family home temporarily acquired a stirrup pump, the presence of which was signified by the painting by the council of the letters 'S' and 'P' on the outside wall of the house – evidently a source of great pride to the inhabitants. For some unaccountable reason it was later decreed, since one member of the household was a fireman, to be inappropriate to keep the street's stirrup-pump there and, to Eric's chagrin, it was subsequently relocated elsewhere and the distinctive painted letters had to be erased from the wall.

Ada was an avid letter writer, writing several communications every day, mainly to relations. She maintained a list of such correspondents, crossing the name of each person off the top as she completed the next missive and adding it to the bottom, so that the regular flow of letters never ceased.

When Eric's grandmother died in 1956, at the age of 81, her son Harold (Ack) took the opportunity to make some drastic changes within the family residence. He demolished the piano, dismounted the scores of family portraits and photographs that lined the walls, and threw out thousands of sheaves of papers and letters that Ada had accumulated over many years. In his view, it had been like 'living in a bloody art gallery' all those years. He also reduced the Christmas card list by about 80%, the correspondence list by 99%, and stopped most of the family visiting, both home and away.

HAROLD MIDWINTER (ACK) (1901-1968)

The nickname Ack apparently came from a somewhat tortuously derived foreshortening of his real name Harold, probably by Eric's brother Bryan. He had a profound influence on the young Eric's development and interests, and he is very fondly remembered and mentioned in several of his books. Ack was born in 1901 in Sale and used to help his father, Harry, with several newspaper rounds. He started his schooling at Springfield, then moved to Sale Central School at the age of twelve, before leaving school at 14 to become an apprentice heating engineer. Ack sang as a chorister in St Pauls Church choir, in Springfield Road, one of several Anglican churches in Sale. He played at inside left for Sale Holmfield FC, and was a keen supporter of Manchester United Football Club and Lancashire

County Cricket Club, with their famous grounds at Old Trafford, conveniently situated only a few miles away.

In 1918, when he was 17, Ack joined the Royal Flying Corps, but the First World War was almost over by then and he soon returned home. He worked as a botanical/heating engineer for a number of years, attending to the heating systems of greenhouses, but later, in 1938, became a full-time fireman. In 1926 he married a local girl, Edna Ashworth. Several references to Ack's career as a fireman, as related by Eric, are included in Francis Beckett's excellent book *Firefighters and the Blitz* (2010), and Eric has also spoken on camera about his father's experiences in a documentary film about the fire service made by Winstan Whitter, as yet unreleased.

For many years, Ack was the scorer for Sale Cricket Club, for whom he served as Secretary, and he was also the Manchester Association scorer. He was evidently one of the first of the 'modern scorers', using a collection of coloured pens and pencils to illustrate how runs had been scored around the ground, and how each batsman got out, in addition to recording the straightforward numerical facts and figures of each innings. At one time he was offered the job of scorer for the Lancashire Second XI, with a view to taking over the First XI, by Major Rupert Howard, Secretary of Lancashire CCC, who had seen and been impressed by his Sale CC score books. This was obviously a considerable honour and opportunity for such a cricket lover, but, as his mother pointed out, it would have been quite impracticable to combine this post with his regular job in the fire brigade. Economic Determinism clearly won the day.

Ack was a stocky man, usually to be found with a cigarette between his lips and ash accumulating around his person. As described by Eric in *The Rhubarb People*, he was 'the distillation of a line of sires carefully bred with the strain of male chauvinism, and his pedigree was impeccable.' He evidently got away with murder by being widely regarded as a bit of a 'card', stimulating responses such as 'what a character' to his frequent, probably outrageous, utterances.

In addition to his love of cricket and football, Ack also had a great affection for the music hall. As luck would have it, he ended his fire service career as fireman to the Palace Theatre, Manchester from about 1947-1950. He had been taking young Eric to variety shows since he was four and now he was able to give his young son free access to one of the nation's leading variety venues. Here Eric witnessed many of the great acts he was later to describe from first-hand experience in his writings. This early exposure to the world of Music Hall and Variety Theatre certainly had a profound effect on Eric and led to his enduring interest in and passion for the many performers who have striven to keep people entertained and amused over the years.

Ack evidently bore a strong physical resemblance to the great comedian Jimmy James, both being well-rounded, barrel-chested northerners of a similar vintage, constantly with a cigarette on the go, and with a similar conversational style. This striking convergence of features is described in some detail in Eric's book *Make 'em Laugh* (published in 1979 and dedicated posthumously to Ack), in which he also confesses that Jimmy James was his all time favourite comedian.

Ack is described by Eric as being anxious to communicate and socialize with people he met, always striving to identify some common connecting thread of shared interest and uncover conversational links with complete strangers. This characteristic, apparently shared by Jimmy James, is perhaps worthy of the epigraph 'only connect', as coined by E.M Forster for his novel *Howard's End* (1910).

In retirement, Harold and his wife Edna moved to Cleveleys in 1967, unfortunately only a year before he died at the age of sixty seven. Two newspaper reports on his death refer to his twenty one years as scorer to the first team at Sale Cricket Club; his retirement from that position in 1957 had been noted in an earlier newspaper report, the event being marked by the presentation of an inscribed watch and a pen and pencil set to Harold by grateful club members.

Ack, Bryan, Edna, Grank and Eric (in school uniform)

Eric's grandfather Harry, son of Fred Midwinter, was born in 1872, in Sale, one of four brothers, and he died in 1940. He left school at 13 and started work in the newspaper retail trade, initially as an assistant on the bookstall at Sale Station, and he remained in the railway station newsagent business all his working life, arising at 3.30 every morning to sort out the papers ready for sale to the early passengers.

After Harry and Ada were married in 1899 they had two sons, Harold (b. 1901) and Albert (b. 1903), but the younger of these died in infancy at the age of about 18 months.

According to Eric, Harry was a jolly grandfather, recalled with affection and described as a 'mettlesome and well-humoured man', complete with ginger moustache and leather leggings. He was recognised as a man fond of both drinking and gambling, who became a 'well-known figure' in the local community. Having been one of the first choirboys at St Paul's Church, where he later became a 'volunteer organist', he was also organist at the St Paul's mission, a smaller place of worship in a poorer part of the town. On one notorious occasion in the church, it was necessary for him, very diplomatically, to point out to Lady Kilvert, patroness of the living, that she was the victim of what might described as an unfortunate 'garment malfunction' whilst she was up a ladder making preparations for harvest festival. His tactful handling of this potentially embarrassing situation – reputedly he said at the time 'M'Lady, I think your cuffs have dropped ' – did not go unrewarded.

Even though Eric was only eight when Harry died, it was evidently from him that he learnt one of the golden rules of story telling: 'Never lie, but always embellish the truth!' This was a lesson that he clearly took to heart and has put to good use ever since, entertaining and amusing a variety of audiences in numerous different situations.

Eric's mother, Edna Ashworth, was born in 1904 and went to Springfield School. After leaving school, she worked in a dress shop with her sister, May, before moving on to a textile firm in Manchester. She met Harold Midwinter at a church dance and they were married in 1926.

Edna was a very caring and dutiful wife and mother, carrying out all the many essential, but often mundane, tasks that such a role entails uncomplainingly and without demur. She clearly played a very important part in Eric's upbringing and early development, providing much needed support in many practical ways, yet seems, somehow, to fade quietly into the background in his later accounts of family life. Perhaps she was, by nature, rather shy and diffident, or was simply overshadowed by the overtly stronger personalities of Ada, Harry and Harold. She died in 1979, having returned from her retirement bungalow in Cleveleys to spend her final days in a nursing home in Timperley, near Sale, close to Bryan and his family

Eric's older brother Bryan, born in 1927, was never a troublemaker, but he had a feisty edge to his character and never flinched from any sort of confrontation with other youngsters in the area. So in any of the sporadic skirmishes and childish street fights that broke out in and around Lynwood Grove in the 1930s, Bryan was Eric's dependable protector and when he was around no one ever dared to lay a finger on him. However, he was evidently not above using the seven-year-old Eric as a decoy on one occasion, in order to trap two boys who had, until then, persistently escaped his summary jurisdiction for their perceived misdemeanours. Bryan secreted himself behind a garden gate and sprang out when the miscreants started to 'bash up' the sacrificial lamb left standing on the corner as bait. He then proceeded to mete out the appropriate justice, albeit somewhat later in the unfolding course of events than Eric himself might have wished at the time.

Bryan left school in 1941 at the age of fourteen and spent his first week's wages on an air pistol for four shillings and sixpence (equivalent to twenty two and a half 'new' pence), thus dramatically changing the balance of power in the local political landscape. Having 'accidently' shot Eric in the leg with this lethal weapon whilst practicing his marksmanship skills, he bent over and generously allowed Eric to fire a shot at his backside by way of compensation. This decidedly foolhardy gesture, which, according to Eric, resulted in Bryan breaking the unofficial world high-jump record, was presumably designed to prevent him from reporting the initial firearms incident to higher authority.

The nature of Bryan's work on the production of essential military equipment at nearby Metropolitan-Vickers meant that the start of Bryan's National Service was postponed until 1949, when he was twenty-one, at which juncture he commenced an eighteen month spell in the Royal Artillery. The timing of this sequence of events meant that Bryan was de-mobbed from the army just as Eric was conscripted for his National Service, as an inexperienced eighteen-year-old school leaver in 1950. At least this allowed the more street-wise Bryan to pass on some useful tips to his younger brother and be available for advice and support if required. Bryan later returned to Metro-Vicks where he worked until his retirement in 1992.

Many years later, in 2012, when Eric spoke at his brother's funeral, he referred to Bryan's inner steadiness and his ability to sustain firm, life-long friendships. He never moved more than a mile from his birthplace and lived his entire life in three houses, two of them close to one another. He was always extremely interested in the local area and was a memorable raconteur of tales, both tall and truthful, much like his father and grandfather before him.

Although Eric and Bryan were dissimilar from one another in a number of ways, and certainly pursued very different career pathways, it is clear that there was always a strong bond of brotherly affection between them.

Starting in the January term of 1937, Eric attended Springfield Council School, like his brother before him, but did not initially take kindly to the experience. On the first day, accompanied by his mother, he attempted to run away before even being registered as a pupil. When they eventually got Eric to the

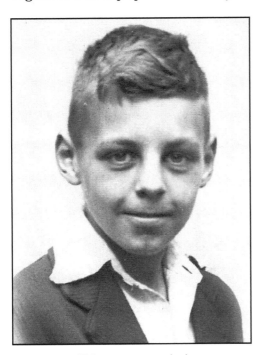

classroom, the reluctant young scholar had to be restrained physically by the teacher, Miss Smart, so that his mother could get away to return home. Soon tears replaced other more violent forms of protest. When Miss Smart instructed all the pupils to go into the hall and 'sit on a nail', young Eric became even more terrified. Not realizing that she was referring to brass studs on the floor, he crawled around, bawling, on his hands and knees looking for a nail, whilst the rest of the class sat quietly in their neat rows with folded arms. So, Eric's schooldays seem to have started badly on day one, and then apparently deteriorated; his was a definite case of school phobia, the local barber having occasion to remark later, 'Many's the time I've seen his mother drag him on his back to school.'

Eric as a young lad

Eric's attendance at infant and junior school seems to have been somewhat intermittent, interrupted both by occasional attempts to escape and by a series of childhood ailments that regularly struck during the winter months, with the result that he was ill in bed for six consecutive birthdays. These episodes included tonsillitis, whooping cough, measles, mumps and scarlet fever, all requiring the patient to spend time at home in bed. On the credit side of the equation, however, they provided the perfect excuse for non-attendance at school. It is not hard to imagine that he used much of this enforced non-school time quite profitably by reading widely.

Despite the problems with the 'refusenik' Eric's early schooling, the experience did not have too deleterious an effect on his educational progress since he went on to win a scholarship to Sale Grammar School, where he started in 1943. This was a great achievement, both for him and his family, and had an enormously beneficial effect on the subsequent course of Eric's life.

GRAMMAR SCHOOL

Eric attended Sale Grammar School from 1943 to 1950. He was the first of the Midwinters to go to grammar school, later becoming the first boy from Sale Grammar School to go to either Cambridge or Oxford University, and the first member of his family to go into higher education after leaving school.

Eric has written in characteristic Midwinter style, some of his recollections of 'Going to the Grammar'. It was produced in late 2013 for inclusion on the Sale Grammar School website, currently under development by Dave Walmsley, and part of this essay is reproduced below.

> There is evidence that many working class children who 'get on' have what is called an 'aspirer' in the family or neighbourhood - it might be a thoughtful uncle of a kindly neighbour; in other words, not necessarily one's

parents. In my case it was my grandmother with whom I lived. Not that my parents were unsupportive, more that my grandmother had the time and the nous to encourage me to read and write and think. Years later, when heavily involved with home/school relations and attempts to exhort parents to help their youngsters, I used to tell groups of mums and dads about 'Grank' as she was lovingly known, and how 'I had done an hour at home before the others buggers had started when we all got to school'.

So it was Grank who, on Sunday walks, would occasionally wander down Ashton Lane and Moss Lane to this building site at the top of the Avenue. The grammar school was under construction. She would explain to me that, if I worked hard, I might go there some day. Which I did do and I did go - in 1943. Grank was delighted, as were all the family. Nor did it halt there. Consequently she used to make copies of all my school reports and dispatch them throughout the extended family.

I had not particularly enjoyed junior school, feeling rather diffident and uneasy about it, and much preferring the warm haven of the home. In retrospect, what I find curious is the assurance I felt about 'going to the grammar', in spite of the fact that I was a first-generation entrant. Moving from being in the 'top class' at elementary school to being a 'maggot' at the secondary school, where the sixth formers, albeit there were but a handful then, wore long trousers and seemed to be grown men, might normally be viewed as a daunting process, but not so. I had a surge of confidence. Whether it was bred in the sheer knowledge that I had passed the much-hailed 'scholarship' or simply that I felt very much at home from the beginning, I cannot tell. Whatever it was, I experienced a sense of belonging that I had not known at my previous school. I wore the uniform with some pride.

When my mum and dad had attended the pre-entry meeting for parents, Mr Norrish (the headmaster) on greeting them had said, 'Ah, Midwinter; we are expecting great things of your boy', which was a bit perplexing – and this is the first time, seventy years on, that I have ever confided that to anyone outside the then family. Well, I did give it a go, cheerfully and solidly, and I tended to be there or there abouts at the head of the lists, certainly for the first three years, as well as playing rugby for the junior XV and captaining the junior cricket XI, with, crowning glory, my first ever published pieces appearing in *The Salian*, the school magazine.

Courtesy of Peter Day

I went off the boil in the fourth and fifth years. It was partial rather than full-blown. There was a general side to it, including playing in the local amateur soccer league, a sin if not a crime in grammar school eyes, and going out in the evenings and not doing a great deal. Perhaps it was a tad hormonal. Fortunately, it was subject rather than knowledge based. I completely lost interest in science and maths and also languages, while even geography was temporarily abandoned. I pursued English and History with the same vigour and purpose and, by now a 'senior' member of the Sale Library, I continued to read avidly, not least in politics and allied topics, with H.G.Wells and George Bernard Shaw given leading spots in all that perusal.

It meant that I ended up with a skew-whiff School Certificate. A pass in English Language and six other subjects was the criterion and I achieved that easily enough. I had distinctions in English Language, English Literature and History but, frankly, had I sustained my output of the first three years I would have copped for a few more. It was something of a wake up call for me as I entered the sixth form, whilst the dropping of the subjects for which I had lost affection was a major point by way of happy release. I had to do School Certificate Latin, which I enjoyed, in the first year of the sixth, and also French, but in my second year I had only English, History and Geography. I couldn't get enough of the first two and the 'human' side of 'jogger' – I was less enamoured of the 'physical' side – was also of much interest to me.

Sixth forms in those far-away days were very small. Most pupils left after the statutory five years to begin careers, many of which involved evening classes or correspondence courses where now there would be a degree course. There were two groups, 6Modern and 6Science. When I inform you that both years of 6Modern were located in what was originally a stockroom between the gym and the dining room you will gain some idea of our minute numbers. There were just six of us in my Lower 6Modern.

Mr Walton was the 6Modern form teacher. He has since been absolutely vindicated, as far as I am concerned, in his proposal to place above the stockroom portal a notice reading 'Abandon hope of earning any money all ye who enter here', compared with the boffins in 6Science.

I have never worked so hard in all my life as I did in the sixth form. I used to do a slow trail home, usually chatting to friends on the way, eat a hearty meal and read my brother's *Daily Mirror,* then a vibrantly campaigning newspaper of some quality, and then settle to work at 6.00 p.m. I would often work until 1.00 a.m. I would have some time off on Monday evening to go the famous Montague Youth Club of happy memory; I would always listen to *Take It From Here* for half an hour on Thursday evening and I would work some twelve or fifteen hours on the Sunday. Saturday was the one free day, on which I sometimes played, at least in the first year sixth, rugby for the second XV in the morning and football for Sale Oakfield in the afternoon. I made the first XV in my final year, which scuppered the football as we toffs in the first XV turned out in the afternoon, and I played cricket in the summer. Then it was the cinema in the evening with a bunch of mates, John Hough and Graham Clegg, as a rule, usually Sale Palace, for, by the time we were out and about, the other three cinemas were packed to overflowing.

The routine was to start the week with Geography, move through English Literature and then on to History, fulfilling the work that had been set and, as we were severely advised, 'reading round' the subject as well. In a normal week I suppose I did some thirty hours of 'homework' in complete contrast to my lethargic efforts in the fourth and fifth form. Yet I contrived to be in the school play, *The Miser*, starring Robert Gillespie, who went on to become a successful actor, in the title role with Bob Greaves, later Granada's chief newscaster, and I, as the servants. I was Head Prefect in my final year and also captain of the first cricket XI and editor of the school magazine.

Left: Eric in costume in school production of The Miser

Below: Eric as Head Prefect in 1950, seated next to the Headmaster, P.L.Norrish

It was a busy and eventually successful two years upon which I look back with considerable pleasure and pride. I recollect occasionally that, in my last year at Springfield council school, two or three of us were sent to Manchester Grammar School to do the entrance exam there. At that time MGS had three feeder preparatory schools, Manchester North, Manchester South and the old Sale High School. This left a handful of 'free' places and 'entrance' (that is, you had to pay the full whack) places. I won one of the latter. My family could not afford it – I remember the tiny detail that the dinners alone were 12s6d a week when my father's fireman's wages were about a fiver a week. There was never a moment of concern or lamentation; it was never discussed; there was never a mention of 'oh dear, isn't it a pity ...'; my family played it perfectly on key. It was something I had attained, a prize in itself. Congratulations were heaped on me as a victor; I felt good about it and never for a second felt about it as a lost opportunity.

Nor have I had any such thought since. I still remain convinced that Sale Grammar School ideally suited me. Maybe it was, and I do not mean any disrespect to either establishment, something about being a larger fish in a smaller pond. For example, not much chance of me captaining the MGS first XI; think Michael Atherton, John Crawley . . . Although as an educationalist, I have been severely critical of the selective ethos and other elements of schooling then and now, there have never been any sour grapes. I have abidingly enormous affection for the old school, the lifelong friends I made there – still in touch with, inevitably, Peter Day, John Hough and Brian Eldred – and with a great sense of appreciation for my mainstream teachers, among them P.L. Norrish himself, 'Bill' Shepherd, Harold Christian (I was guest speaker at his retirement speech day) Doc Urwin, 'Wally' Walton. Frank Johnson, Frank Burke and my history master, Roy Hope.

I was privileged to share the duties of speaking at the school's fiftieth anniversary dinner with Dave Walmsley, as ever displaying his distinct brand of sparkling eloquence. Then, barely months later, they knocked the bloody school down.

I went to look at the wreckage. It was a building site. It was rather like the scene Grank had taken me to see fifty years before.

Eric and his fellow pupils were fed awareness of Harold Wilson at school, for their head had previously been his history master at Wirral Grammar School when he won his Oxford Scholarship. Many years later, in 1987, shortly before going up to do a speech at the school's 50th anniversary, Eric went to the House of Lords to see Michael Young, and Wilson, by this time suffering badly from dementia, was standing on the steps. Eric took a chance and asked him if he recalled Mr Norrish, the headteacher in question, and Wilson sprang to life, for twenty minutes giving a marvellous reverie of school, his scholarship, Norrish and Oxford where he said he shared rooms 'with a student who became treasurer of the Welsh Conservative Party and tried to commit suicide'. Wilson's fabled long-term memory was clearly still intact. When his car arrived, they shook hands and Eric said 'the last time we shook hands was when you gave me the 4th form progress prize at Speech Day when you were President of the Board of Trade.' The next time Eric saw him was at the 25th anniversary of the Open University; he sat in a corner with his wife both looking isolated. Eric went over to have a word with him and Mary Wilson explained, as Harold sat there eating a crisp and sipping a glass of red wine, that his mind had now completely gone – she was really nice and thanked Eric very graciously for his attentions.

The crowning achievement of Eric's school career was to be his attainment of an Exhibition to read history at Cambridge University.

When Eric came to sit his entrance examinations for St Catharine's College, Cambridge, he did the four written papers at the school during the half-term holiday. This was invigilated by the second master, Mr Shepherd, who kindly gave up two days of his holiday for this task. Eric describes what happened:

> I had one stroke of luck. I was doing (as ever since) 19th century history, but I had recently read an enthralling biography of Joan of Arc and followed up that with some more reading and scribbles. I spotted a question on Joan of Arc in the medieval section and took a chance on going outside my 'period', normally a grievous sin, and I think that may have helped by showing a wider grasp.

It is worth noting that not one of the staff of Sale Grammar School, which had opened just a year or two before Eric started there, had any experience or knowledge of Oxbridge. He was the first pupil even to try for entry to Oxford or Cambridge as well as being the first to succeed.

A few weeks after sitting the examination papers, early on a Sunday morning, a telegram arrived at the Midwinter house. Continuing the story in Eric's words:

> My dad was in the lavatory and I can hear my mum now rattling the door handle, crying, 'Harold, Harold, there's a telegram', not daring to open it (and not noticing it was addressed to me) as, in her mind, TELEGRAM spelt DEATH. It invited me for interview at Cambridge on the Tuesday, so I cycled round to the head to tell him. He said exactly the right thing psychologically– 'it looks as if someone has dropped out and you've been called up as a late replacement', which stopped me from being too confident or having high expectations. I only found out much later that everybody had received a similar telegram.
>
> I was interviewed by the kindly historian E.E.Rich, who was later to become Master of the college, but

we both spoke in alien tongues. I told him I had done 'subsid', in other words Higher School Certificate (HSC) subsidiary exams. He had never heard of that and was more used to students doing their HSC and then Oxbridge scholarships in a 3rd year in the 6th form. He told me my French translation was weak, but I have ever been a poor linguist and was not doing a language for HSC. He even took down a history book in French and asked me to translate a passage, a most humbling experience. He kept asking me about state and county scholarships but I didn't quite catch his drift and thought he was saying it's touch and go whether you can have an exhibition because of a lack of a foreign language; that is, touch and go whether I would get in.

Thus Eric was very much relieved to hear a few days later, in March 1950, that he had been elected an exhibitioner. His 6th form colleagues greeted him with an Oxbridge type mock boat of rowers and he was hailed before the school. The granting of a half-day holiday in celebration made him, understandably, extremely popular. The Parents' Association, who paid his expenses to go to Cambridge for the interview, presented Eric with a monographed briefcase. The £40 exhibition meant that he qualified for the equivalent of a state school grant – he never realised that he could have left school there and then but, instead, stayed on and grafted away and got two distinctions in Higher School Certificate and one in the State Scholarship exams which he also passed, plus a County Scholarship and the local Borough Exhibition. Eric was only allowed to hold one of these awards, although the County and the Borough did give him a few useful extra pounds a year as a pleasing bonus.

Eric's great success certainly did not go unnoticed in the Town Hall, and on 8th May, 1950 the Mayor of Sale wrote to him as follows:

Dear Eric,

At the monthly meeting of the Town Council on Tuesday last it gave me much pride and pleasure to refer, from the Chair, to the open Exhibition which you have been awarded to enable you to proceed to Cambridge to take up your Honours Course in History.

The Council were most gratified to learn of this success and have asked me to express in their name, and mine, their warm congratulations upon this fine achievement, and their best wishes for your continued success and future career.

The Mayor's letter concludes:

I hope you will be very happy at Cambridge, and take up your place there in the knowledge that your town is proud of you.

These were fine and warmly felt words and, no doubt, Mr Frank Highley and his successors as Mayor would continue to feel pride in Eric's growing list achievements in later years.

The former history master at Sale Grammar School, Mr Roy Hope, wrote touchingly many years later, in 1999, in which he says in response to a letter from Eric:

I was fascinated to have the details of your Cambridge Exhibition. It was an exciting time and though it is now some 50 years ago I remember many of the details with great pleasure of your success. I was not aware, however, that it was only after your Army service, and on taking up your place as an Exhibitioner at St Catharine's, that you realized the true measure of your achievement. And your subsequent academic and professional career has fully justified it. You were always a pleasure to teach and, like you, I have much enjoyed our association and friendship and continue to do so.

Roy Hope died in 2000 but his daughter, Penny Dynan has kindly sent the following recollection of the schoolboy her parents knew as 'Middy'.

You are correct that my father was Eric Midwinter's history teacher at Sale Grammar School, which opened shortly before the war. My father taught there from 1946-1953/4 and was Senior History Master. It was during this time that he encountered 'Middy' as he was apparently affectionately known. He taught Middy for six years, including the time when he was in the 6th form.

My father considered Eric to be his star pupil and thought a great deal of him. He always described him as having 'a wonderful mind'. Eric was entered to apply for a scholarship at Cambridge and he was the first pupil from the school to attain such an award – in his case to St Catharine's College to study history.

Middy was apparently renowned for his sense of humour and my mother recounts an anecdote illustrating this.

When in Sale, Middy belonged to a youth club, the Montague Club. My father was asked to give a talk to the club, where he met its leader, William Ellis, and subsequently both my parents and Middy were invited to a Christmas party at his house. Mr Ellis happened to be a monumental mason who had his workshop behind his house. My parents arrived at the house on a dark December evening to find the long driveway lined with tombstones. They arrived at the door and rang the bell to have it answered by Middy with the words 'Hello, how are you? Pull up a tombstone and make yourselves at home!'

Mum has never forgotten this and it makes her chuckle to this day. I do also remember my father recounting the same story so it obviously left a lasting impression on both of them.

Eric's childhood activities outside of school included sport and amateur dramatics but he was also in the cubs for a short while but he was never, by his own admission, a wholehearted participant. In fact he became overtly anti-scout in his opinions in later life. Clear evidence of this can attitude be found in his book *The People's Jesters* (2006) when describing the popular Ralph Reader *Gang Shows* that were produced between 1936-1974. He wrote: 'They were naturally laundered to the sentimental, ultra-patriotic, excruciatingly jolly mood of scouting, with its emphasis on the Boer War uniform and, indeed, Boer War values, espoused by its oddball founder, Robert Baden-Powell, that strange assortment of atavistic credo and propagandist wiles'. As he went on to admit, that statement did betray something of a revulsion against the concept of scouting and its offshoots.

MEMORIES OF FRIENDS

Several of Eric's old school friends remember him vividly from his early days in Sale. One of these, Brian Eldred, recalls:

> I first met Eric in 1941 after my family were 'bombed out' of our home in Old Trafford during the Manchester 'blitz' and moved into the road where Eric lived. We immediately became good friends after he called at our home and made himself known.
>
> He was always extremely keen on cricket and we would spend hours in Sale Park playing. I believe that was where he made his one and only double century. We propped up half a plank of wood as a wicket. To improve his batting, Eric attached a rope to his mother's washing line to which he tied a sock with a tennis ball in it. The ball was suspended about a foot from the ground and as he hit it with his bat it came back at all angles.
>
> Following the amalgamation of Sale Grammar School for Boys and Sale Grammar School for Girls there is no longer an Old Salians Association. So, unfortunately, there is no Annual Dinner, but at this event Eric always made the final speech and it was eagerly awaited and appreciated by the gathering.
>
> I shall always regard it as a pleasure and a privilege to be counted as one of Eric's friends.

Another school friend with whom Eric has kept in touch, John Hough, has written:

> Eric and I have been very good friends for seventy five years, though our lives went their separate ways when we were in our early twenties.
>
> We first met at Springfield Road School in 1936, my abiding memory of this period was from about 1938 having to carry our gas masks in a cardboard box to school and the awful smell of the rubber during emergency practice. We then both went to Sale Grammar School for Boys in 1943.
>
> We were both from working class backgrounds - no telephones or TVs - but had generally happy formative years, both sports mad, from about twelve years of age we would cycle the few miles to Maine Road, Manchester City football ground, to watch our beloved Manchester United, leaving our bikes in local back yards for threepence.
>
> Around this time, even though Sale GS was a rugby school, out of school we played soccer; in fact we set up our own team - Sale Oakfield - and entered the local league. We wrote to prominent local people for donations to purchase a set of shirts and Eric's mother, a lovely lady, embroidered an oak leaf badge for all the shirts, it must have taken her hours, and his father, Harold, became our manager.

Another good friend and contemporary, Peter Day, was also a neighbour in Sale and went to the same schools as Eric, and he has provided the following entertaining reminiscences of their early days together.

> We were brought up living in back-to-back terraced houses on Oldfield Grove and Lynwood Grove. Eric was leader of the Lynwood Grove gang. We often played a game to see who could get control of the summit of the air raid shelter built in our back garden. One day,

one of our gang, my brother Billy, was pushed off the top by Eric and Grubber Gordon, as a result of which he fell and damaged himself seriously on some railings. Grubber Gordon put a note through our door the next day addressed to my mother apologising for killing Billy – such was the rivalry and respect in the relationship between the two gangs.

One of our favourite tricks was to get toffee bags from the local sweet shop, fill them with soil so they made cluster bombs, and lob them over the fence into the Midwinter family's garden. On one occasion, the second such missile deposited itself on the football column of Ack's newspaper as he sat in the garden and never in the history of warfare have hostilities been brought to such an abrupt end.

But some of our play was collaborative. We used to play in a large deserted house together and Eric would lead us shouldering chestnut palings as weapons on manoeuvres; we would stand guard on the railway bridge and carry out drill exercises. Here, against the background of the Second World War, we were Middy's Home Guard.

We were at Springfield Elementary School together and were both the victims of Mrs. Sharrocks who would frequently take delight in battering us over the knuckles with a heavy ruler. Eric was once instrumental in organising a joint action to face down a school bully; this was so effective that he never troubled us again.

A group of us were involved in starting a youth club at the local Congregational Church, with a lay preacher, Walter Hagenbach, who also tried to interest us in religion. We met every Monday evening for typical youth club activities, but Middy had other ideas – the church hall had a small stage in it and this fired his imagination. Soon we were organised into a theatrical performance company – Middy wrote the scripts for the sketches and the songs and took charge of the direction and I recruited and managed the stage hands and organized ticket sales and programmes. My mother and Grubber Gordon's did the costumes and someone else's mum did the refreshments for the interval. Meanwhile, the local memorial stone mason and church worthy, Walter Ellis, looked after the business side and the scenery. And so the Montague Club was born – a regular part of our lives, drawing audiences from parents and friends and the church congregation. The hall was packed for nearly every performance. On one occasion, a scandalised head teacher in the shape of Mr. P. L. Norrish, first head of Sale Grammar School, sat transfixed on the front row, mouth wide open as he saw his pupils cavort across the stage in some Midwinter inspired number – dressed as Suffragettes!

Eric (right) on stage with Peter Day (centre) and Duncan Mercer, as 'Suffragettes' in the 'Pastymes' revue produced by the Montague Players

The Montague Club was the centre of our social lives and where many of us met girl friends and future wives. And soon it was to be woven into the life of Sale Grammar School. Every year, after the annual summer fete there had been an attempt to stage some sort of diversion for the parents. Bill Shepherd, the stern first deputy head teacher of the school, got wind of the deeds of the Montague players and they were offered the opportunity to entertain parents and others on the evening of the school fete. So, indeed, began a tradition that was to remain with the school until just before it closed in 1990.

At Sale Grammar School, Eric was popular and well-known for his academic prowess and he thrived under the tuition of Doctor Glen Urwin, his English master, and others. Eric went on to be a prefect and head boy and to win an open exhibition to Cambridge University – although none of this went to his head and he was always approachable. He was a great friend of my brother Billy while at school – they were two rascals together. Academic excellence was not for us all – I recall one of my classmates on the receiving end of this unflattering admonition from one of his teachers, 'If by some chance you do get through the school certificate, it will have been as the result of divine intervention.'

After school, Eric became a regular for a time in the rugby and cricket teams of the newly formed Old Salians Association. In rugby, he largely played for the second and third teams at centre or full back. In keeping with his theatricality, he was excellent at throwing a convincing dummy – but also at avoiding the more physical aspects of the game, often ending a game with spotless shorts, even on pitches which appeared to be quagmires, like the legendary bog at Nelson and Colne. I recall that one outrageous dummy which Eric threw against Toc H resulted in three opponents ending up in what could loosely be described as the crowd. Old Salians was probably best known for its rugby but there was a cavalier and rather rustic cricket side as well with Eric as its social beating heart. Eric was a captain of the cricket side, a shrewd tactician and steeped in cricket, and he was also a good batsman at this level, stylish and

THE WORLDS OF ERIC MIDWINTER

correct. The social life of the team revolved around Eric and his humour and he retained his immense popularity despite the character assassination of his confederates – especially myself and Brian Eldred.

Eric Midwinter (centre left) enjoying a drink after speaking at an Old Salians' Rugby Club dinner. The group includes Eric Evans, former Sale and England rugby union captain (far left), Bob Greaves, Chief News presenter, Granada Television (centre right), and Peter Day (with cigarette)

But Eric's greatest contribution to the Old Salians was his after dinner speaking at the annual Old Salians' dinners. He spoke at 33 of the first 36 Old Salians dinners – as well as at the 50th birthdays of the school and of the Old Salians in commemorative dinners - and at the 150th anniversary dinner of Sale Cricket Club, held at Old Trafford cricket ground. As organiser of those dinners, I could not have been luckier than to have had a speaker to call on of Eric's brilliance – he was witty, could build a great narrative and had great timing and animation. The butts of his humour became legends in the folk lore of Old Salians – my bladder; Duncan Mercer's eyesight; and Stan Whitehead's wallet. Other characters in the narrative were Jack Gilks – a figure so skilfully created that he seemed to be a figment of our imaginations – and Ken Derbyshire, whose pipe and flasher's mac prompted many a good tale. Underpinning the gentle mockery and storylines, Eric's left wing radicalism shone through in irreverence and a chiding of the establishment. Eric's speeches were loved by the faithful but also drew praise from guests to the dinners. Geoff Green, rugby correspondent of the *Manchester Evening News* never missed a dinner – and Eric Evans, an England international and captain, said that Eric was the best after dinner speaker he had ever heard.

It is clear from all the testimonies reproduced above that Eric was, and still is, greatly admired and respected by his old school mates. Another Old Salian, Dave Walmsley, has written that he was 'an inspiration to many of the few academically minded and aspirational pupils at Sale Grammar School as his was one of the first names on the honours board which was placed on the wall at the back of the assembly hall, recording his open scholarship to Cambridge, although the school never exploited the opportunity to use as role models those boys who had been so stunningly successful in the early years of the school.'

At the time when Eric won his Open Exhibition in 1950, Cambridge insisted on those studying 'useful' subjects like medicine or engineering doing National Service after university, whereas those doing 'useless' ones like history were expected to do their National Service beforehand, in the vain hope that they might gather some maturity. Far from being dismayed by this approach, it may well have been an advantage for someone from Eric's background, as he has observed:

Incidentally, I have often been asked what was it like for a working class boy going to Cambridge then in class terms – although there were occasional discomforts, often due to lack of money, the more patent division was between those who had been in the forces and those straight from school - we were not so dreamy-eyed and we were more sceptical about the strict social disciplines etc - there were parts of it I loved and I am one of those who thanks his lucky stars for his university education every day, but there were parts I didn't like.

So, after an eventful, industrious and happy childhood, despite the intervention of the Second World War and its aftermath, Eric's schooldays came to a triumphant end in the summer of 1950. Along the way, he had absorbed important influences from his family, especially Grank and Ack, but also other relatives, as well as from some of his more enlightened school-teachers, which were to stand him in very good stead as he entered the various worlds through which he was destined to pass in succeeding years. During these early years, he had also started to develop his great love for sport, literature and the theatre, as well as his ideas about religion, politics and social justice, and the significant habits of regular reading and writing. This was to be an intriguing and unusual journey, during which Eric met and befriended an extraordinary number of loyal friends and associates.

Top: *School First XV in 1949/50 season*
(Eric back row, third from right)
Middle: *School First Cricket XI in 1950*
Eric (captain) in centre front row

Bottom: *Sale Oldfield FC*
Eric seated second from left

THE WORLD OF GROWING UP:
THE SOLDIER AND THE STUDENT

NATIONAL SERVICE

In 1950 Eric went from school to the army to complete two years of National Service, before taking up his place in Cambridge. He enlisted at an infantry training camp at Chester, where, as was customary, he underwent twelve weeks of basic training and square bashing. Having some interest in teaching, Eric had developed the notion of joining the RAEC (Royal Army Education Corps), otherwise known disrespectfully in the army as 'Run Away Enemy Coming'. More flatteringly, when trying to explain the meaning of the letters on the shoulder flashes and, perhaps, to impress people at dances or other social functions, they occasionally became transmuted to 'Royal Atomic Energy Commission'.

Six of the young recruits amongst Eric's intake were put down as potential candidates for RAEC, but, in the event, and to their considerable horror, on the very day of passing out they were informed that their services were not required for this purpose. Instead, they were to be transferred to the Lancashire Fusiliers. The unhappy young soldiers were given seventeen days embarkation leave and told that on their return they would be shipped out to Khartoum to guard oil installations. As the six disappointed would-be RAEC recruits walked miserably through the barrack gates, a regimental policeman suddenly shouted after them 'are two of you Kenyon and Midwinter?' They were instructed to see an officer who, after apologizing for 'buggering up' their leave arrangements, informed them that they would, after all, be joining RAEC and were being sent forthwith to Bodmin for training. As Eric later reflected, seventeen days leave would seem to have been rather poor compensation for spending the next eighteen months protecting oil pipes in Sudan. It was never explained why Kenyon and Midwinter were selected for this posting in preference to the other four candidates, two of whom were trained teachers, but it seems likely that knowledge of Eric's forthcoming Exhibition to Cambridge played a decisive part in the army's decision-making in his case.

Whatever the reasoning, this was undoubtedly a lucky break for Private Midwinter. The three months of training in Bodmin was spent living in wooden shacks during a very severe winter, and living conditions were challenging. The Education Corps was in the process of being moved to new quarters at the Army Education Depot in Beaconsfield, and Eric's group was the last company remaining at Bodmin. Facilities were very basic, with hot water only available on Thursday nights and little or no heating in the huts. Even the bread supplies ran out on one occasion.

Only sixty of the 120 men undergoing training were actually required for the RAEC, the remainder being returned to their units and eventually sent to other duties, such as those of the infantrymen, some to fight in the Korean War (1950-53) with the Middlesex and Gloucestershire Regiments. The lucky winners in the selection process would become sergeants, since such 'schoolies' needed this more senior rank in order to teach and instruct other soldiers. They were, in fact, amongst the few non-regular (i.e. National Servicemen) sergeants in the army. One of the considerable advantages of being a sergeant was better pay without the higher expenses of the officers, access to a decent sergeants' mess, and what was sometimes described as a 'cushy number'. For example, when Eric was stationed in Germany he was able to play cricket four times a week during his first summer there.

Private Eric Midwinter sorting out his kit

The critical choice of individuals to remain in the RAEC has been described by Eric as the most extreme win or lose situation in which he has ever found himself. They were allocated to 'syndicates' of twelve or fifteen men and the practical work consisted of the group pretending to be a class of squaddies, with each of them taking turns to teach a lesson. This scenario made it necessary for each individual to strike a reasonable balance between mucking up someone else's lesson and running the risk of that person seeking revenge when it was his turn to perform in front of the class.

When, on the final morning, they lined up on parade to learn their fate, the names and numbers of those who should fall in on the other side of the drill shed were called out. It took a while for them to realise whether the names shouted out were those of the winners or the losers. Eric freely admits that he has never been so glad to be a winner, and he went on to spend a rather wasteful, but never uncomfortable, 18 months or so with the British Army of the Rhine (BAOR). His companion from Chester, Percy Kenyon, was less fortunate and did not make the cut.

One day during his time in Germany, Eric was delighted to receive a huge parcel from home. Anticipating that the contents might include a valuable assortment of delectable things to eat and drink, some of which might even be traded to his advantage, he eagerly tore open the package. It is not hard to imagine his disappointment when he unwrapped 120 pages of handwritten papers, painstakingly copied by his grandmother, the inveterate letter writer. A large pamphlet concerning grants for post-military education had arrived at the family home, none of which actually applied to Eric's particular situation, but since it was an official document from HMG, it must obviously have been of great importance. Accordingly, not wishing to risk the possibility of the original document falling into the hands of the country's recent enemies, the 76-year-old Ada Midwinter had faithfully transcribed every page and sent this duplicate copy to Eric in Germany. It must have taken her many hours to complete; we sometimes tend to forget the advantages of modern inventions, such as the photocopier.

Eric spent the first fifteen months of his time in Germany in Herford (not to be confused with the English towns of Hereford or Hertford), before moving about 20 kilometres North to Bad Oeynhausen for the last six months of his tour of duty.

At Herford he ran the unit library and led some map reading classes, to the great amusement of his family back at home, who were aware of his rather poor sense of direction. He also prepared the weekly current affairs briefing for officers to read and discuss with their troops, went on periodic field exercises, and produced a daily news-sheet for distribution to the soldiery. Eric and colleagues were the 'News-sheet and Anti-propaganda' personnel, the term 'Anti-propaganda' being at the time the British term for 'Propaganda'. These activities were fairly leisurely, allowing plenty of time for games of cricket, soccer and rugby.

Sergeant Eric Midwinter R.A.E.C

Things were rather more formal when Eric arrived at Rhine Army HQ at Bad Oeynhausen. He even found himself having to salute General Eisenhower on one occasion as the great man was saying farewell to the troops before leaving to become a presidential candidate in the USA. Work consisted of teaching regular classes, some of which were directed at the Army Certificate of Education, 1st, 2nd and 3rd Class, required by non-commissioned officers for substantive rank and promotion. Fortunately, he did not suffer quite the same fate as one callow youth who went straight from school into the army and had just arrived as an RAEC sergeant. When faced with a class of WRAC girls, some of whom had recently been away on exercises, he asked 'hands up those who missed the last period'. It is not hard to imagine the cries of mirth echoing down the corridor, to the huge embarrassment of the innocent young sergeant.

During this last six months at BAOR HQ, when Sir John Harding was CO, there had been some security breaches and alarms, so security was tight at the weekends when the main building was empty. Eric found himself on duty as Guard Commander one Saturday evening, together with two of the twelve sentries under his command, when a car drew up at the steps leading to the main entrance. Out of this taxi stepped the famous actor Robertson Hare, accompanied by two or three actresses, and Hare grandly invited them to follow him with the words 'this way ladies' as he swept up to the front door. Eric and the sentries, complete with fixed bayonets, had to repel them and deny access to the building, much to their consternation and shock. Fortunately, it was quickly realised that the visitors were actually heading for the Officers' Club next door and peace was soon restored. They were evidently part of a touring company of actors who were performing one of the Ben Travers farces around BAOR. As Robertson Hare, who was noted for his many appearances in theatrical farces on stage, might have remarked, "Oh Calamity!". Little did the young Guard Commander on that evening, Sergeant Midwinter, know that many years later he would be called upon to write his first of many notices for the Dictionary of National Biography (DNB) about John Robertson Hare (1891-1979).

Whilst stationed at Bad Oeynhausen in 1952, Eric happened to meet another National Serviceman called Anthony Pearce, who was working in HQ 1st Corps in BAOR, based in the same town in North Rhine-Westphalia. By a strange coincidence, and to their mutual surprise, they discovered that they had both been awarded Open Exhibitions in History at St Catharine's College, Cambridge, and would soon become fellow undergraduate students after their army service days were over. So, having done their bit to protect Western Europe from the threat of Russian invasion, the way of life of these two bright young national servicemen was about to undergo a radical change as they entered the hallowed Groves of Academe.

The opportunity for Eric to study at Cambridge was clearly a major factor in his life, not only as an educational experience that allowed him to develop his knowledge of, and life-long interest in, history, but also because it provided opportunities to experience a very different way of life from his earlier days in Sale, and to indulge some of his passion for other things, such as football, cricket, debating and the stage.

St Catharine's College, Cambridge, is situated in Trumpington Street and was founded in 1473 by Robert Woodlark (or Wodelark), then Provost of King's College. As of 2013 there were approximately 436 undergraduate students and 165 graduates, including both men and women, but at the time when Eric joined the College in 1952 only male students were admitted and considerably fewer students in total, probably less than 300, were enrolled. The Master of the College at that time was a military man, Donald Portway, author of *The Militant Don* (1964), *Military Science Today* (1940) and *Memoirs of an Academic Old Contemptible* (1971). When the College Fellows, to their Master's disgust, voted to install a smooth pathway round the cobbles surrounding the quadrangle because of the damage the cobbles did to ladies' shoes, Portway wrote a letter to *The Times* objecting to what he called the 'popsification' of the college.

When Eric arrived at St Catharine's College, commonly abbreviated to Cath's or Cat's (pronounced 'Catz'), there was a notice requesting all scholars and exhibitioners to attend a meeting in the study of the Junior Dean, Mr Lacey. Expecting to find a large group of people crammed into this room, he was somewhat surprised to discover that there were only about 12-14 attendees, two scholars and a small bunch of exhibitioners. They were informed that it was their duty to take turns in reading the Latin grace before dinner in 'hall', a task which Eric fulfilled without fully understanding the meaning of the words, although he can still recite them parrot fashion to this day.

Eric as first year undergraduate at Cambridge 1952/3

Until he got to Cambridge, Eric admits that he had not appreciated the fact that the undergraduate intake included only a relatively small number of scholars and exhibitioners like him, together with a much larger number of commoners who managed to obtain admission by other means. He had actually thought that the only way to gain admission was by winning a scholarship or exhibition. Because nobody from his family or school had any previous experience of the ways in which the older universities, like Cambridge and Oxford, operated, everything was very new and unfamiliar to him. The penny then dropped and he belatedly realized the significance of the remarks made by Teddy Rich during his 'mesmerising' interview, when he told Eric that he could have a place if he could also win a state or county scholarship. Rich evidently understood sympathetically that there were insufficient parental means for Eric to rely on for financial support. After that interview, Eric had waited anxiously for about two weeks before a letter arrived from Cambridge confirming that he had got in with an exhibition, even though he had been 'in' all the time.

The delayed recognition of the significance of being a scholar or exhibitioner rather than a commoner, was something of an Epiphany moment for Eric and it had a marked psychological effect on his outlook. As he has explained to the author, this new feeling of confidence was evident the next day when he first met his history tutor: 'rather than being someone who had just scraped in via a late call as a replacement and a dodgy interview, and likely to be clinging on by the skin of my academic teeth, I was one of whom quite a bit was expected, one of three in the history group of about a ten or so, who was looked upon with some aspiration. It was very bracing for me.'

The tutorial file about Eric in the St Catharine's College archives contains basic information about his family, schooling and examination attainments, and also notes that he had under-taken military service before coming up to Cambridge. It goes on to record that he studied History and gained a 2:1 in Part I of the History Tripos in 1954 and a First in Part II of the History Tripos in 1955 (one of only seventeen students in the whole University to gain a first in Part II that year). He was awarded the prestigious Figgis Memorial Prize by the College for his First in Part II (worth £40) and he was also made a lifelong Scholar of the College.

An extract from a reference written in 1955 by Eric's Pastoral Tutor, J.N. Gooderson, reads: 'He is one of those men whom it is impossible to recommend too highly and for whose successes superlatives are appropriate. He is a brilliant after-dinner speaker. As a personality he is cheerful, unassuming and thoroughly sound and reliable. He is popular with his colleagues and with the teaching staff.'

During his last year at Cambridge, whilst Eric was Secretary of the College Football Club, he sat next to the Master, Donald Portway, at the club's annual dinner. Portway greatly appreciated Eric's after-dinner speech, telling him it was a 'lost art' that he had revived. He particularly enjoyed Eric's reference to the Dean, Stanley Aston, who was responsible for a new residential complex for the College, and the suggestion that it should be called 'Aston Villa'.

The tutorial file also notes that 'while at St Catharine's he was a full back in the College XI, was a member of the Midnight Howlers (a College revue society), for whom he wrote scripts and regularly performed on stage.'

Eric's tutor at Cambridge was an Irishman, Oliver MacDonagh (1924-2002), who had studied History and Law at University College Dublin, graduating in 1944. He was a Fellow of St Catharine's College from 1952 until 1964, before going on to enjoy a brilliant career both in Ireland and Australia.

During his distinguished academic career, MacDonagh published over a hundred papers and thirteen books. His main early work was concerned with the ongoing debate about the amount of government intervention in British administration and the pattern of government growth. Oliver McDonagh's *The Passenger Acts: A Pattern of Government Growth*, published in 1961,was a seminal study in the inexorable expansion of state bureaucracy in the 19th century. Eric, who had caught on to this line of enquiry under McDonagh's tuition, was to be one of several to make this important issue the basis of their own academic research.

The history students at Cath's attended Oliver MacDonagh's weekly tutorials in pairs, and Eric's partner for this exercise was the man he had first met in Germany whilst they were both doing National Service, Tony Pearce. According to Tony :

> We shared the same Supervisor and we were required to write an essay to read to him once a week. My essay would be written in about 45 minutes immediately prior to the Supervision and would rarely gain more than five minutes of his attention. The only praise I received from him in three years was that he admired my epigrams. I would then spend the rest of the Supervision listening to a dialogue between two first-class minds.

According to Eric, Tony is being overly diffident about himself in the above description. In his opinion, his former study partner has a rare mind but never really got on with their joint supervisor and rather lost interest in proceedings, leaving most of the discussion to Eric and MacDonagh. With regard to procedure, the students evidently took turns to read their essays on alternate weeks, the non-reader simply handing in his work for written marking.

Away from the tutorial environment, Tony Pearce recalls that their main mutual interest was football, in which pursuit they both obtained College colours. He describes Eric as a doughty defender who read the game very well and who always managed to be in the right position to foil an opposition attack.

Tony and Eric also spent some time together in the College Revue Club, 'The Midnight Howlers', about which more later. He comments that they had an enormous amount of fun rehearsing for and performing a new show each term. The concerts were evidently very popular since a lot of the material was not only very funny but also quite outrageous. Tony particularly remembers Eric producing some excellent sketches and performing in them in his characteristic 'deadpan' style.

Eric and Tony Pearce have remained good friends since their Cambridge days in the 1950s and, although they went their separate ways, they have managed to meet regularly for lunch with a small group of other former St Catharine's men (originally seven, now reduced to three). They usually meet at Simpson's in The Strand, or at one of their London clubs, and rarely talk 'shop', but these occasions have allowed Tony to discover something about Eric's unusual and interesting career progression over the years. As he comments:

> One of the many things I admire about Eric is that he was never seduced into seeking a career in the public eye. Instead he preferred a 'portfolio' career, moving horizontally into a new field when he felt he needed a new challenge.

This perceptive analysis of Eric's unusual pattern of career progression anticipates much of what will become apparent in later chapters of the Midwinter story. Tony concluded his comments by saying:

> Eric has been a friend for 60 years and I value very highly the experience of such a penetrating intelligence, concealed behind a veil of modesty and the same bluff, down-to-earth exterior.

Like many of Eric's friends, old and new, Tony Pearce has always been glad to receive one of his occasional postcards and the fiendishly difficult Midwinter Christmas crossword puzzles ('Chrissy Chrossies'), which he claims only to have completed a couple of times in over 40 years.

Another student friend and lunch companion of Eric's at Cambridge was Mike Brookbank. He went up to St Catherine's College in 1950, two years ahead of Eric, so they were not exact contemporaries, but their time did overlap because Mike stayed on at the college for two years after graduation for further post-graduate studies. Mike was reading engineering, so their academic work did not overlap, but they were both keen footballers. As Mike recalls:

> When Eric arrived at the College in October 1952 I was just starting my year as captain of the club and would

have met Eric in the first week of term when we were trying to find players among the freshmen for the College teams. I cannot remember our first meeting, but Eric very quickly established himself as a regular and solidly reliable full-back in our 1st Eleven. We had a very successful team in those days. In his first year we were top of the inter-college league, which was played in the autumn term, and were finalists (losing to Emmanuel) in the inter-college cup competition (the 'cuppers'), which was played in the spring term.

St Catharine's College Association Football 1st team (1953/54). Eric seated far left next to Doug Bowler. His close friend, Tony Pearce, standing second from left

In Eric's second year the 1st eleven had a good league run and also reached the semi-finals of the cuppers, whilst in his third year they once more reached the final (under Doug Bowler's captaincy), eventually losing to Emmanuel again. This occasion was the one and only time that Eric played at Grange Road, the University football ground for both soccer and rugger.

Although Mike Brookbank was not himself a cricketer, he remembers a story that involved Eric's friend and sometime room-mate, Douglas Bowler. When Doug came on to bowl for the college team, the scorer would immediately shout out 'Bowler's name?' to which the response would be 'Bowler' and then 'Yes, bowler, what's his name?', 'Bowler', etc. No doubt Eric subsequently made good use of this episode in some of his many after-dinner talks to various organisations. Mike also observes that Eric, even as a university undergraduate, was a man of diverse interests including, among other things, the college debating society (The Lightfoot Society), and the University Labour Club.

What shines through in all of Mike Brookbank's recollections is Eric's sense of humour. However dire or serious the occasion might be, he could invariably be relied upon to find and bring out some comical element hidden in it.

MIDNIGHT HOWLERS AND THE LIGHTFOOT SOCIETY

During his time at St Catharine's College, Eric was heavily involved with the activities of both the Midnight Howlers and the Lightfoot Society. The Howlers put on light-hearted satirical revues, also known as smoking concerts, to which Eric regularly contributed as both writer and performer. As a reviewer wrote in the 1955 Society Magazine after a particularly funny performance, in which 'Eric Midwinter (with his elastic face) and others made marvellous fun of spiritualisms "Happy Mediums", after which it is evident that no one is really safe from the Howlers' winging shaft of wit'.

One of Eric's successful sketches for the Howlers, which became part of the canon, was a Hollywood skit with a biblical epic done as a Western, 'The Sons of Israel'.

Debates at the Lightfoot Society also seem to have been witty occasions, as reported in the Society Magazine accounts of some of the 1954-56 meetings. For example, in the 1954 issue:

The first debate of the Michaelmas Term – 'That Royalty should be abolished' – was remarkable mainly for an exceptionally fine speech by E. Midwinter. His points were that he was a Socialist, but not an active anti-Royalist; that he deplored the cost of maintaining the Royal Family, and hoped the Queen would 'do something about Manchester's public lavatories'.

After the other speakers – including D.J. Bowler, who confessed that there was little left for him to say on behalf of the Motion – had delivered their speeches, the Motion was evidently soundly defeated.

In the 1955 Society Magazine, it was reported from another meeting of the Lightfoot Society that 'Floreat Mancunium proved most popular, with Mr Midwinter renewing our acquaintance with Manchester's public lavatories.' A year later, the description of another meeting in the 1956 Magazine, involving a cross-talk act by two gentlemen from Birmingham, 'recalled the past glories of the famous Manchester act of Bowler and Midwinter'. It would seem that the public sanitary arrangements in Manchester provided a rich source of material for some of the debates staged by the Lightfoot Society during Eric's time.

Eric's evidently enjoyable and successful three years in Cambridge came to an end in the summer of 1955. He had achieved perhaps the main objective by obtaining a very good degree in history which, if things had worked out differently, might well have led him on to the first rung of a university academic career. However, as will become apparent, his somewhat unusual career pathway was to take him in other directions. The Cambridge experience also allowed Eric the opportunity to indulge his enthusiasm for sport, particularly football and, to a lesser extent, cricket, participate in light theatrical productions (as writer, performer and producer), get involved in debating and public speaking, to write, and to develop his interest in politics, all activities that he has maintained ever since. And so, at the tender age of twenty-three, the young man from Sale, the first member of his family to go to grammar school or to university, was now ready to dip his toe into the world of paid work.

THE WORLD OF WORK
1: THE TEACHER AND LECTURER

Eric Midwinter's professional career followed a highly unusual pathway in that it demonstrated a mainly horizontal trajectory rather than the more usual vertical progression through different levels of seniority within a circumscribed field of activity. He worked in education and teaching in various capacities, held posts in consumer and public affairs as a 'consumers' champion', and was engaged as a social gerontologist concerned with the social aspects of older age. He has also made numerous contributions as a social historian, with a particular emphasis on British comedians and comedy, and the history of sport. Throughout this interesting and diverse career, and continuing long afterwards and during his so-called retirement, Eric has produced a steady and impressive stream of books, articles and reviews on a wide variety of topics, as well as giving countless lectures and talks, both serious and more light-hearted, all over the country.

During his last year at Cambridge, Eric was accepted by Manchester University to study for a Post-graduate Education Certificate, then the prescribed route into the teaching profession. However, when he achieved a First in his final university examinations, siren voices, including those of some of his former teachers, whispered that teaching was possibly a little unambitious for someone of his potential. Accordingly, he pulled out of the offered Manchester place and sought other employment.

He was eventually taken on for a fast-track post-graduate post in the City of Manchester treasurer's department in the autumn of 1955, with the prospect of a grand career in local government unfolding before him. In the event, he soon found the work he was involved with extremely boring and absolutely hated it. He quickly realized that he had made a big mistake and that he should have stuck to his original idea about a career in teaching. Within a few weeks of commencing this unsatisfactory and unfulfilling local government appointment, he wandered into the Manchester education offices during one of his lunch breaks and was offered a temporary post at Manchester Central Grammar School – not to be confused with the more famous Manchester Grammar School.

EARLY SCHOOL AND COLLEGE TEACHING EXPERIENCE

Eric worked at this school for two terms, teaching history, English and games. Unfortunately, at this particular time it was what he describes as a dreadful, failing and undemanding school, but it gave Eric his first insight into how poor a school could be and, perhaps, stimulated him to look for ways in which secondary education could be improved in future.

During his short stay at the Manchester school, Eric applied for and was appointed to the post of history teacher at the newly opened Oldwood School in Wythenshawe, at the time the largest council estate in Europe. This was decidedly not a cosy suburban environment and it provided important early experience for Eric, which he was able to apply to his subsequent work in the Liverpool Educational Priority Area. He taught there from September 1956 to December 1958 and, in addition to teaching history, also became very involved with putting on pantomimes and musicals. He wrote and produced these in alliance with the music teacher, Jim Fairbanks, and their productions included intriguing titles such as 'Alpine Magic', 'When in Rome', and 'Cross Your Teas'. Eric had spotted that the usual school plays performed elsewhere were often not very attractive to either pupil or parent, particularly when the works of Shakespeare or other famous playwrights were gabbled unintelligibly and heard uncomprehendingly by the audience. Lots of children and almost all the teachers became involved in these Midwinter productions in a very enthusiastic way, and they received a huge and friendly response from the public who saw the shows. This was, Eric noted, his first major venture into community education; it also demonstrates that he was putting to good use the knowledge gained from his earlier experiences in the field of drama and entertainment at school and university.

Eric's propensity to ensure his teaching was enjoyable as well as informative did lead to questions being asked. Two teachers, both friends of Eric, who assumed major responsibility for the school's discipline, upbraided him because his classes used to emerge in a bubbling, excitable mood and sometimes create havoc for their next, perhaps weaker, teacher. They accused Eric of 'playing popular Jack'. On one occasion when Eric was dramatising some historical event to great amusement, the headmaster walked in. He immediately left without comment but sought out Eric at the end of the lesson and apologised for the interruption. He wryly explained that he had entered the classroom because he had heard loud laughter and his experience had always been that laughter meant trouble. Eric has never shifted from his basic position that, for children or adults, there can be no proper education unless it is being enjoyed.

Whilst working at Oldwood School, Eric made good his teaching qualifications by obtaining both the Educational Diploma of the College of Preceptors (now, since 1998, known as the College of Teachers) and an external Post-graduate Certificate in Education from the University of London, with a distinction in the practical. In the evenings he did drama in a youth club run in another Wythenshawe school and, later, with an operatic society in a Gorton school, both under the auspices of the local further education service. He also spent four or five years lecturing on international affairs for the Workers' Educational Asssociation (WEA) in nearby towns, such as Macclesfield, Irlam and Mossley. Since 1903, the WEA, a charity, has provided educational opportunities through locally organized part-time courses, for adults facing social and economic disadvantage.

All this activity, both in and outside the school, stood him in good stead with the educational authorities and he was advised by senior officers in the further education department to apply for a post as a lecturer in the Liberal Studies Department of the Manchester Regional College of Art. He took up and fulfilled this position from January 1959 until July 1961.

During his time at this college, Eric's Head of Department (Liberal Studies) was Bob Osbourn. Bob has fond memories of Eric as a friendly, effective and popular teacher and the two men have kept in touch ever since, even though they have not had an opportunity to meet since Eric left Manchester.

It was while he was teaching at the Manchester College of Art that Eric found himself lecturing in the very room where Neville Cardus, the famous cricket correspondent and music critic, had been married. This event allegedly took place during a match at Old Trafford, from which it is said that Cardus had absented himself temporarily in order commit 'the most respectable and irrevocable act in a mortal man's life' at Chorlton Register Office, before returning to the cricket. Unfortunately for lovers of a good story, in reality Lancashire were playing an away fixture on the day in question, so it seems that a certain degree of 'artistic licence' may have been applied to Cardus's amusing recollections of his nuptials. Eric recalls an occasion when a seminar was in full swing on the topic of Louis XIV when a young man stuck his head round the door and enquired "Is this where I register my Auntie Edna's death?" It transpired that the Old Chorlton Town Hall was an annexe to the college next door and had, for many years, housed the Chorlton Register Office.

In his last year at this college, Eric undertook the teaching of the entire liberal studies component for the first year introductory course at the Openshaw annexe. During this time, as well as giving a weekly lecture to all the students and looking after seven groups of students for a half day of liberal studies teaching, he was also able to 'knock together' a cabaret group from amongst them.

Teacher Training

1. Edge Hill College of Education

Eric became increasingly interested in education per se whilst at the Manchester Regional College of Art and spent a little time in the education department of the college during his last year there. He eventually applied for the post of history lecturer at two or three teachers' training colleges, including Edge Hill College, Ormskirk, where he was appointed in 1961 and worked until 1964.

Two significant things were happening to Edge Hill College of Education at the time that Eric was recruited to the staff in 1961; the original two-year course was being extended to three years, and the college had recently changed from being a women-only to a co-educational establishment. In addition to being the main history lecturer, ably assisted part-time by a very friendly and supportive vicar called William Hope, he was also the warden of the first men's hall of residence. From the viewpoint of a living-in member of staff, who also happened to be a social historian, Eric was able to observe how a long-standing female establishment reacted to being threatened and revolutionized by the invasion of male staff and students.

Eric has kept in touch with a number of colleagues from his days at Edge Hill in the 1960s. Amongst these is Brian Walsh, who started work there on the same day as Eric and has remained a close friend ever since. Brian comments on their time together at Edge Hill, as well as offering some more general, personal recollections about their long friendship.

Brian Walsh in 2014

I imagine I must be one of Eric's longest-standing acquaintances having enjoyed his friendship and that of his family with mine for the best part of a half-century. I count myself fortunate to have had access to his humanity, intellect and humour at frequent intervals over those years.

My years of closest contact and the basis of the friendship is our time together on the staff of Edge Hill College of Education (EHTC, since then the University of Edge Hill). Eric was appointed Head of History as part of the 'new wave' of staffing in response to developments then in teaching teacher training, specifically the introduction of male students to EHTC as it then was and the lengthening of the course to three years.

Whether there was a policy decision by Lancashire County Council to 'shake up' a rather cosy all-female training college for teachers of young children or not, this in retrospect was one effect of the staffing influx and I was appointed to the English Department, alongside John Martlew (English), Maurice Craft (Sociology) and Louis Cohen (Education and Sociology). Though there was little formal contact between the departments, I know that Eric steadily revolutionised the work of the History Department bringing in an emphasis on social history and the use of local records and primary materials making for a popular, rigorous and well-recruited course.

Eric broadly had an important impact on the development of the college professionally having the confidence of successive principals (Dr Bain and P.K.C. Millins). He also enriched the wider life of the college by introducing staff cricket and football teams, which fostered staff and staff/student links as well as relationships with neighbouring schools whose staffs we played. At this time Eric was a single man and he accepted the post of Warden of the men's hall of residence, which he oversaw with characteristic geniality and a blend of firmness and tolerance. As an aside, he flirted briefly with golf and we paid a few visits to the local municipal course but the game wasn't for him as he tended to hit every tee-shot like a cover drive.

Meanwhile, on a personal level, our own relationship grew from being involved in the wider life of the college and centrally from our mutual interest in Lancashire cricket and its varied fortunes from the war years onwards and in particular the many characters we enjoyed remembering from those times. To escape from the cloistered life of Warden of Stanley Hall, he appreciated being a frequent visitor to our home where he became an unofficial 'uncle' to our three children, two of whom to Eric's amusement, still refer to him as such. He struck an immediate chord with my wife, both being aficionados of Gilbert & Sullivan, she being, though I say it myself, an outstanding performer of alto leads in numerous amateur productions, and Eric a well-informed authority on the pair.

I suppose our shared interest in sport, with Eric's beloved Manchester United, and my Blackpool FC, old rivals though they be, our support of the eternally disappointing Lancashire County Cricket Club and a taste for old-time comedians such as Billy Bennett, Frank Randle, Robb Wilton and others have helped shape our long acquaintance.

To end on a personal note, over the years, visits to Fenner's, Lord's finals, Old Trafford and family occasions have helped maintain our friendship. I regard it as an enormous privilege to be in Eric's company. While he wears his vast intelligence and deep knowledge lightly, Eric likes a sounding board for his ideas and on occasion I have been able to act as that while watching the action 'in the middle'. In addition I think he needs the means of expressing his buzzing headful of thoughts and views beyond writing them down in his manifold collection of books, copies of most of which I have.

Continuing the Edge Hill story, the three other colleagues mentioned by Brian Walsh have also responded to requests for recollections about the time they shared there with Eric. Louis Cohen has written:

Eric and I arrived at Edge Hill College in 1961. The College was in the process of very rapid expansion. It changed from an all female institution to a large mixed group of students following a whole range of subject specialisms including some new disciplines such as Sociology and Social Work. The staff grew very quickly and included many male lecturers. Several older, female heads of department witnessed these changes with undisguised horror. I can still recall the looks of incredulity on the face of the head of English as she watched Eric entertaining his male colleagues with a mime he had once seen on the variety stage. Eric was totally extraordinary – someone who arrived at Edge Hill, out of the blue, and became almost overnight, the centre of attention.

Eric with Rev William Hope, his colleague at Edge Hill, in the 1960s

I recall the Vicar of Euxton, William Hope, a small, grave little man who did part-time teaching in Eric's Department, coming up to me in the Senior Common Room and pronouncing that Edge Hill had acquired a history scholar of high repute, a graduate with a first-class history degree from Cambridge. There's no doubt that Eric was singularly able. Some of his staff were more bemused by his behaviour as Head of Department but recognised that he had a powerful presence as a lecturer. The students worshipped him.

I had the dubious honor of sharing a large room with him that served as an office and a place to conduct tutorials with our respective student groups. It was rarely the case that his student groups arrived for tutorials at the same time that my Sociology groups were there. On one occasion, however, when I was struggling somewhat with an explanation of the provision of a national framework for state school education in the 19th century, a voice came from the other side of the room – "No, no, no, Lou"; Eric then gave an account of the three relevant Acts of Parliament with a virtuoso, neo-Marxist account off the top of his head!

Eric was single at the time we were at Edge Hill. I was married with a four-year-old son and we had a small apartment adjacent to the College. Eric used to come across for a meal with us on occasions and I recall one evening when Eric was doing a sort of clog dance on the low central heating radiator in the bay window and singing at the top of his voice when he stopped suddenly and walked over to David my son. 'Do you think I could get the whole of that pork pie into my mouth?' David said 'No', then Eric put the whole pie in his mouth and went back to resume his clog dance.

The College hierarchy soon adapted to Eric's unusual behavior. He charmed the Principal, a delightful, kind, genteel medieval French scholar. She seemed utterly impervious to the rapid changes going on about her. Eric was very fond of her. 'A vacuum in a velvet glove' was, I believe, one of his descriptions of her leadership.

Inevitably, we both moved on and, as is so often the case, lost touch.

Years and years ago, I saw Eric in the bookshop on one of the main London stations. He was engrossed with a copy of *Wisden*. I crept up behind him and said, 'I hope you are going to pay for that.' He turned round, looked at me, and said, 'You've done all right for yourself.'

After leaving Edge Hill College, Louis Cohen later became Professor of Education at Loughborough University and is co-author, with Lawrence Manion and Keith Morrison, of the book *Research Methods in Education*, first published in 2000.

Another former colleague, the sociologist Professor Maurice Craft, who went on to hold professorships at Exeter and Nottingham, and eventually became Dean of Education and Pro Vice-Chancellor of the University of Nottingham, has provided the following thoughts.

I met Eric Midwinter during the 1960s at Edge Hill Teacher Training College in SW Lancashire, where we were both on the staff. Edge Hill was founded in 1885 in Liverpool, and moved to a 34-acre campus outside the nearby small town of Ormskirk in 1933. After the war years when it became a military hospital and the staff and students were evacuated to Bingley in Yorkshire, it grew very rapidly during the 1960s and subsequently, eventually becoming a multi-Faculty, degree-awarding University of more than 20,000 students a few years ago.

Eric and I were among the growing number of young men appointed during the early 60s. Eric lived-in and dined in hall, as the only male among a group of older, long-established, unmarried women staff. Both he and they found this a new (and astonishing) social change, requiring much mutual adjustment. But with just one or two exceptions, Eric became much admired and respected, and with a great deal of charm, courtesy and tact he developed excellent relations with his new colleagues.

Eric was quickly recognised by us all as an extremely able Head of the History Department, and as a very affable fellow with a sharp and perceptive sense of humour, who was very well liked by both staff and students.

Eric's talents – as demonstrated in his subsequent career – went beyond the academic. In a College debate on the Common Market where he and I led opposite viewpoints he deployed incisive analysis and a broad and informed perspective. But in a brilliant College revue, which he wrote and directed, he also displayed a skilled understanding of humour and brought the house down. He might well have become a university professor, and I was delighted (but apprehensive) to encounter him once when we were both shortlisted candidates for a chair appointment. Instead, he progressed from directing an outstanding Liverpool project on educational underprivilege (he was resolutely egalitarian), to the Directorship of one of the UK's leading national charities for the aged, as well as writing authoritatively on cricket and on humour, amongst other things. I well remember passing a smart television retailer's in Lewisham, South London on one occasion and observing that all ten screens in the window were filled by Eric, talking about his current work in Liverpool. It was difficult to resist button-holing passers-by and declaring, 'Look! I know this famous chap!'

But Eric never got 'lift-off', he remained profoundly down-to-earth. At Edge Hill College, when several of us were writing our PhDs, I recall asking him why he had decided to do this. "I want to be called 'doctor'," he said, in his inimitable Manchester accent. How true that must be of so many doctoral candidates.

In a lifetime spent working in universities around the world, Eric Midwinter stands out memorably for me, and I consider it a privilege to have known him.

As well as covering the formal history syllabus at Edge Hill, Eric became very involved in both the teaching of history, about which he had somewhat avant garde views, and the history of education. He felt strongly that the latter was very necessary, properly done, for the students' understanding of the system in which they would work. At the same time he started work on his DPhil at Liverpool University, to which the college was affiliated.

Another of Eric's colleagues, John Martlew, has provided the following comments:

I first met Eric at Edge Hill College where we both arrived in the second wave of male staff at the previously all-female college. Most of the staff had been elderly ladies, almost aristocratic, who always took 'afternoon tea' together. There had been three all-female hostels, each run by elderly, unmarried ladies. Some had lost boy friends in the Great War.

When I first met Eric I thought he was quite formidable to look at, big, dark, almost Italian-looking. My initial thoughts were 'I don't much like the look of that bugger'. This was not entirely due to his size, but he looked a bit sulky - he isn't really, but has rather a 'dark look'. He was not inelegant in appearance and never looked a mess, although he was not very interested in clothes. My subsequent memories are of him always talking, laughing, discussing things, but with some element of comic narrative. There had been discussions about the possible problems of having boys and girls together in the same college and practical solutions about sleeping accommodation. As Eric said: 'They always imagine that you can only have sex at night.'

He thought of himself primarily as a historian, and was always referring to history; this often gave him the ability to see two sides to an argument. It was all part of the 1960s, more radical, approach. He was conscious of the need to present a more social view, this, along with his working class background, governed and conditioned his thinking in many ways. He was intellectually quite brilliant and, also, very good at handling people.

Previously, male staff had been 'nice' to the ladies (some of whom were very good) but slightly indulgent. Eric managed to get on with them (or most of them) extremely well, but he understood - as others didn't - what it must have been like to have this sudden invasion of new, self-centred and arrogant people thrust into this society. He was, therefore, much more sensitive to them than some, even though he might not have struck you as particularly sensitive on first acquaintance.

He is very political, I always thought that he should have gone into politics, perhaps to become an MP. I don't quite know why he didn't, maybe he did not like politicians or the political scene, but he never discussed it. I always felt that he would have been a very good politician, he knows how to be 'political'. He was strongly passionate about his socialist beliefs and influenced by various radical thinkers, as many people were in that new generation of people who went to university (for the first time) – we all were. My background was more middle-class (teachers), but we were all new to university. Eric's roots were different and he was very anxious to preserve them and, because of this, he has this awareness and functions very much intellectually. He got on very well with his colleague in the history department, the Revd William Hope, even though Eric was not religious himself and their political opinions often differed.

Intellectually, Eric can be very rigorous. He caused a minor problem at Edge Hill (over the performance of weaker students) because the college hardly ever got rid of students (on academic grounds – some occasionally had to leave for other reasons). He and Louis Cohen decided that there were some who really ought to be failed; four or five students were not up to it or had done insufficient work. His main concern was that children ought to be properly taught by competent/properly qualified teachers. There was a bit of a 'mother hen' attitude amongst some of the staff, especially towards student who were training to teach infant/junior children, and they tended to protect their students. All in all, intellectually, he was very stringent and demanding.

John and Eric wrote a show together for Edge Hill College called 'Book Me a Penguin'. They did it with students and included some so-called 'louts' in the production, that is students who did not quite fit in with the traditional ethos and gentility of the College. This was not done provocatively, but because Eric saw another side to them. In fact, he was anxious not to distress the older staff, but by the time the revue was staged they were so enamoured of him there was little danger of upsetting them, but, nevertheless, he was careful. The two of them were encouraged to put on this revue because they and the Principal had been disappointed by the students' own somewhat abject efforts to produce end of term shows that were overloaded, undiscriminating and generally awful. They decided on a small team of about ten students, plus a pianist, and they contributed a couple of duos themselves. The whole thing lasted about 40-45 minutes, without an interval, and they did four shows, two on each of two consecutive nights, all well attended.

The combined programme and ticket (free to staff and students) was in in the four-sided form of a Penguin book cover, using the different Penguin genre colours (i.e. blue, green, red and brown), as if the title was 'Book Me a Penguin' by Mildew Martwinter. Each scene/sketch was named after a book title, such as 'Withering Slights', and there was a series of spoof TV advertisements based on well-known songs from Gilbert and Sullivan. A protest march, speech and song on behalf of 'The Campaign for Sociological Rearmament' went down particularly well, perhaps because Maurice Craft had only just introduced Sociology as a subject into the college. Eric and John did a sketch about how medals were given out in the British, American and Chinese armies, and then a cabaret-style version of 'Back in the Old Routine', each with a brush as a prop. As far as Eric can remember, the whole show went off brilliantly and was very well received by the audiences.

Eric has provided a couple of amusing tales about school practice whilst he was working at Edge Hill. His very first visit to watch a student-teacher work was during a PE lesson for juniors at a school in Walton, Liverpool. As he walked into the playground, the first thing he heard was the young lady student cry out 'All grip your balls tightly'. Unsurprisingly, perhaps, under the circumstances, he felt unable to follow her instructions to the letter.

In Eric's own words:

> Actual teaching practice was a real culture-shock for students; one or two gave up altogether (mind you, when I was Warden of a hall of residence, one student didn't

get that far. I was at the entrance, mine host, smiling and welcoming, when a car drove up; a mum and dad got out and half carried half dragged their son towards me, rather as if some drugged prisoner was being pulled to the scaffold. I thought he had fallen ill en route but no, it was culture shock – we took him to the sanatorium to recover and then they took him home and that was the full weight of his college life). Anyway, a school practice was on and I was sitting in my study one evening and one of my history students (but not one I was supervising on the practice) knocked on the door and burst in smoking a cigarette, which was rather frowned upon in the college, and collapsed in a chair. She was in something of a state. She told me this horror story of teaching art to a class of rumbustious lads at a secondary school in a mining village just outside of Wigan. The boys seemed to prefer physics, finding it interesting to roll the jars of water in which paintbrushes were supposed to be dipped across the floor. Just as one of the college art tutors walked through the classroom door to watch her teach, she stepped on one of these rolling jars and went base over apex to ribald cheers and an encouraging cry of 'pick tha bluddy feet oop, miss'.

I tried to sympathise, despite being distracted by her smoking, especially as she was using my waste paper basket (I was a non-smoker) for an ashtray. She lit ciggy after ciggy and the room was filled with a blue haze. I spoke to her on the subject, asking her how many had she smoked since getting back to college from the scene of this unfortunate incident about two hours before. Lighting another from the stub of the last, she blurted through the smoke rings, 'thirteen'. 'Thirteen', I said horrified, 'how many do you normally smoke? Taking two or three more long deep inhalations, she answered, 'I don't smoke'.

One of Eric's mature students at Edge Hill was Tony McGrath, who started as a student there at the age of thirty. His particular course included a history lecture every Monday and a tutorial on Fridays. His group was made up of about thirty students and they were expected to produce one essay per fortnight, with no messing about or excuses. As Eric had told them, 'You've come here to work'. It was made perfectly clear that their careers depended upon them doing their best.

According to Tony, Eric always had a firm grip on things; he worked hard himself and he made the students work hard too: 'Work was work and socializing was socialising'. They did have occasional 'hot pot' evenings, at which Eric was revealed as a great entertainer. As a well-balanced lecturer, Eric was dedicated and efficient – 'He brought the subject alive and made it live'. He was much valued as a teacher, offered encouragement and incentives to students, and generally made things possible. He was also strikingly honest with everybody.

After completing his course, Tony McGrath went in to the field of Special Education, working at a residential school for children with epilepsy. On a personal level, over fifty years since he was a student at Edge Hill College, he commented that Eric stood out as a teacher to remember. He had a wide interest in many fields, putting his heart and soul into everything he did, and was altogether, 'An unforgettable person in my life'. Very sadly, Tony died shortly after providing the above summary of some of his memories.

It seems clear from the extensive and generous testimonies quoted above from his contemporaries at Edge Hill that Eric created quite an impression on everyone at the college, even though some of the older female members of staff may have been rather shocked by his more 'progressive' methods and attitudes to education. He was promoted to Senior Lecturer after only one year in post, indicating that he was highly thought of by the principal and senior colleagues, and he began to build up a small staff in the History Department before moving on to his next position in Northumberland.

2. NORTHUMBERLAND COLLEGE

Eric left Edge Hill College in 1964 to help open and establish the newly created Northumberland College in Ponteland, near Newcastle, and so he found himself working in yet another new institution. He was appointed as Principal Lecturer and Head of History, but as the college deliberately had no vice-principal, the principal lecturers acted as a kind of advisory council, with added responsibilities. In Eric's case, these involved having some control over a mixed group of staff and students at a college annexe in Hexham. So, in addition to his teaching commitments, Eric was also gaining valuable administrative experience.

Whilst at Northumberland College, Eric devised an educational approach whereby a principal lecturer, such as himself, formed a team comprising an education tutor, a humanities tutor, an art or music tutor, and a science or mathematics tutor. Such six or seven person teams were required collectively to organise the education studies of a group of students and to supervise their work in schools. This original attempt at such a modular approach, involving small teams of staff, seemed to work successfully in Northumberland and Eric developed this idea further in the various places where he subsequently worked.

Having enjoyed a most congenial and rewarding time at Edge Hill, Eric found this post at Northumberland College rather less satisfactory and enjoyable. In retrospect, he considers it to have been comparable to taking some unpleasant medicine that was probably good for him, but he was glad when he had finished taking it.

It was during his time at Northumberland College, despite his other responsibilities, that Eric was able to complete the work for his doctoral thesis.

Whilst he was working at Edge Hill College, Eric decided that the intellectual sort of life beckoned and that he ought to further his academic qualifications. He had always enjoyed study, especially when it had a purpose, and he was attracted by the idea of gaining a doctorate. The University of Cambridge, where he had studied as an undergraduate, did not allow graduates to take external degrees, so he was forced to look elsewhere in order to register for a doctoral degree. Many universities would only deal with their own graduates; some, like London, required potential candidates to take their own BA and MA degrees first, and others either set distance limitations (e.g. Sheffield) or required that you either lived in their home city or chose something about that city as the subject for the dissertation (e.g. Leeds).

Eventually, he found that Edge Hill was linked with the University of Liverpool, as all the training colleges had to be grouped around a university, and there was a clause in the regulations that allowed aligned lecturers to register for Liverpool degrees. So Eric was able to register as an external postgraduate student and had completed about two years of study when, in 1964, he was offered the new post in Northumberland. His laid-back Irish tutor at Liverpool University, Dr W.J. Rowe, Reader in Modern History, initially advised Eric that because he had got so far with his studies, it would be quite acceptable for him to complete the degree whilst working elsewhere. Unfortunately, after he had accepted the new job, it transpired that this advice was wrong and he was barred on geographical/residential grounds from taking the Liverpool degree.

To make matters worse, most universities made it clear that doing two years work somewhere else under the direction of some other supervisor was not acceptable and Eric was faced with the possibility of having to start all over again in a new place with a different subject. Newcastle University, to which Northumberland College was linked and which was conveniently situated nearby, did not at that time make any appropriate provision for college lecturers to register. Fortunately, Eric struck lucky at York University, which was established in 1963 and had only recently opened for business. The tutor who interviewed him was very helpful and, although they had not yet fully sorted out the regulations, they took on Eric as an external student. As he already had two years research under his belt, Eric was able to complete his work between 1964-66 and he became, possibly, the first successful DPhil graduate in the arts faculty at York University. Incidentally, once the degree regulations had been formalised and issued after Eric's registration, he would not have qualified on residential grounds, even though the 90 or so miles distance by rail between Newcastle and York was not particularly far. So it was a stroke of extremely good fortune that after all the earlier disappointments he had managed to register for the DPhil degree before the new regulations had actually come into force.

Eric's major school studies were in 19th century history and his interest in political science and theory, including concepts of government, had already started to develop at that early stage. At Cambridge the course was much more widely ranging and included a course in political thought from the Greeks onwards. He was fascinated by a final year course in 'Theory of the Modern State', and became very interested in Benthamism and Utilitarianism, especially in their social effects on actual administration. Eric's tutor at St Catharine's College, Oliver McDonagh, was a 19th century specialist, and his own work and publications involved arguments about laissez-faire and state intervention in Victorian times, control of passenger shipping being his particular research area.

Eric's interest was more on the social than the commercial side of the story and he decided to look at governmental efforts, both central and local, to cope with the social effects of industrialism and urbanisation. It seemed to him that Lancashire, where he was at the time situated whilst at Edge Hill, offered the perfect cockpit for this, since it was the world's first major industrial region. Helpfully, Eric was able to incorporate his research interest in this aspect of social history into some of his teaching at the college, with students undertaking small, related projects of their own, which made life a little easier.

The original intention was to trawl the Lancashire local press for coverage of reactions to the three great evils of poverty, sickness and crime, each of which was exacerbated by the effects of urban overcrowding and industrialisation. However, this approach was considered to be too narrow and Eric was encouraged to embark on a mainline study of how these great central issues actually played out on the ground. Inevitably, such studies involved detailed consideration of the effects of new Poor Law that was passed in 1834, as well as the 1835 Municipal Corporations Act, the 1839 Rural Constabularies Act and the 1848 Public Health Act, and the important influence of Edwin Chadwick, secretary and disciple of Jeremy Bentham, in all three areas of interest.

Eric's timetable was to cover one main theme per year, with a fourth year to polish, finalise and draw parallels between each section. In practice, notwithstanding the problems of changing jobs and switching his registration to a different university, this plan worked very smoothly and he was able to start the fourth year of study with three mini-themes already completed. Five copies of each were kept in different locations in case disaster struck and all the material was somehow lost, as had happened to an unfortunate colleague.

Fees for postgraduate students were relatively modest in the 1960s, Eric recalls that they amounted to less than £200 in his case, so the main cost associated with carrying out the research lay in the travel expenses, since the sources of information were widespread. These included the Lancashire Record Office at Preston, the Manchester Central Reference Library, which was already Eric's intellectual spiritual home, and the Public Record Office in London. Many local libraries retained their own records, such as the minutes of poor law guardians' meetings and public health board minutes. As a result, numerous visits had to be made to town halls and libraries in places like Blackburn, Darwen and other Lancashire towns in order to gather the evidence.

In Wigan library Eric discovered the first minute book of the Wigan police. This find was sufficiently interesting and 'Will Hay-like' in character to be written up separately as a booklet that was published by the Borthwick Society. This led to Eric being interviewed in his own sitting room by John Humphrys when he was a young BBC North reporter. The two men met again years later when both of them were considerably older and in a different way of life.

Both W.J. Rowe, Eric's initial tutor at the University of Liverpool, and Professor G.A. Williams, his fiery and energetic Welsh tutor at York, recommended that Eric should mark out his academic claims by publishing articles on his work. Accordingly, four such papers were published in various journals between 1965-68. One outcome of this was an invitation from a commissioning editor, Patrick Richardson, who had read some of the articles, for Eric to write his first book – *Victorian Social Reform* – which was published by Longman as one of their 'Seminar Studies in History' series in 1968. This book endured in print for 22 years, and he was subsequently asked to do a second volume on *Nineteenth Century Education*, which appeared in 1970.

Gwyn Alfred Williams (1925-1995) was a Marxist historian who later, in 1974, moved on from York to the Chair in History at Cardiff University and did great things for Welsh history from a left-wing viewpoint. His activities there included

E. C. Midwinter

Victorian
Social Reform

writing and presenting a 13-part television series on Welsh history with Wynford Vaughan-Thomas. He was known as an exciting lecturer who was able to draw large crowds from across the university to his presentations. According to Eric, he was enormously encouraging and full of gusto, and the two of them got on really well. His line comments on Eric's drafts were evidently very good; on a particular page that was concerned with the effects of cholera he scribbled 'Oh God, I can feel it coming on'. When Eric applied for his next job, the Vice-Principal's post at Ethel Wormald College, he wrote a reference for Eric which Williams described as 'a piece of controlled hysteria'. He clearly had a very influential effect on Eric's thinking and it is unfortunate that he did not survive long enough to be invited to contribute some pertinent, Welsh-flavoured comments to this biographical study.

Social
Administration
in Lancashire
1830–1860

POOR
LAW

PUBLIC

HEALTH

POLICE

E C Midwinter

It is not easy to summarise the contents and conclusions from Eric's extensive doctoral studies in a few words, but, fortunately for those wishing to learn more about it, his thesis was published in book form under the title *Social Administration in Lancashire, 1830-1860* (Manchester University Press, 1969 – and can also be accessed on-line).

The external examiner for Eric's oral examination in York was the very distinguished historian Professor Asa Briggs (now Lord Briggs), who wrote in a letter to the author 'I was impressed by Eric's D.Phil, but do not even have a copy of my report on it. I knew that our interests converged.' Lord Briggs also kindly expressed pleasure in learning that someone was writing a biography of Eric. It was on Asa Briggs's recommendation that the thesis was published. Some years later, the two men were to meet again under rather different circumstances when Lord Briggs presented Eric with an honorary doctorate from the Open University, of which he was Chancellor from 1978-94. The York DPhil degree was actually awarded to Eric after he had returned to Liverpool to start work at his next job so, ironically, he was back in the same collegiate grouping from where he had originally started his doctoral studies.

After successfully completing his DPhil, Eric went on to do an MA (Ed) at Liverpool, in order to ensure that he had strong educational qualifications and because he enjoyed the business of purpose-based research. For this degree he continued with similar methodology to that used for his DPhil and examined the development of public education in Lancashire, especially in terms of the 1870 Act and up until the 1902 Education Act. This work included some case-studies of particular School Boards and other 'attendance' authorities, where, once again, he was keen to assess the impact of a major piece of legislation and its reception locally.

Eric confesses that the whole issue of the place of local government in respect of the individual and the state has been a continuing area of interest throughout his adult life and it has also been at the heart of much of the work he has done professionally in various capacities.

3. ETHEL WORMALD COLLEGE

As part of the Government's policy of expanding access to education in the 1960s, especially for those who had missed out on earlier opportunities due to the lasting effects of the second World War, or because of motherhood and childcare responsibilities, it was decided that every large area of population should have a day college for mature students. One such college created during this period was Ethel Wormald College in Mount Pleasant, Liverpool, named after Dame Ethel Wormald, a Liverpool City Councillor who served for a number of years as chairman of the Education Committee and became Lord Mayor of Liverpool in 1967-68. Dame Ethel was also chair of the governors of the college that bore her name.

Eric applied for the post of vice-principal at Ethel Wormald College and was duly appointed, serving there from January, 1966 until July, 1968. In passing, this may be noted as yet another instance of a 'new' institution in Eric's eventful and somewhat tortuous career pathway. After the appointment, the Chief Inspector of Schools, Tom McManners, took Eric to one side and told him that he had pressed for his appointment, having been very impressed by his brightness. In response to a question about why he had changed jobs so often, he had astutely replied 'in order to gain the experience intensely and swiftly so that I could apply for a post such as this', and the panache of this approach had evidently pleased Tom McManners. He confided to Eric that the principal had really wanted to appoint someone else, who had been on the short list with him when he was chosen as principal, but the appointments committee thought otherwise. Tom concluded this conversation with a big smile, saying 'If you move again within thee years I'll kill you, I'll ruin your career'.

It transpired that Tom became something of a kingmaker for Eric and he was a most important element in his early career. Eric admits that he has never known anyone so objective about talent and commitment – he regarded most of what Eric got up to as crazy and did not believe in half the things that he did – but he backed those who had the confidence and the wit to have a go at what they believed in. Eric has never met anyone else with that degree of stepping back and giving people the practical liberty to be faithful to their beliefs.

Ethel Wormald was a small college, beginning with just a first year intake of students and Eric ran the history course for a year, in addition to his other administrative duties. He also worked closely with the education department, where he made two very close friends, Norman Garner and Ron Palmer (sadly both now dead), and everything went 'swimmingly' well. Eric also did some work for Tom McManners on courses for Liverpool teachers.

Another former colleague, Harry Pepp, who first met Eric when he was just about to leave Ethel Wormald College, has sent the following reminiscences:

> Eric, unlike me, was blessed with an amazing memory and I marvelled at his ability to tell a story, offering a narrative or recollection in great detail and richness. Unfortunately I can remember very little of the detail of what he said but I do recall his favourite subjects: the Midwinter family history in and around South Manchester, working class culture, especially the music halls and the comedians and the history of Manchester United and Lancashire Cricket club. As an American with no background in any of these subjects, I could only listen in amazement.

> I didn`t actually work with Eric at Ethel Wormald College because, as I came in, he left. I met him on the day of my appointment and he advised me that I would

be invited to dinner at the house of Alec Walters, the principal, and that I mustn`t eat the curried eggs. The last one who did died a few days later. I took his advice.

We became friends subsequently as we learned we were near neighbours. Our wives were in the same baby-sitting circle and our boys went to the same primary school. Friday night at the Crow`s Nest, our local pub, with the Costigan brothers, who continually expressed their disappointments in teaching, became a regular event as did Saturdays in our garden playing football and then on to the local football club, Marine, in the northern premier league I think, with the kids in tow. We would bunk in at halftime so we didn`t have to pay.

I can remember a few pieces of wisdom: Eric knew there would never be a Third World War. If the Russians wanted to invade across the German border in the 1950s there could be no weaker spot than the British manned border on a Saturday night when no one was sober. He advised me to leave Liverpool because it had no future. Eric has a great enthusiasm for everything that interests him, and great wit, intelligence, determination, generosity and a propensity for friendship.

After a happy and successful time at Ethel Wormald College, things were about to change once again as another new opportunity presented itself to Eric, this time in the form of the Liverpool Educational Priority Area Project. In the relatively few years between 1956 and 1968, Eric had gained considerable experience of teaching in schools and several different colleges, he had successfully completed his DPhil, he was the youngest vice-principal in the country, and he had started his distinguished career as an author. The time was clearly now right for another new challenge.

THE WORLD OF WORK
2: THE COMMUNITY EDUCATOR

ANOTHER NEW APPOINTMENT

One Friday in the early summer of 1968, just a term short of three years after he had started working at Ethel Wormald College, Tom McManners came to see Eric and asked him bluntly why he had not applied for the post of Director of the Liverpool Educational Priority Area (EPA) Project. Eric had actually seen the advertisement and quite fancied the job, but, typically, responded with a question of his own: 'Who was the rotten bastard who threatened to kill me if I moved jobs within three years?' Tom's face was the picture of injured innocence – 'would I do a thing like that?' – and he suggested that if Eric were to do this job well it would help to complete his CV nicely and set him up to apply for a job as principal of a college at a remarkably early age. When Eric proposed to have an immediate word with the principal about applying for this new post, Tom's response, in Thomas Cromwellian – or even Machiavellian – fashion, was to say 'Not today, otherwise he'll associate it with my visit – tell him on Monday'.

Inconveniently, the following Monday was the very day of the interviews, so Eric had to write an essay about his thoughts on the job over the weekend and hand it in with his application to the Liverpool Education Department offices early that morning, before going to the college to explain to the Principal that he was just off for an interview. Fortuitously, both sites were within central Liverpool, so he had time to do all this during the morning. One or two of the other applicants had already been interviewed for the London EPA post and were also short listed for the Liverpool one, but Tom McManners wanted, if possible, to have one of his own lads *in situ* rather than some 'jackanapes' from outside.

The candidates gathered in the ante-room at the appointed time and Tom came out to announce that they were going to be interviewed in alphabetical order, apart from Dr Midwinter, who would be seen after lunch. Although he advised them not to read anything into this unusual arrangement, the other candidates all looked at Eric incredulously and feared the worst, no doubt wondering why the selection committee was going to all this trouble if there was no particular reason. In fact the explanation was that, because of Eric's last minute application, some of the interview committee, most notably Professor A.H. (Chelly) Halsey and Her Majesty's Inspector of Schools (HMI) John Gregory, had not yet had an opportunity to see his application or to read his essay. They were thus able to catch up with the paperwork over lunch.

According to Eric, the interview was the best of his life. He and Professor Halsey evidently got on from the start like a pair of houses on fire, at one point Chelly Halsey even remarked 'You are appealing to my prejudices', and Eric continued to ramble on merrily in full flow. Tom McManners never said a word, but after a while he signalled – ever so delicately – that it was time for Eric to stop waffling by slightly jerking his head towards the door and mouthing the words 'bugger off'. Never slow to take a hint, Eric finished the sentence he was on somewhat abruptly and quickly beat his retreat, realising afterwards that he might have grown a touch over-confident and had been rabbiting on needlessly. As Tom succinctly remarked later 'You'd talked yourself into the job, there was no need to talk yourself out of it'. Following this selection interview, Eric was duly appointed in 1968 as Director of the Liverpool Educational Priority Project; all in all, he says, it was a very Liverpool-style appointment.

Thus started a very important phase in Eric's career, during which he and others were to break new ground in the world of education, by encouraging the involvement of the local community into the process. However, before attempting to relate some of his experiences and achievements in Liverpool over the next few years, it might be useful to step back for a moment and consider the background to the creation of the Liverpool Educational Priority Area.

THE PLOWDEN REPORT AND EDUCATIONAL PRIORITY AREAS

The report of the Central Advisory Council For Education (England) into Primary Education in England, entitled *Children and their Primary Schools*, was published in 1967 and is unofficially referred to as 'The Plowden Report'. The report was commissioned in 1963 by Sir Edward Boyle, the Conservative Education minister at the time, and was chaired by Lady Plowden. Bridget Plowden (1910 – 2000) was described in *Education Unlimited* as a 'consensus-seeking committee chairman whose controversial report changed the course of primary education' and was renowned for her enthusiasm for 'getting things done'. As there had been a change in government during the period when the council was carrying out its deliberations, the final report was presented to the new Labour Secretary of State for Education and Science, Anthony Crosland, in October, 1966.

The 1967 report was notable for praising child-centred approaches to education, stressing that 'at the heart of the educational process lies the child' or, as the educational commentator Sandra Jones has put it, 'making the child the centre of the educational process, not the outer edge of it.'

Michael Young, a member of the Plowden council, wrote the three chapters of greatest significance to this account, on educational priority areas, home-school relations and community education: legend has it that he completed these in a single stretch of many hours, fortified by frequent doses of black coffee.

As is fully described by Eric in his book *Priority Education*, which was published by Penguin in 1972 (as one of its *Educational Specials* series), the national Education Priority Area (EPA) project arose out of the Plowden Report's concern with the problems that characterized certain underprivileged areas of the country. One particular recommendation was that 'research should be started to discover which of the developments in Educational Priority Areas have the more constructive effects, so as to assist in planning the longer term programme to follow'. In response to this advice, the Department of Education and Science (DES), together with the Social Sciences Research Council (SSRC), awarded grants for action-research in a number of areas. Michael Young, Chairman of the Institute of Urban Studies and of the SSRC, was appointed Chairman of the National EPA Steering Committee, and A.H. Halsey, Head of the Oxford University Department of Social and Administrative Studies, was appointed National Director. In view of Halsey's academic base, Oxford University was designated as the national headquarters of the EPA project. The £180,000 grant was, at the time, the largest sum ever awarded for one educational programme. As Eric walked through the mean streets of Liverpool 7 and 8 in the years following his appointment, he sometimes chuckled to think that, for pay and conditions, he was on a par with a Reader of the University of Oxford.

The remit for these EPAs outlined four main aims: to raise educational standards, to lift teacher morale, to strengthen home and school links, and to assist in giving communities a sense of responsibility. Altogether quite a stiff challenge, prompting Eric to ask his colleagues at Ethel Wormald College 'What do we do in the second week?' Eric was allocated thirteen schools in which to operate, for which he created a programme whereby each did a curriculum project, a home/ school project and a community involvement project, thus giving rise to 39 mini-projects in total. Each school was also asked to appoint a Project Liaison Teacher and Eric arranged a dedicated link with a local College of Education.

Mothers in the classroom for a coffee morning in a Liverpool school

A detailed and extremely useful analysis of the history of the Northern EPA Projects has been published recently by Dr Keith Williams, Senior Lecturer in Education at Edge Hill University, in his PhD Thesis entitled 'The North of England Educational Priority Area Projects 1968 – 1971 (University of London, Institute of Education, 2012). Sincere thanks are due to Keith for making this and other related documents available whilst researching this book. In correspondence, he also remarked 'I would say that every person I met was very complimentary of Dr Midwinter – charismatic, stand-up funny, persuasive and approachable. Professor A.H. Halsey said that he relied on Dr Midwinter to generate the high profile for community education he and Michael Young wanted'.

Chelley Halsey (1923 – 2014), aged over ninety when he responded to the author, kindly contributed the following comments:

> I am delighted to learn that you will write a biography of Eric Midwinter. I wish I could be more helpful but my memory has deteriorated these past few years but I do remember him most vividly in an episodic and unsystematic way. For the latter I can only urge you to go through the EPA literature and thereby put Eric into place as an important, if individualistic, contributor to the whole field of education in modern education and its urban slum dwellers. Tony Crosland suggested to Michael Young and me that we should explore current theories of education for the urban poor with special reference to the then new American 'Headstart' programme in Britain in the late 1960s. Crosland was Secretary of State for Education, I was his adviser, and Michael was the first Chairman of the newly formed Social Science Research Council.
>
> Our plan was to start parallel projects in London, Birmingham, the West Riding and Liverpool, with a fifth Scottish project in Dundee. Each was to be pretty much autonomous but I was to coordinate the research aspect from Oxford. I toured the country looking for a project director in the four chosen English places, and so I met Eric. He interviewed brilliantly and he was an immediate enthusiast with a lively set of ideas for Liverpool. We quickly became close friends and I knew he would produce a really exciting and useful analysis of the Liverpool scene. And he did.
>
> At the end, and after I had presented our five volumes to the new Secretary of State for Education, Margaret

Thatcher in 1980, the chair of education at Cambridge became vacant and I tried hard to persuade them to elect Eric (apparently this plan was unknown to Eric himself at the time). They failed to do so. But perhaps that was a triumph rather than a disaster because, as you know, Michael had also noticed Eric's diverse talents and was instrumental in starting him on a new and successful career in London, firstly as a champion of consumers, and then of older people.

Eric had a constant flow of really amusing jokes. Just before Christmas, on the morning that I was off to deliver a lecture on the EPA projects to a conference in York attended by Edward Boyle, Eric sent me a postcard depicting two men in full Arab dress outside the Lodge at Nuffield College. The porter asked one of them for a name. 'HEROD' was the reply.' We want to see Professor Halsey: we have a solution to the pre-school children problem'.

It is a characteristic of many of the responses the author has received from people when commenting about Eric and his work, that they recall his sense of humour and unerring ability to find a suitable story or joke for every occasion.

As pointed out by Keith Williams in his thesis, the late 1960s was an opportune time for the EPA project, since primary education had become the focus of much research and policy interest. The Plowden Report had sustained this focus and helped to create an opportunity for Chelly Halsey and Michael Young to pursue some of their ideas on education and their ambitions for restructuring the relationship between school and family.

The next few years of Eric's working life in Liverpool, as he got to grips with the challenges of carrying out ground break-ing educational work within an area beset with social and economic problems, were highly significant and he himself regards this time as the crux of his career. The contributions to education that Eric and his team made during this period were to achieve national recognition and this certainly helped to raise his personal profile in a number of ways, through his writing, lectures, radio and television appearances, thus opening the door to other opportunities in later years. The two main television opportunities were the first of a new Sunday afternoon series simply called 'The Education Programme', and, later, having a Thames Television 'This Week' programme devoted to the Liverpool EPA.

The early stages of the LEPA project were mainly taken up with building a small and active team, establishing good working relationships with a number of local schools, and planning the different aspect of the work to be carried out. A key staff appointment was that of Keith Pulham, who joined Eric's team as his Research Officer and second in command.

The project team went on to develop a number of the innovative activities and, in his book *Priority Education*, Eric describes four case studies as examples of some of the activities of the LEPA.

THE PADDINGTON PLAYMOBILE

In order to develop some form of pre-school provision for the many under-fives (and their parents) within the Liverpool EPA who had no access to such educational opportunities, the team managed to obtain and convert an old bus from the Transport Department. After sorting out various logistic problems associated with insuring, garaging, running and maintaining the vehicle, the task of converting the bus was undertaken by the boys and girls from Paddington Comprehensive School, supervised by the technical and art staff of the school, as a piece of 'community service'. Some of these children were involved mainly with metalwork aspects of the conversion, whilst others preferred working with wood or more general tasks. Potential vandals amongst the young workers may particularly

PRE-SCHOOL PRIORITIES

A short history of
alternative
pre-schooling in Liverpool

have enjoyed the task of stripping out the passenger seats and other fittings from the old bus, without fear of prosecution!

Clearly great ingenuity was shown in the design and creation of the Playmobile, which included such child-friendly features as dummy steering wheels at the front, infant-sized desks, a ladder and slide, and a Wendy House. The whole creative exercise was much appreciated by the children and teaching staff involved, to the extent that Eric later wrote 'I always maintained that, had the bus never left the school campus, it would still have been a worthwhile project. It fulfilled the two vital necessities of community education at secondary level; that is, it contributed a benefit to the local community and, at the same time, it was of educational value to the children involved'.

The initial three standpoints where the completed Playmobile was deployed were outside the house of a lady who had already tried to establish a playgroup but failed to find suitable accommodation, another was outside an eleven-storey block of flats where no pre-school facilities were available, and the third was in a space amongst a solid and dreary pre-war flat development. In each case, after its presence became known, the big, brightly coloured bus attracted the attention of local mothers with young children and it quickly became over-subscribed. In some instances, it acted as a stimulus for the initiation of a playgroup in a particular area prior to the group being relocated in a more permanent location with a larger capacity.

The Playmobile evidently made a big impact wherever it toured and was a fine 'publicity-monger' for the whole LEPA project. It was featured more than ten times on television and a thick file of newspaper cuttings had soon been accumulated. The idea has subsequently been much imitated elsewhere, and Playmobiles or Playbuses have been introduced into many parts of the country since the original experiment in Liverpool, with interest in this approach to the delivery of pre-school activities continuing to the present day. As Eric has pointed out, the Playmobile showed that its flexibility allowed it to meet the various and swiftly-changing patterns of pre-school needs and that it was potentially as viable in rural as in urban environments. All in all, this was an important and effective innovation, with obvious advantages for areas lacking other forms of pre-school provision, and its conspicuous success helped to raise the profile of what Eric and his LEPA team were trying to achieve.

Keith Pulham has added some of his own recollections about the Playmobile:

> Every child coming on board could don a busman's hat and ring the bell.

The bus was officially launched by a local councillor, Mrs Margaret Simey, utilising a bottle of 'suitably diluted' welfare orange juice for the ceremony. It is reported that it went off to its first assignment wearing a smug expression on its bonnet.

The concept of, as Eric put it, 'Taking the mountain to Mahomed' worked very well. Families with very young children, many on low incomes, and with no local authority nursery place within walking distance, were delighted to find a playschool on their doorstep.

The news spread throughout the land, and, as one outstanding example, a playbus appeared on the streets of war-torn Belfast, and at the height of the troubles.

'THE DAY OF THE DISASTER'

The Liverpool EPA team received a grant from the Gulbenkian Foundation to set up a 'Theatre-in-Education' group, which worked full-time with them. As part of their activities, in accord with their keen interest in encouraging community education, 'The Day of the Disaster' project was devised. It was carried forward with the help of the Educational Director of the Liverpool Everyman Theatre who led the group, Paul Harman, and a small group of three actors. Unusually, it was designed for use within primary schools, in contrast to similar attempts at introducing community-based education projects into the curriculum in other places, which were more commonly aimed at secondary school pupils.

Two educational themes came together most vividly here, the need for social purpose and the value of creative expression. The story that formed the centre piece of the project and was to be acted out by the participants, was based loosely on the invasion of Liverpool by Irish immigrants after the potato famine of the mid-nineteenth century, and the resulting conditions in the city that led to overcrowding and friction between different communities. The disaster, modelled on an actual event that occurred in Liverpool in 1969, was the collapse of a house overcrowded with poor families. Two top junior classes in the participating schools were prepared to take on the roles of 'Country' or 'City' people and the actors then brought them together and led them through the playing out of a number of conflict situations. Teachers and parents who had watched the dramatic presentation by the children were invited to act as the jury and help decide who was to blame for the disaster that had been enacted.

As described by Eric in *Priority Education*, the project was an overall success from all points of view, including the huge enjoyment of the children, their lack of self-consciousness, their enthusiastic and gifted responses to the challenge, the approval of the teachers and the splendid follow-up work that ensued. The team was quite startled by the aplomb with which nine-year-old children handled complex social issues such as rents and unemployment and were able, with a minimum of supporting props and stage equipment, to describe and act out the terrible living conditions symbolized by the story.

The evident success of this project was in no small part due to the skill and enthusiasm of the actors involved, who turned out to be excellent and committed teachers. The whole thing helped to exemplify Eric's personal faith in the creative media as a vehicle for social or community education, and it had the added advantages of being both attractive to parents and highly diverting for pupils.

Eric's great friend and educational colleague, John Rennie, was the external adviser for the theatre-in-education team in Liverpool and he had attended a performance of the 'Day of Disaster' show. During the oration he gave at John's funeral in 2013, Eric recalled:

> Once, when in Liverpool, I had obtained funding for a theatre in education team, working with parents and young children, for which John acted as the external

adviser. It was successful enough to warrant renewed sponsorship and John and I met with this young group of actors to discuss the application. We felt very strongly that, good as they were, they would benefit from an author to sharpen and craft their scripts, but the only actor who could drive their van had obtained another post, and they were obsessed with including a driver rather than an author in a pretty tight budget. As the argument continued, I could feel John growing restless, his natural reaction when those in his immediate circle showed signs of not agreeing with him totally and utterly. As so often, he closed the discourse with one decisive statement; he suddenly stood up and turned on this startled band of talented if pedestrian Thespians and fiercely cried:

'Look, when have you ever been in the theatre to witness, as the curtains fell at the end of an absolutely riveting, magical production, the audience rose to its feet as one man, applauding wildly and calling for the driver?' We got our author and one of the actors learned to drive the van.

THE T.J.HUGHES EXHIBITION

In some ways, the T.J.Hughes Exhibition formed the climax of the various activities that Eric's team undertook as part of its home-school programmes, which were aimed at developing home and school relations. All of them involved attempts to place the parent in a learner situation so that they might appreciate better the educative processes being experienced by their children, and to find natural social foci for that situation. As Eric has written, 'The important premiss was the saleability of education and the fact that, granted the use of correct techniques, working-class parents could be interested and engaged in education'.

Prior to embarking on the actual event, a large survey of parents' knowledge of, and attitudes to, education was carried out in five areas nationally, including Liverpool, as reported by Keith Pulham in a section of *Priority Education*. The survey confirmed the real interest of parents in their children's education, whatever their background, and demonstrated that they were a potentially valuable force within the educational process.

So, after trying a number of smaller displays of children's school work in local shops, it was decided to put on a much larger educational exhibition in the departmental store, T.J. Hughes. As the manager of this store said when Eric first approached him about the project in June, 1969, 'You might as well do it here; it's where most of your children do their shoplifting'. Without wishing to denigrate the good citizens of Liverpool further, this comment is rather reminiscent of a big oral health campaign carried out in the city at around the same time that apparently resulted in a dramatic recorded increase in the theft of toothbrushes from Woolworths.

The Liverpool EPA eventually took over the exhibition area and theatre at this large departmental store for a fortnight in March, 1970 for their exhibition. T.J. Hughes – affectionately known as 'The Harrods of the Liverpool EPA' – attracted shoppers from a wide catchment area, so there was potential for a large audience to view what was being put on display. This included an 'Education Shop', a Pre-School Corner, a Secondary School Display, an Adult Education Section, and a varied selection of normal lessons taught by teachers, with the audience watching, usually with accompanying handouts to instruct them further. Eric was particularly impressed by a young teacher who conducted a P.E. lesson with 40 infants that could have been, as he said at the time, 'like Gallipoli with milk', but she was evidently magnificent. Many people were involved in putting on an exhibition of this size and scope, in addition to the LEPA team. These included staff and children from participating schools, a team of students from the C.F. Mott College of Education, a Liverpool teacher who was seconded to the project by the LEA for the duration of the exhibition and who acted as Chief Steward. In addition, there was some important practical input provided by design and technical staff from the store itself.

The exhibition was titled 'Child in the City' and it emphasized the idea of the community-orientated curriculum, one of the important themes of the LEPA's approach to education. Questions from the public were answered in the Education Shop, either directly at the time or by mail as part of an answer service. An important part of 'Child in the City' was the staging of live demonstrations, which gave parents and others an opportunity of observing the educational process at work. As might have been expected, activities such as music, drama, and dance were rather more popular than the more academic subjects, with which many parents were less comfortable. One of the star daily attractions was the Paddington School Silver Band, kitted out in their smart, modish uniforms.

On the afternoon that the exhibition was opened by the Director of Education for Liverpool, Mr C.P.R. Clarke, only a rather disappointing 350 visitors were recorded as attending, but the numbers soon picked up and by the closing day 10,000 visitors had been registered. According to the store, this was the most successful exhibition they had ever staged in terms of attendance numbers.

Three main points emerged from Eric and the team's 'post-match analysis' after the event. One of these was the need to look for better ways of 'selling' the basic subjects, such as reading, writing and arithmetic, in a lively and more visually attractive manner. As a result, the debut show subsequently put on by the theatre-in-education team was about reading. Secondly, the child-centred nature of some of the work on display clearly enlivened the awareness and enjoyment of parents and other visitors to the exhibition. Thirdly, if parental support is truly to be valued, ways should be sought to involve them more in planning and delivery of the school curriculum, in order to encourage their continuing interest and help.

All in all, the substantial investment of human and material resources in this exhibition was amply repaid in terms of audience response, and the viability of education in the market place had been demonstrated. As Eric remarked, 'The school and the community had been drawn closer together'. Keith Pulham commented that it was one of one of the LEPA's most successful experiments.

One of the Chatsworth School murals

Keith also recalled with pleasure the creation of the Chatsworth School Mural. In his words:

> Chatsworth was a gaunt and forbidding Victorian school enclosed by a high brick wall, housing infant and primary departments. The playground was transformed by a huge wall mural representing the Liverpool 'Kop', for which every child painted a face in the crowd with careful attention to a balance of red and blue, so as to placate Everton supporters.

Eric has pointed out that they had paid half price for damaged pots of paint from Woolworths, some of which had actually been kicked by the salesman to ensure that there were enough damaged, half-price tins for the project. There was also a handy collection of old shirts available to use as overalls.

Keith's comments continue:

> The message was clear, and as relevant today as in 1970, children were being dignified in their own environment and respected for their culture and rich dialect. Many had written them off as failures; the traditional curriculum had failed them; their territories written off as slums only fit for demolition. Eric spoke of 'making the known more knowable' from a starting point of the child's family history, the geography of the street and not forgetting their natural abilities in subjects such as maths, where they could calculate 501 or 180 on a dartboard and the betting odds on the racecourse rather more rapidly than those of us with qualifications in the subject.
>
> Familiarity with these and other aspects of their lives, might enable our socially and educationally disadvantaged children through a relevant curriculum to master the three Rs and proceed creatively to compete on more equal terms with their more privileged suburban middle class peers. Academics attacked us from their 'ivory towers', accusing us, as one Professor of Sociology put it, of 'providing a slum education for slum children'. We didn't bother to reply to such wrongheaded critiques.

ADULT EDUCATION

On the adult education front the usual problems of formality and institutionalism existed. Again it was necessary to break down the barriers and let education advance into the community as a normal everyday occurrence. Initial attempts by the LEPA's adult education officer, Tom Lovett, to get adult education activities working in Liverpool 8, with its potential study population of 170,000, were fraught with difficulty. For example, an imaginative and well-thought-out course on 'Football Appreciation' might have been considered as an ideal topic for the soccer-mad Merseyside area, but, despite the distribution of thousands of leaflets, only one person actually enrolled.

Much more success was achieved when Tom regularly visited a well-patronised pub in Everton every Tuesday night. At what he judged correctly to be the opportune time he took with him one Tuesday a professor of zoology from Liverpool University and they struck up a robust discussion on 'are we naked apes?' Over a couple of hours the discourse ranged in lively fashion with some people leaving and others joining the debate and the professor having more and more bottles of Double Diamond procured for him. Every Tuesday night for eighteen months thereafter Tom Lovett introduced a speaker and a topic at what proved to be a popular and well-attended occasion. No register; no fees; no curriculum; just a very successful and profitable 'evening class'.

TOWARDS PRIORITY

By the final year of the original LEPA three-year project, things seemed to be going well and Eric was asked by the Local Education Authority to draw up plans to take the work forward beyond 1971. He responded by producing a Project Extension Plan and the recommendations in this plan were eventually supported by the LEA, thus enabling the work of the LEPA to continue for an additional year.

The publication of a pamphlet entitled *Education – A Priority Area*, written by Eric for the National Union of Teachers (NUT) in 1970 created a great deal of beneficial publicity and helped to raise his personal standing with teachers in Liverpool. It was widely reported in the local, national and educational press, putting Eric's name and the work of the LEPA firmly on the map. On the actual day of publication the telephone never stopped ringing and reporters even came to the door; that morning Eric realized that LEPA and its work had gone 'national'.

One particularly notable event in 1971 was Eric's meeting with Margaret Thatcher, at the time the longest serving Secretary of State for Education since the Second World War. He received a call from the Education Office inviting him to come to a lunch the following day at the Town Hall, as Mrs Thatcher had asked to see him during her forthcoming visit to Liverpool. She was coming to give the then Polytechnic its charter in the morning, attend a buffet lunch with local dignitaries in the Town Hall at midday, before opening a comprehensive school in the afternoon. Eric discovered that Lady Plowden, on hearing from Mrs Thatcher of her planned trip to Liverpool, had recommended that she should meet Eric whilst she was there.

Eric was booked to travel in her car for the 40-minute journey from the town hall to the school on the outskirts of the city. He was understandably anxious about the prospect of climbing into her car with so many police and bodyguards about, in case he was mistaken for a terrorist, but was relieved to find at the lunch that he knew her personal secretary, who made sure that the logistics worked out without untoward incident. Eric had not previously realized that a car ride with a government minister was such a highly prized opportunity, much more useful than communal events like buffet lunches where there are many people jostling for his or her attention. So, in preference to various local MPs and other politicians anxious to bend her ear, some of whom were actually trying to get into her car, Eric was the chosen one granted a private audience on this occasion.

During the ride, Eric and Mrs Thatcher talked chiefly about pre-school provision and she evidently listened intently. It is hard to assess the real effect of this conversation on her thinking, but in her subsequent White Paper on Education, pre-schooling, especially for socially deprived children, was the only area where she was really positive. It is known that when Mrs Thatcher later visited Liverpool as Prime Minister, following the Toxteth riots, she asked what had become of Eric's valuable work in the city. Mrs Thatcher was well known for her capacity to master a brief with acute rapidity, and Eric was impressed by her obvious ability to absorb information, although, overall, he felt that she had massive intelligence but little wisdom. In his opinion, she was far, far more than the token woman in Edward Heath's cabinet, although he wrongly predicted at the time that she would soon become Home Secretary and bring back hanging and flogging.

PRIORITY (1972-75)

The EPA project was initially set up for three years (1968-71), then extended by one year, but as it neared its end thoughts were turned both locally and nationally towards the extension of the work that had been started so successfully in Liverpool. To this end, the charity Priority was created with Eric Midwinter as its Director and with funding from various sources, in order to provide an example of community schooling in action and to act as a national shop window for this approach to education.

The Local Education Authority (LEA) provided premises for Priority at Harrison Jones School, plus furniture, stationery and other essentials, as well as money to employ a warden and a grant towards public relations at EPA schools. As a result of the successful 'Project Extension Programme', there were now scores of schools involved in Liverpool. Funds from several other sources were also added to the pool of resources that could be drawn upon for the project, including the John Moores Foundation, the Workers Educational Association (WEA) and Liverpool Social Services.

The Advisory Centre for Education (ACE), based in Cambridge, contributed legal, financial and employment services to the new enterprise, and Eric became a Co-director of ACE, together with the educational reformer and writer Brian Jackson (1933-83). Along with several of the other organisations for which Eric worked during his career, ACE was yet another brainchild of its founder, Michael Young. Brian Jackson, like Eric, was a graduate of St Catharine's College, where he took first class honours in the English Tripos, although apparently the two men hardly knew one another during their undergraduate days. Jackson was well known for his influential book *Education and the Working Class*, written jointly with Dennis Marsden (also a St Catharine's graduate) and published in 1962. Tragically, Brian Jackson died just after taking part in a charity run in his native Huddersfield in 1983, at the early age of fifty and Eric had the unhappy responsibility, at very short notice, of writing his obituary for *The Times*.

When the Home Office decided to promote twelve Community-based Development projects, Eric was taken on as Educational Consultant, which necessitated him spending three days per month visiting these projects around the country, including Coventry, in addition to the two or three days he spent in Cambridge on ACE business. He was also made an independent co-opted member, with voting rights, of the influential Liverpool Schools Sub-committee of the Education Committee. During this period, the Gulbenkian and Van Leer grants to the Theatre Education team and another initiative, Home Link, which was an ambitious venture into support for young parents based in a council flat on the Netherly housing estate in Liverpool, were extended or renewed and the various training college connections that had been established were maintained.

Nationally, Eric and his team established a one-day conference programme, which they ran in dozens of places all over England and Wales, and they also organized a big three-day course on community education at Edge Hill, with a panel of expert speakers who were involved in project-related activities. The team, led by Eric, continued to produce books, journal articles, a periodical and many other publications, and there was a considerable amount of coverage of their output in the educational press and the broadcast media. As an example of this recognition, Eric became the educational adviser for the Granada TV programme *This is your Right*. There were many visitors to Priority, to the extent that it became necessary to set aside a day a month to receive them, and to take them on a coach trip around the project landmarks.

Eric in a TV studio

One of the other significant initiatives supervised by Eric around this time was the 'ASK ACE' project, which was held for three or four consecutive years at four different Butlins Holiday camps. For the four main weeks of the summer holidays they had teams of four people on hand for twelve hours a day offering educational advice to the campers, and the interest this stimulated was evidently amazing. Eric officiated at the opening ceremony at Pwllheli holiday camp, then said to be the biggest holiday centre in Europe (this camp operated from 1947-1998 and is now used as a caravan park, renamed Hafan y Mor); it was on the first Sunday and there were 10,000 new visitors and 2000 day visitors in attendance on that day. The children were provided with ASK ACE balloons that they released as Eric cried 'as the balloons fly away, let your educational problems fly away'. A rather snooty *Guardian* headline appeared the next day, along the lines 'The coming together of two meretricious national institutions; state education and Butlins.' This project was one of the main collaborative efforts between Priority in Liverpool and ACE in Cambridge.

A solid foundation had been achieved by Priority, and the project gained further publicity with a 'Support Our Schools' week in 1973. Around this time there was much involvement with Radio Merseyside, a special signature tune was composed by local band 'The Scaffold', and a huge party was held for teachers, schools and parents, with entertainment provided by the famous local comedian from Knotty Ash, Ken Dodd. When Ken was once interviewed on the radio about education, he talked eloquently and spontaneously about the teacher-child-parent relationship, referring to it, in variety terms, as a 'trio'. Eric has explained that they used to invite Ken Dodd to some of their functions because he related more to the community, far better than typical speech day dignitaries like the Earl of Derby or the Vice-Chancellor of Liverpool University, and he also seemed to understand more about education.

Eric has subsequently written much about popular entertainers and comics, including Ken Dodd, and the two of them evidently got on well together. A telephone conversation with Ken whilst researching this book revealed that he still had fond memories of Eric and he recalled with pleasure the times they worked together in Liverpool in the 1970s. Now well into his 80s, in an amazing display of show business longevity, Ken Dodd continues to fill theatres to capacity wherever he travels around the country, reducing audiences to tears of laughter during his almost heroic one-man shows.

Returning to some of the comments sent to the author by Keith Pulham, he clearly has fond and vivid memories of a number of particular moments during the years that they worked together, especially drawing attention to Eric's skill as a raconteur and public speaker.

Addressing a conference of Merseyside teachers and in elaborating on the concept of 'community', Eric said 'Once we lived in caves, lit only by the light of fires designed to scare off wild animals. Today we live in a lounge lit only by the light of television sets designed to scare off thought!'

In discussing the notion that the community hardly changes over time, and that whereas as a species we have hardly reached first base, Eric noted that grasshoppers had been around for 215 million years, and observed 'I would like to take this opportunity of wishing grasshoppers the best of luck for the next 215 million years.' As he succinctly summarized with a typical illustration of 'the time changing but the melody lingering on', Eric drew on his fund of comedic illustrations, and recalled finding a paperback edition of a Dickens' novel on a railway bookstall. The cover was adorned with the picture of a semi-dressed sexily posed and alluring honey. Draped around her body in dripping red letters, it read 'Oliver Twist: he asked for more.' Readers will have found that the contents were true to the original edition.

Moving on to matters educational, Eric was once querying the usual hand-raising preface to trips to the toilets.

He was challenged by a primary teacher who declared that, were the practice to be abolished in her classroom, one particular child she knew would spend all his school term in the lavatories. Eric's quick reply was to ask the question as to 'What was more fascinating about the urinals than your classroom, madam?'

Eric probably missed his vocation, he ought to have been a music hall performer, as he once readily admitted to me. He thoroughly enjoyed humorous interchanges with his teacher audiences, as exemplified by another occasion when addressing a course with members drawn from an area wider than Merseyside and representing an all-school age spectrum. On addressing the issue of how teachers might cope with the extra year of schooling occasioned by the raising of the school leaving age in 1972, he was interrupted by a voice from the back of the hall 'No problem for us in Wales, we will just teach more slowly.'

Much of the success of our collaboration in Liverpool is down to our mutual love of British comedy, especially stand up, the Music Hall tradition and, of course, cricket.

Other specific episodes that stand out in Keith's memory include Eric's rendition of the famous George Formby song 'When I'm cleaning windows,' accompanying himself on the ukulele, and the music hall party held for Project schools at Paddington Comprehensive. The entertainment included Keith playing the role of chairman, dressed in his grandfather's old frock coat and checked trousers, and Eric, who rendered most of the acts, as well as performances from the aforementioned Paddington School silver band. According to Eric, this all took place at their 1969 Christmas party, during which they had a Victorian menu for the food and everyone joined in singing a set of music hall choruses. As Keith notes 'The wheels of innovation in our schools were oiled, and teacher morale lifted.'

Keith describes the years he and Eric worked together in Liverpool as rich and productive, and remarks that they cemented for him a lasting friendship with an extraordinarily talented fellow educationalist, for whom he has great admiration. He ended his affectionate comments with one further memorable episode.

> I drove Eric to a day meeting with education staff at a Midlands University. On our way we were seriously slowed by fog and, in order to pass away the time, we lapsed into song. I was brought up a Baptist and know every hymn and verse in the *Baptist Church Hymnal*, from cover to cover. (I am in good company; the ex-Chancellor of the Exchequer, Sir Stafford Cripps, once claimed to know every hymn in *Hymns Ancient and Modern* off by heart). So I started up with the wedding hymn 'Dear Lord and Father of Mankind, forgive our foolish ways'. Much to my surprise, Eric was able to go along with me for much of the way. He has such a wonderful memory and I still don't know where he acquired his knowledge of church music. I must ask him some day [Keith was evidently unaware of Eric's Anglican upbringing, under the firm guidance of his grandmother].

THOSE WERE HAPPY DAYS

As a postscript to the hymn-singing car ride experience, Eric has added:

> With regard to hymns, what I most memorably recall is our joint mirth, accompanied by a combined appropriate action, to the line in 'Jesus shall reign where e'er the sun' - 'the prisoner leaps to lose his chains' - I'm laughing now thinking about it - it was pre-Pythonesque.

Before moving on to the next developments in the Liverpool story, some further comments from Harry Pepp add an interesting personal dimension to how Eric came across to others during the time when he was working in the Educational Priority Area.

> Eric was at this time piloting the Education Priority Area project, which was well underway when he brought me

in. An abiding Midwinter characteristic was to involve his friends in most of what he did and this led to a great mutual loyalty. Eric`s projects seemed to have an octopus like characteristic in that they spread in all sorts of sometimes unlikely directions. Over the next few years I found myself leading at least three school projects, with three school governorships, some minor publishing activities and a week-long Easter event for educational priority schools at Butlins in Minehead. Although Eric turned up for a day, all of the Eric volunteers from Liverpool worked to provide daily drama, art, music and writing activities for around 500 primary kids who had mostly never been away before. I was exhausted but enriched.

Every activity and everyone I met through Eric was something I probably never would have encountered on my own. Eric had an inevitable ability to make unlikely new friends and contacts. He managed to befriend the taciturn Peter Robinson the secretary of Liverpool Football Club, and John Moores Jr was a regular dining partner. And Eric loved his interviews with Ken Dodd who normally only entertained large audiences. Eric had several meetings with him and I am sure Doddy was as fascinated by Eric as Eric was by him.

I was privileged to listen to Eric`s musing on a range of subjects over the years he was in Crosby. His politics were apparent. I didn`t hear him theorise or politicise working class culture à la Stuart Hall or Raymond Williams but he held it very dear and of great intrinsic value. He knew all the comedy and music hall routines and could offer them whenever the opportunity arose. He has a great rich sense of humour and a love for repartee and was always great company. He was useless at DIY, and not in the least interested in material things, aside from a good telly. The piece of grass in the garden was for sports. He kept his aesthetic sensitivities under wraps and was no lover of nature. I remember walking with our families through Freshfield pinewoods and he produced a football for his son Matthew to dribble around the trees with the comment 'That`s what God put them there for'.

I remember Eric saying how he would like to give lectures on commuter trains. I couldn`t imagine myself ever doing it but I`m sure Eric did, and loved it. He said he was too old to go into politics and I think most who really valued him were relieved he didn`t. His talent for comedy and acting were probably fulfilled by teaching and meetings and I think he liked the idea of following different lines of inquiry, such as different modes of employment, more or less at the same time.

Eric has a great enthusiasm for everything that interests him, and great wit, intelligence, determination, generosity and a propensity for friendship.

CHANGES IN THE AIR

Shortly before Christmas 1973, the Warden of the teachers' centre at Walton left abruptly and unexpectedly, and Eric was called in for a long meeting with the Chief Education Officer, C.P.R.Clarke, to discuss the situation. It was suggested that Eric might apply for the post and that his other staff could also fit in, with the whole team assuming a wider role. The outcome was that, with such high level backing, Eric was duly appointed to the vacant Warden's position, even though this went against the wishes of one deputy head teacher, chairman of the teachers' committee, who had wanted to see a serving teacher get the job. However, in typical Midwinter fashion, Eric immediately went to talk to this dissenting individual in order to clear the air and, despite their initial differences, they soon formed a really good working relationship.

So it was that Eric developed the biggest teachers' training centre in the country, one described by the *Times Educational Supplement* (TES) as a 'Rolls Royce' of a teachers' centre. It embraced the existing centre at Walton (mainly concerned with curriculum development) and the Harrison Jones site (also involved with curriculum, with added home and school activities), but, as an additional aspect, Eric took on overall responsibility for the Garston in-service training centre for teachers, which had its own warden and assistant warden. Priority, together with its mainly pre-school adjuncts like the Playmobile, the John Moores' Pre-school Fellowship in support of a key worker in this field, and Homelink, was given a rightful place as a kind of ally. All the mainline members of staff were given tenured jobs with the Local Education Authority so that altogether, with one or two additional individuals on second-ments, Eric now had a staff of about twenty people working in the enlarged centre.

Together with his new friend, the initially reluctant teachers' committee chairman, Eric formulated a new constitution for the centre. A governing body was proposed, which included teachers' representatives from all the relevant unions, and Eric's title as head of the organization was changed from 'Warden' to 'Principal', in order to give him parity with the training college principals. Three sub-committees were intro-duced, variously responsible for curriculum development, in-service training, and home-school relations, with officers from the centre staff in attendance as relevant at their meet-ings. As a result of the activities of these sub-committees, the teachers' representatives gradually came to understand that Eric and his team were not 'anti-teacher' as they had once suspected, but that they actually believed that the proper professional status of teachers was a major aspect of what was needed in education if progress was to be made.

A dramatic shift in emphasis of the work of Eric's team occurred in the field of in-service training. They developed courses that were largely based on teachers' contributions and in 1974/75 the course programme was massive; it more or less trebled the usual output and, significantly, the proportion of teacher-led courses rose from less than 30% to 90%. Hitherto, education advisers been responsible for organizing such courses and they had also been the major contributors – it seems likely that some of them did not like the changes that had been introduced. Eric personally ran a weekly full-year course, with colleagues, for deputy heads, the intention being to influence the next generation of school leaders. This appeared to go well and it was observed that candidates for senior teaching jobs were often asked if they had attended the course. Eric and his team also became heavily involved in a national pilot on the probationary year for new teachers, with Garston being used as one of the bases of the Liverpool contribution to this study.

The way things were going around this time in the mid 1970s seems in retrospect to represent the apex of Eric and his colleagues' achievements in educational research and innovation in Liverpool. The common belief about educational experimentation at the time was that, having achieved a promising result with a project, the critical thing was to get it embedded in the LEA and thus achieve continuity. A weakness of many such experiments was that, even if successful initially, they somehow failed to be sustained and become an integral part of the everyday fabric.

Eric's view was that his team's efforts over a number of years had been conspicuously successful on many fronts. Very helpfully, Stan Thorne, Chairman of the School Sub-committee, found some additional money for various small projects, including the idea of awarding £150 public relations grants to every one of the 100 or so EPA schools for use in the development of improved home-school relations. The only catch was that Eric and his team had to approve and sign off all the payments under this scheme, thus providing one or two amusing incidents. Some recalcitrant heads did not wish to get involved with anything so *avant-garde* as seeing parents, but the thought of having the chance of £150, quite a large sum in those days, going to waste was anathema to them. One head teacher wanted to buy a new carpet for her office so that parents would feel more comfortable if (an unlikely event in her case) they visited. Another had asked his colleagues for suggestions at a staff meeting and the only thing they could think of was a new teapot. Eric's response to this was 'I'll have Arthur Negus round first thing in the morning to price one for you'.

So, by this stage, Eric and his team had direct working relationships with EPA schools; they had developed effective templates for pre-school and adult education activity, where little or none had existed previously; they controlled the in-service training, home and school relations and curriculum development of the entire Liverpool LEA, and were able to give a community education branding, style or message to all three of these activities. They also had the enthusiastic support of the leading political party, chief education officer and chief schools inspector; the local training colleges were all energetically supportive, and, to cap it all, their work was recognized and lauded nationally.

A COLD WIND (OR 'MORE TROUBLE AT T'MILL')

At a Saturday discourse around this time, run by Eric for the whole Liverpool Education Committee, the question of how to develop community education within an LEA was considered and discussed. During this meeting one of the councillors, a Welshman tipped to become the next chairman of the education committee, hinted privately to Eric that the two of them might make a good double act. This was the first indication that Eric was being considered as a possible candidate for the post of Director of Education that was about to become vacant.

When C.P.R. Clarke did retire, it was suggested by some Labour Party insiders that Eric should apply for the vacant position of Director. He found it a difficult decision to make since, apart from realizing that he possibly lacked sufficient high-level administrative experience, he would be taking risks if he did apply. Failure to get the job could result in a distinct drop in 'pull', as he soon found, but he was also in danger of disappointing and upsetting those who were supporting and encouraging his candidacy if he did not apply. On balance, he felt at the time that he could make a good job of being Director of Education, primarily because of his wide experience as an educator, provided that he could appoint an excellent administrator as his number two. He knew that a comparable situation was already the case in the West Riding, where the educator Sir Alec Clegg was Director of Education, working with an efficient deputy to look after most of the administrative aspects.

Eric in a classroom

Unfortunately times were changing and the strong position that Eric had striven to achieve in Liverpool for himself and his team was starting to show signs of unravelling. His chief political backer, Stan Thorne, highly influential and supportive on both the main Education Committee and the Schools Sub-committee, went off to be MP for Preston South – a big loss. Also about this point there were important local political changes; the Labour group lost control of the Council and the Liberals took rather messy, indeterminate control in their place. Significantly, Eric's other great supporter, Tom McManners, who had talked him into applying for the LEPA post in the first place, had left in 1974, even before Clarke's retirement, and his successor as Chief Inspector of Schools in Liverpool was far less favourably disposed towards Eric and his 'new-fangled' ideas. As a result of this change of personnel, doors that had mysteriously been opened were now, equally mysteriously, beginning to close. As Eric has said, 'Tom was the *éminence grise*, quietly pushing a door open here and shoving a foot in another door there – I never realized how much until he had gone'.

Another important factor at this critical time was the temporary power vacuum created by the absence of a director of education in post. This inter-regnum allowed the new Chief Inspector and his team of advisers, some of them actively opposed to the project, to rule the roost, with devastating effects on some activities.

Eric has given several examples of the unnecessary pedantry and unpleasantness of the new regime under Tom McManners' successor. On one occasion, during the above-mentioned course that Eric ran for deputy head teachers, one of the participants wrote an amusing parody of an A.A. Milne poem about honey for tea, in which he made gentle fun about being a head teacher. On hearing about this, the new Chief Inspector hauled Eric into his office and gave him a severe reprimand for allowing such a display of indiscipline and disrespect to happen. This reaction seemed to be a completely unwarranted and 'over the top' response to a minor and insignificant episode, hardly worth the time and attention of the Chief Inspector.

Tom McManners and C.P.R. Clarke had always encouraged Eric to accept invitations to travel around 'spreading the gospel' about all the good work that was being carried out in Liverpool, supporting his participation in advisory work for the Home Office, ACE in Cambridge, various television and radio appearances, and attendance at conferences, even though these activities took him away from Liverpool quite frequently. They, very sensibly, thought that such outside exposure was good for Liverpool and attracted positive publicity. In stark contrast to this constructive and supportive approach, Tom McManners' replacement rebuked Eric for leaving Liverpool one day without his permission, even though he was the Principal of the Liverpool Teachers' Centre and had, incidentally, informed his Chairman of Governors about his absence. This all seemed very petty, and Eric believes that the man regarded him as a threat to his own position, which might well have been the case had he actually been appointed as Liverpool's next Director of Education.

DECISION TIME: A NEW OPPORTUNITY

In the event, Eric was not appointed as Director of Education for Liverpool, but another opportunity presented itself when Michael Young offered Eric a new post to work with him in London, albeit on something completely different to the educational work he had enjoyed so much up until then. Whilst weighing up his options and deciding whether to accept this new direction in his career, he reflected that he had by this time completed seven years of intense work on the various educational projects in the Liverpool EPA, in retrospect probably the hardest he had ever worked, and he began seriously to wonder if he might be growing a bit stale. Eric's original long-term plan was to prepare himself for an eventual post as the principal of a college, as had been suggested some years earlier by Tom McManners, but he liked the idea of the post that Michael Young was now offering, it sounded both different and very attractive.

Eric recognised that the problems he was experiencing in Liverpool had a strong personal element, with he himself being cast in the villain's role of the unwanted rival who was thought to be stealing all the limelight in the educational arena. If that was indeed the case, things might work out better for all concerned if he was to go, leaving behind a strong foundation for his successor to carry on the good work in Liverpool. The proposed contract for the new job in London made provision for Eric to maintain a link with Priority, such continuity being something that Michael Young strongly supported.

So, in 1975, Eric resigned as Principal of the Liverpool Teachers' Centre in order to take up his new job as head of the Public Affairs Unit at the National Consumer Council in London. Sadly, however, things did not continue as hoped in Liverpool after he had left. In Eric's own words: 'Basically, what I had built over eight years from 1968 to 1975 was destroyed in about eight weeks. All that was left was the Priority charity aspect, chiefly pre-school work, which continued much as before, and a legacy of suggestions, ideas and aspirations.' In fact, the vacant post of Principal was never advertised; the three centres were separated and one closed; the advisory staff regained control of the in-service training; and Eric's former colleagues were effectively demoted.

However, notwithstanding the obvious disappointment at this unfortunate turn of events that must have been felt at the time by Eric and his colleagues, it is true to say that the beneficial effects of much of the pioneering work they undertook on home and school relations as part of the Liverpool EPA project remain and are now so widely accepted nationally that they are almost taken for granted. This applies particularly to the level of communications between schools and parents that is now standard, but perhaps less to some of Eric's ideas about the curriculum that are clearly out of step with the current concepts of a national curriculum and the need for frequent and intrusive testing of young children. Happily, there is also a substantial body of published books and papers about the work in Liverpool, making the innovative work of the LEPA and Priority available to anyone with an interest in education.

The history of the Liverpool Teachers Centre between 1973 and 1976, and Eric Midwinter's pivotal role within it, is described in far greater detail in a recent paper by Keith Williams, published in the journal *History of Education*. As one would expect in such a scholarly article, it gives a full list of relevant references for those interested in pursuing the subject further. Whilst acknowledging that 'Midwinter came very close to establishing the administrative machinery which would have impacted on the city's entire teaching force', Williams also sounds a word of caution about the whole approach to teachers' centres as adopted in Liverpool:

> Part of the success in Liverpool can be attributed to placing the right people in the right roles. Yet, this apparent strength reveals one of the fundamental weaknesses of the teachers' centre as a vehicle for challenging dispositions and practice. It is questionable whether it would be feasible to staff hundreds of centres with the same blend of dynamic, ideologically motivated individuals. Any policy that relies on the commitment and ideological motivations of a handful of individuals will eventually run out of steam.

Perhaps there are just not enough Eric Midwinters and his ilk to go around in an ideal educational world? It would certainly appear that the world of office politics reared its ugly head with vengeance at a crucial juncture in Liverpool's history, thus destroying much of the educational framework that Eric and his team had so carefully and energetically constructed over the previous eight years. Fortunately, much of the good work on community education that had been started in Liverpool, incorporating many of Eric's own ideas on the subject, was continued in Coventry, under the direction of Eric's great friend and colleague, John Rennie.

So, with the ending of the Liverpool episode in Eric's constantly evolving career, the story moves on to London. Although his new job opportunity would seem to have come rather out of the blue, Eric had been in regular touch with Michael Young throughout the Liverpool years, since Young was national chairman of the EPA projects and also had his fingers in many other pies nationally. As a result, he would have had a shrewd insight into Eric's particular abilities and achievements and was in a good position to see his potential for making significant contributions in other fields of activity.

Eric with Michael Young in 2000

THE WORLDS OF ERIC MIDWINTER

THE WORLD OF WORK
3: The Consumer Champion

So it was in 1975 that Eric moved to London to start his new job, and embark upon a completely new career direction with the National Consumer Council (NCC), once again turning his talents to another aspect of community service. Shirley Williams was Secretary of State for Prices and Consumer Protection in the Labour Government from 1974-76, and it was whilst she was serving in this capacity that she set up the NCC, with Michael Young as its founder chairman.

Michael Young had long been interested in consumer affairs and had earlier established the Consumers Association in 1957 as a consumer campaigning charity. The first issue of its famous magazine *Which?* appeared in October 1957, initially published from a small converted garage in Bethnal Green in East London. From those humble beginnings it has grown to become a widely read and respected publication with over a million subscribers.

Michael Young: Innovative Thinker and Social Entrepreneur

Since Michael Young's name appears quite frequently in this account of Eric's life and as he was so influential at critical stages in his career, it would seem appropriate at this juncture to pause for a moment and add a few words about this remarkable man. The headline over his obituary in *The Guardian* newspaper on 16th January, 2002 was 'Innovative thinker', and this would seem to be a very apt description that can hardly be bettered for either accuracy or brevity.

Michael Young was born in Manchester on 9th August 1915. He was the son of an Australian musician and his Irish wife, who was both a painter and actress and, by all accounts, something of a Bohemian character. Michael's early years were spent in Melbourne, before he returned to England after his parents' marriage broke up, at which point he was just eight years old. He attended several schools, eventually arriving at the progressive Dartington Hall School in Devon, founded by Leonard and Dorothy Elmhirst in the 1920s. Michael had a long association with this school, firstly as a student and in later years as trustee, chairman and historian and was greatly influenced by the Elmhirsts, by whom he had been unofficially 'adopted'. He went on to study economics at the London School of Economics (LSE) and also became a barrister, called to the Bar in 1939.

After the war he was very involved in shaping Labour Party thinking, serving as secretary of the policy committee when Clement Attlee was party leader, and he was responsible for drafting the party's manifesto for the 1945 general election, at which Attlee's Labour government was elected with a majority of 146. Michael later returned to the LSE to undertake research for his PhD, based on studies of housing and local government policy in East London. He founded the Institute of Community Studies in Bethnal Green as an urban think tank and this became his base and principal vehicle for exploring ideas about social reform, from which he created more than sixty institutions and charities over the following years. These included, in addition to the Consumers' Association, *Which?* and the National Consumer Council mentioned previously, the Advisory Centre for Education (ACE), the College of Health, the Open University, the National Extension College, the Open College of the Arts, Language Line, and Grandparents Plus. Together with Eric Midwinter and Peter Laslett, Michael Young also founded the University of the Third Age (U3A), an organization that continues to thrive and grow to this day.

Michael Young was a prolific writer, producing many books, papers and pamphlets. Two of his most influential publications were *Family and Kinship in East London*, which he co-authored with Peter Willmott in 1957, and the dystopian satire *The Rise of the Meritocracy*, first published in 1958. The latter work has been much quoted and often misinterpreted over the more than fifty years since it first appeared, and has given rise to a commonly used 'new' word in the English language.

He was was made a life peer in 1978 in recognition of his work, sitting in the House of Lords as Baron Young of Dartington. Amongst his many appointments over the years, he was a fellow of Churchill College from 1961-66, and President of Birkbeck College, University of London, from 1989-92. When he died on 14th January 2002 at the age of 86, a number of eminent public figures made comments about his many important contributions to national life. For example, Tony Blair said 'Few people have made such a contribution to our society in so many different areas as Michael Young. He was that rare combination – not just a great thinker but also a great doer'. Lord Denis Healey, who had worked with Michael Young at Labour party HQ in the 1940s commented: 'The things he did changed the whole approach of the Labour party and other parties to housing, the environment and the consumer movement'. To this list he might well have added the words 'education' and 'older people'.

As a close friend and colleague, Eric organised Michael Young's NCC retirement party, and some years later gave the opening talk, a review of his life, at the heavily attended celebration of his life after he had died. He has also written a moving tribute to Michael in his book about the U3A, *500 Beacons*. In this he writes:

> A devout egalitarian, he retained to his dying day (during which, in the shadow of imminent death, he contrived to do six hours work) an unbudgeable belief in the capacity of the man, woman and child on the Clapham omnibus to organize their own affairs in localized concert with one another, if only they were allowed the resources, the tools and, perhaps most important of all, the encouragement. In every one of his manifold enterprises one may trace this sterling, humane and deeply moving faith in his fellow men and women.

Eric continued:

> Diffident in many ways, he was defiant and robust in his defence of this principle and enormously resourceful and agile in putting it into practice. The track record of previous utopian socialists was not too dazzling, and perhaps his extra ingredient was constantly to find a spot in the existing social fabric where he could insert his innovative communitarian notion and enable it to adhere in reasonable comfort. That degree of superb judgement, allied to a colossal intellect and that energy in the cause, made Michael Young the supreme craftsman of social invention.

Without doubt Michael Young was a remarkable man and his influence on Eric's life and work can hardly be overstated.

NATIONAL CONSUMER COUNCIL

There were just a few people working at the NCC when Eric first started there as head of the Public Affairs Unit, but the numbers soon grew. Two of its remits were to consider the consumers of public services and the needs of poorer consumers. The activities of Eric's unit embraced the public services, such as education, health, social services, and local government services, and it was intended that he could do for the consumers of such services what he had started to do for the consumers of education services in Liverpool. Eric was also responsible for the annual National Consumer Congress, of which he eventually ran five, the first two being in Manchester and Birmingham, chosen because they were also the venues of the first and second Trades Union Congresses. Other responsibilities of the job encompassed public relations, including parliament and the lobbying of politicians, running the press and media office, publication of *The Clapham Omnibus* and all the NCC's other publications. On one occasion a Consumer Awareness Week was organized in Preston, complete with the Lancashire Police brass band (brass bands being one of Eric's passions) and a team of clog dancers in attendance. Eric also found himself secretary of the Bulk Buy Bureau and helping with the 'Brain Train', where commuters shared lessons and experiences from their daily journeys to and from work.

Eric soon found himself with a team of ten people, one of whom was Wendy Toms. Wendy has kindly provided some recollections of her experience of working at the NCC.

> I first met Eric in 1977 when I was appointed as the National Consumer Council's first permanent press officer. Eric was head of the Public Affairs Unit, of which the press office was part. My over-riding memory of him is that working under Eric was fun and when he left NCC, we who had made up his team really grieved.

This collective grief was underlined some years later when Eric spoke at the annual general meeting of a charity. Whilst introducing him, Jill Pitkeathly (later Baroness Pitkeathly, who was CEO of the National Council of Carers from 1986-98), recalled that she had started work at the NCC on 1st September, 1980, the day after Eric had left. She said the place was beset by gloom and that the question on everybody's lips was 'who is going to organise the Christmas pantomime?'

Wendy also mentioned two amusing memories of working with Eric that she and other former colleagues particularly cherished. One of these was the occasion when, after a very hard-working team meeting, held in an office facing Queen Anne's Gate, Eric suddenly leapt onto the low window sill and shouted at a startled passer-by, 'Help, help! I am being held prisoner by five women from the Rumanian Embassy!' The other was his foolproof technique for ensuring that when he and his team were travelling by train to organise the annual Consumer Congress, no strangers entered our carriage. (This, of course, was in the days before the large open-plan carriages that are the norm now.) At the first sight of passengers in the corridor, he would stuff a sandwich into his mouth and then, mouth wide open and full of sandwich, would grin manically at anyone who had the temerity to open the door of our carriage. It invariably worked, with shock and disgust written large on their faces, passengers would hastily close the door and move further down the corridor after which, of course, Eric's team collapsed with laughter. Wendy did not consider this unauthodox behaviour to be childish because his light-hearted approach was a deliberate management technique stemming from Eric's conviction that a happy team would work efficiently and meet its deadlines – and she believed that, in this, he was absolutely right.

Wendy Toms listed a number of other points about what were obviously happy and productive times working together with Eric and his team at NCC. She applauded his efforts to create a united consumer movement via the Consumer Congress, while at the same time recognising that such a disparate body of people, representing such a variety of mainly specialised interests, could not be expected to provide a meaningful voice on issues of the day by passing resolutions. This was something that always puzzled the media, used as they were to run of the mill conferences. But she believed that Eric was right – Congress went downhill after he left, from the moment that voting on resolutions was introduced and more and more consumer reporters stopped attending.

Wendy went on to comment on Eric's editorship of *The Clapham Omnibus* – whose name was later changed to *Consumer Voice* after the Scots complained that the title was too metropolitan and English, and his gifts as a radio or tv interviewee, pointing out that there was no need to send him for training in the art of a good interview, since he was a natural. She also applauded his attempts to encourage the Nationalised Industries Consumer Councils (NICCs), largely unheard of by the consumers they were supposed to represent, to make themselves known via stalls in shopping precincts, complete with balloons.

Wendy noted that Eric's ideas on education and parental involvement were ahead of their time – voting for parent governors in the pub, for instance, and publishing schools' examination results, but alongside details of the educational achievements of adults in the local community. This would often have shown that a school regarded as excellent was actually not achieving as much as might have been expected, given the environment in which the children were growing up. Conversely, one in another area with a lower percentage of examination successes was actually doing remarkably well, given the non-academic background of parents. Alas, that idea became impossible to implement once parental choice of schools was introduced, resulting in children often travelling miles outside their local communities to school. Wendy remembered, too, that Eric had foreseen the problems that giving parents local choice of schools would bring and argued forcibly that making each school as good as it possibly could be and giving parents a real say in their children's education, was a much better idea. Eric's mantra was 'Choice within schools, not choice between schools', meaning the nearest school.

Eric was forever arguing that it was not enough just to carry out research into consumers' problems and needs and to advocate reform, they had to actively campaign for change, otherwise all that they were doing was filling one another's bookshelves. He was very active in helping consumer bodies of all kinds to do a better job of representing the interests of grassroots consumers.

As well as mentioning 'all those lovely pantos with brilliantly funny scripts', Wendy referred with obvious pleasure to the joint leaving party for Michael Young and John Hosker, the Director of NCC. During this memorable event, Eric persuaded the two men to participate in the reading of three 'original' BBC scripts based on the popular TV programmes Steptoe and Son, The Two Ronnies, and Morecambe and Wise, heavily laden with appropriate 'in-jokes'. The hilarity of the occasion was greatly enhanced by the fact that Michael Young, whilst entering fully into the spirit of things and reading Eric's script with great gusto, had clearly never heard of the individuals in question, nor had he ever watched the well-known television series named after them.

Eric has great affection for Wendy Toms, describing her as the 'best press officer in London', who could make any 'dull as ditchwater' item of news sparkle like champagne. It is claimed she was such a fast typist that Eric had to stand by with a fire bucket in case the typewriter burst into flames, although the veracity of this account has not been independently corroborated. Wendy used to play the part of principal girl in the annual Christmas party pantomime, written and organised by Eric, with great aplomb and she evidently did great impersonations of selected 'important' women, including one former minister of consumer affairs, and members of the National Consumer Council.

When the NCC office was situated in Old Queen Street, the back window overlooked the area where military bands were marching along Birdcage Walk to and from Wellington Barracks. Eric got the press officer's assistant, Dina, to call him whenever the band appeared so that he could move across the corridor from his own room to the press office balcony in order to hear the music more clearly. Brass bands have always been a passion of Eric's, as has been cricket. A former colleague recalls that meetings had to be scheduled to avoid the time of Test matches, whenever possible.

At about this time a Labour MP had argued that, since army bands were costing the country about £3m per year, they should all be scrapped. Eric responded by writing a letter to say that it would be better to scrap the army and keep the bands. On one occasion he suggested to a new recruit that she ought to try to get away once a week from the hurly-burly of the office and listen to the band. One of her colleagues muttered quietly to her 'That's as near as an order that you'll ever get from him'. Clearly Eric chose not to exercise his authority in a bombastic or domineering fashion, preferring to use the art of gentle persuasion wherever possible.

After three years at the NCC Michael Young had finished his contractual stint as Chairman and moved on to other things, as had Eric's close friend John Hosker. Eric had first met John in Liverpool when he and Michael Young visited him to talk about the new body, and they kept in touch over the years. He had what Eric described as a 'pawky' sense of humour and was always very supportive of what he tried to do – John was definitely listed as one of the 'good guys' in Eric's book. John Hosker died in August 2011, after a long battle with Parkinson's Disease.

Eric applied for the vacant Director's position when John Hosker left and was short-listed, but he was not appointed. The atmosphere was changing, partly, in Eric's opinion, because Michael Young had frightened the civil service to death with his unconventional manner with the council and with his unusual ideas about what should be done. He would arrive for the regular Tuesday morning meetings of senior staff with his little diary full of indecipherable writing, ignore the formal agenda, and come up with all sorts of new wheezes and apparently crazy ideas that had to be followed up because they knew of his great track record – one of these 'off-the-wall' notions might actually turn out to be a world-beater. One particular example is when he reported that he had been talking to David Astor over the weekend about its subscribers taking over the *Observer* newspaper.

With the change of Chairman and Director, there followed a marked shift back to conventional consumerism, with more of the *Which?* magazine and commodities element, as befitted the ideas of the new director who came from that kind of 'Office of Fair Trading' background, and there was an altogether less maverick look about the council itself. Eric's vision, like that of Michael Young, was of a mass organisation of consumers electing the Council and becoming the Youngian 'third element' to offset the influences of vested interests such as employers/managements and workers/unions.

Things were still going reasonably well and Eric much enjoyed the company of his NCC colleagues, both professionally and socially, but he started to realise that he was getting somewhat sluggish and it felt as if he was treading water. So, in what was by this time developing into a characteristic and somewhat predictable pattern, he started to look for a new challenge. It was at this stage that he became aware for the first time that his rather unusual horizontal career pathway did not always fit comfortably alongside the more normal vertical route of progression. He applied for four chairs of education at different universities, having been actively encouraged to apply by three of them, but despite being short-listed and interviewed, was not appointed to any of these posts.

Whatever the true reasons, a senior university academic position was not to be offered to Eric at this juncture, even though there were some people in high places who considered him to be an ideal candidate for such an appointment. It is interesting to speculate how different things might have been if Eric had been appointed to a university chair in the mid-1970s, but that did not happen and his subsequent career went in other directions. However, it should be noted that there has always been a strong academic thread running throughout Eric's life, as exemplified by his many scholarly writings, through which his knowledge and expertise as a social historian constantly shines, and he was later appointed to a Visiting Professorship at the University of Exeter.

Eric did have one or two close encounters with opportunities for seeking 'power' during his time at NCC. When he first moved South to Harpenden, he was approached with the idea of standing for Labour in a safe Conservative seat in the home counties. He was initially intrigued by the prospect of running an electoral campaign without the fearful thought that he might actually win, but because this would have necessitated him resigning from his job at NCC, which was a QUANGO, its members appointed and staff employed under Civil Service conditions, he decided not to throw his hat into the ring. The other brush with such ambitions came when the first European elections were organised in the late 1970s. Michael Young wanted Eric to run as the Consumer candidate for the Central London constituency; this was another no-hoper in terms of winning, but would have provided a good opportunity for additional publicity. However, the Civil Service, already anxious about Michael, whom they regarded with suspicion, put its foot down and stifled the suggestion. Eric was told afterwards by a colleague that one of Michael's main reasons for proposing Eric's name was that he would attract the women's vote – a heart-warming notion that he has cherished ever since although, perhaps fortunately, it was never actually put to the test.

THE TRANSPORT BRIEF: LTUCC AND LRPC

One day in 1977, about two years after Eric had started work at NCC, Michael Young sidled into his office and informed him that he had to go that very afternoon to see the Minister of State for Prices and Consumer Protection, but he remained very non-committal about the reason for this unexpected summons. Eric duly attended the meeting that had already been arranged for him with the minister and, after a short conversation, he was offered the part-time, paid chairmanship of the Transport Users Consultative Council for London (LTUCC), which was the British Rail (BR) watchdog for passengers. Although it was never fully explained how this appointment came about, it is most likely that Michael Young had been asked to nominate someone and, once again, he picked his trusted friend and ally Eric Midwinter for the task. Later, when London Transport was taken over by the government, Eric was invited to chair the new committee formed to cover London's buses and tubes as well as British Rail train services in the London Region. This reformed grouping was renamed the London Regional Passengers Committee (LRPC).

Eric's leading colleagues at LRPC was Rufus Barnes, who has pointed out that Eric had been appointed originally as Chairman of LTUCC under a Labour government, serving for seven years from 1977-84. He then served a further twelve years (1984-96) as Chairman of the newly constituted LRPC, this time appointed by a Conservative administration.

Rufus Barnes first met Eric when he was Secretary of the London Transport Passenger Committee, the previous Greater London Council watchdog for tubes and buses, and was appointed after Eric had advertised for a secretary of the newly constituted body. They worked closely together to set up the new committee and get it operational. According to Rufus, Eric was a fantastic chairman, particularly because he understood the role of a non-executive chairman, and successive government ministers recognized his abilities in this role, despite any differences of political persuasion. His main interest was in consumer principles; he was never too involved in the details of transport, but in 'looking after the users'.

Eric's exemplary literary talents were put to good use whenever publications and reports needed to be prepared. Examples of these include:

The Clandestine Railway (about the inner ring of London's underused lines and stations)

Get Staffed (about de-staffing of BR stations)

Inconvenience (about lavatories on public transport)

The last of these three was a particular area of concern and is quoted as a seminal document in consumer circles, where it is widely regarded as a great example of how such public service publications should be written. As fondly recalled by Wendy Toms:

> I remember Eric's work as chair of the LTUCC and especially *Inconvenience*, which not only drew attention to the disgusting state of most of the railway loos inspected, while praising the few good ones, but surely did more to put the London Railway Passenger Committee on the map than anything that it had done before.

Inconvenience is a slim 32-page illustrated booklet, published by LRPC in 1994, and it reports the findings of a survey of lavatories on London's stations. As well as itemizing the detailed observations at each of the stations and the results of questionnaires, the report came up with five recommendations for future action. It would be interesting to carry out a similar investigation today in order to establish whether station toilet facilities have significantly improved since 1994. Certainly the often-used phrase 'spend a penny' needs to be updated in line with inflation these days, at least at mainline stations in London.

THE TRAVEL CARD: A VICTORY FOR COMMON SENSE

One of the key issues considered by LRPC was the development and introduction of the Travel Card in London. Originally, this just covered journeys by bus and underground. Passengers had to buy a separate Capital Card in order to use over-ground mainline trains in London. Eric and Rufus campaigned persistently and hard for these to be combined into a single Travel Card and, according to Rufus, a narrow window of opportunity occurred for this to be agreed by the then Minister.

The satisfactory resolution of the Travel Card debate was the result of tough negotiation and persistence as well as good fortune. It was a case of getting all the basic components on side, including buses, trains, and underground, as well as the government representatives. The eventual outcome of all their combined efforts was a major triumph and, in retrospect, Eric regards the Travel Card as one of the most fruitful things with which he has ever been involved, certainly in terms of widespread benefit to people in the community.

Rufus Barnes has commented on the fact that Eric's own political views did not really matter, noting that he was consistently re-appointed by Conservative Governments. What came through most strongly was his commitment to transport users and their problems. Rufus also noted that Eric was always very popular with members of the committee, who recognized his knowledge and skills. His encouragement for people to be involved with other things and other organizations was a notable feature of his approach.

Rufus, like many others who have known Eric over the years, was greatly impressed by his talent as a raconteur. He recalled one meeting – in Barking Town Hall – when there was an unexpected delay in the arrival of a speaker to address the committee. Eric stood up and entertained everyone by telling a hilarious story, involving a gun, and the scheduled speaker duly arrived in the middle of this performance, possibly wondering what he had let himself in for.

Perhaps the only mild criticism of Eric's manifold abilities made by Rufus was a reference to his 'awful' handwriting, which sometimes caused difficulties for his colleagues. Having experienced similar problems recently, the author can vouch for the veracity of this opinion from personal experience.

WHY LONDON BUSES WORK

Another important area of activity during the time when Eric and Rufus worked together at LRPC, to which they and their committee dedicated a great deal of time and effort, was concerned with tendering for bus services at a time when privatisation of all such public services was very much in vogue with the Conservative Government. The response of the Committee to the Government's 'Bus Strategy for London' is set out in the booklet *London's Buses: The Tender Balance*, published in 1991. In his trenchant and thoughtful Chairman's Foreword to this document, Eric wrote:

> On behalf of a pragmatic laity, the London Regional Passengers Committee sniffs suspiciously at the whiff of excess dogma. The bus contest has been allowed to become something of a head-on collision, between 'regulation' under the aegis of state body or local authority, and 'de-regulation' with market forces in

LONDON'S BUSES

——————

THE TENDER BALANCE

A response from the
London Regional Passengers' Committee
to the Government's
"Bus Strategy for London"

major dominion. Each has its virtue: the uniform pattern of the former; the sharper competitive efficiency of the latter. But each has its attendant vice: the tendency toward anonymous officialdom of the one; the other's proclivity towards instability and lack of coherence. We have witnessed much of this in many of our other public and allied services and utilities. Nothing is ideal. The public sector is better on needs; the commercial sector is better on wants.

After much thought, and no little heart-ache, the LRPC accepted in 1989 that the tendering device, utilized in London, offered the least worst solution for the city's many bus passengers. After even more thought, and a bit more heart-ache, the Committee was prepared to endorse that conclusion and to claim shortly that deregulation would be a retrograde step.

After two further short paragraphs, Eric concludes:

We should be grateful that the tendering process has enabled London bus services to discover some kind of balance between the two extremes – and that is a process of decent refinement. That is the choice the Government should make. It cannot be said too strongly that a move to deregulation would be a backward and antediluvian step, no more glamorously progressive, if no less so, than a bland reliance on bureaucratic statism.

The document continues for a further twelve pages, with thirty numbered paragraphs outlining the detailed responses of the LRPC to the Government's proposals for London's bus services. The whole bus-tendering episode was highly political in nature; LRPC had two members of parliament as advisers, one Conservative and one Labour, who were both members of the House of Commons Select Committee on Transport. Eric and colleagues discussed the issues with them and other politicians, and had to give evidence to the Select Committee. Rufus and Eric also drafted the rubric for the Select Committee's discussions and made the principal contribution to a well-received report on bus control.

According to Rufus Barnes, the big battle was about whether the whole of London's bus services should continue to be provided by London Transport, a nationalised central body, or handed over entirely to private companies who would bid for the right to run them. Eric and his LRPC colleagues were anxious to avoid complete deregulation of the system, as has happened in every other town and city, since the act had privatised buses everywhere in the country except London. As a result of the LRPC's detailed arguments and skilfully constructed written response to the Government's proposals, the eventual recommendation was to maintain central control of the bus services with respect to issues of particular importance to the bus user such as route planning, frequency of services, and fare structures, but to allow the actual provision of those services to be in the hands of private operators. Thus, it was possible to achieve a significant degree of privatisation, but still with overall centralized control of the whole bus system. London is alone in Great Britain in having achieved such working arrangements and is much envied by those in other parts of the country where bus services have been completely deregulated and privatised, often with disastrous effect for local bus passengers. While London bus services have thrived, those elsewhere have seen a doubling of fares and a halving of passengers since privatisation.

Rufus clearly has a great fondness for Eric, whom he describes as 'a fine, amazing man'. From Eric's comments to the author, it is also obvious that there was a great deal of mutual respect between the two men, and they evidently worked very well together as a team. Rufus Barnes has the unique distinction of having had a train named after him; he unveiled it himself at his local station, Gordon Hill, on 19th March 2008 to mark his retirement after 25 years with London Travel Watch, and its predecessors.

ORDER OF THE BRITISH EMPIRE (OBE)

It should perhaps be noted here that Eric's long and greatly appreciated stint at the helm of LRPC started in 1977, whilst he was working at the NCC, and it continued for a further sixteen years after he had moved on to his next job. He finally relinquished the LRPC chairmanship in 1996. In recognition of his valuable and distinguished contributions to London's public transport services, Eric was awarded the OBE in the 1992 Birthday Honours List; the citation simply recorded 'Eric Clare Midwinter, Chairman, London Regional Passenger Committee'. Notwithstanding this brief statement, it seems highly probable that his many other contributions to public services were also taken into account when he was nominated for this award, even though these were not specifically mentioned in the official citation.

By 1980 Eric had spent five years working in the realm of consumer affairs with the NCC, but now, at the age of forty-eight, it was time for Eric to start the next phase, once again in collaboration with his friend and mentor, Michael Young.

THE WORLD OF WORK
4: THE THIRD AGE CAMPAIGNER

Some time in 1979, whilst he was still working at the NCC Public Affairs Unit in London, Eric received a visit from the distinguished Cambridge academic Peter Laslett, who was a friend and sometime 'partner in crime' of Michael Young in several of his innovative enterprises, and whom he had met previously on several occasions. During the visit Peter advised Eric in characteristically forthright manner to forget his prior obsessions with children and youth and turn his attention instead to older people, the new wonders of the age. He declared firmly that the issue of older age would soon be **the** fashionable area in which to work and that any right-thinking (or, for that matter, left-thinking) social analyst should get in on the ground floor.

Having been tipped off in this way by the man who became, alongside Michael Young, one of his twin mentors, Eric kept his eye open for suitable opportunities to become involved in this suggested new area of endeavor. So it was that in September 1980 he applied for a new post and soon found himself appointed as Director of the Centre for Policy on Ageing (CPA), a think-tank devoted to the social challenges of older age (a term these days preferred by those in the field to the words 'elderly' or 'old age'). Although he was not actually 'head-hunted' for this post, it seems highly probable that glowing references from Michael Young and Peter Laslett did little to harm to his candidature.

Thus Eric continued his by now well-established pattern of moving laterally into a new field of activity and being employed to work in newly created posts or enterprises, in each of which he was given the opportunity to build up a team of colleagues who were encouraged to tackle various challenges in an original and innovative way. In this new post he was to become a campaigner for the 'Third Age', that large and important cohort of retired older people who are no longer in full-time paid employment.

PETER LASLETT

Peter Laslett, like Michael Young, had a significant influence on Eric's ideas and career. Laslett was born in December 1915, the son of a Baptist minister, and educated at Watford Grammar School for Boys. After leaving school in 1935 he studied history at St John's College, Cambridge, graduating with a double first in 1938. He returned to Cambridge in 1948 with a research fellowship at St John's College, after which, in 1953, he was appointed to a lectureship in history at Cambridge, and he was also elected as a fellow of Trinity College, where he remained for many years.

From the early 1960's Laslett started an entirely new line of research, historical demography, and with Tony Wrigley he co-founded the Cambridge Group for the History of Population and Social Structure. Also in the 1960s, Peter Laslett and Michael Young worked together to develop the National Extension College, and later the Open University (OU), which was formally established in 1969. Peter and Michael had sold this idea to Prime Minister Harold Wilson, and Peter became one of the members of the committee advising Jenny Lee, Wilson's arts minister, on the shape and structure of the OU. Despite some conspicuous lack of enthusiasm for this newly established educational enterprise from the Conservative government that succeeded Wilson's Labour administration in 1970, the OU continues to thrive to this day, though not necessarily in quite the way that Peter and Michael would have envisaged or preferred.

Peter Laslett eventually became Reader in Politics and the History of Social Structure at Cambridge University in 1966, although, despite his obvious academic distinction, he was never awarded a full professorship by the university. He retired from this position in 1983.

Peter Laslett

Eric has written of Peter Laslett, 'He was one of the busiest and most enthusiastic persons I knew'. He evidently lived three concurrent working lives, the mornings being spent on political philosophy, the afternoons were devoted to the Cambridge Group for the History of Population and Social Structure, and the evenings were used for his Third Age campaigning. The idea of the sequence of four 'ages' or 'stages' of man was something that Peter had helped to introduce into British thinking. Again in Eric's words, 'Peter Laslett remained a trenchant, if affectionate, critic of all the institutions with which he was concerned, fulminating about Cambridge University, about the Open University and, indeed, the U3A'.

CENTRE FOR POLICY ON AGEING

The precursor of the Centre for Policy on Ageing, which was established in 1947 by the Nuffield Foundation, was originally called the National Corporation for the Care of Old People (NCCOP), so it had already been in existence for 33 years by the time Eric joined the staff as Director of the newly constituted CPA in 1980. He was, in effect, the first Director of the new think tank *per se*, which seemed, to all intents and purposes, like a new organisation. The original objectives of the NCCOP included promoting the welfare of the aged and those suffering from disabilities associated with older age, to give donations and support for organisations, places or activities that provided a wide range of benefits for older people, and to undertake the management of property held by charitable trusts for the benefit of such folk. Amongst the activities supported were the provision of residential homes, convalescent and holiday homes, and occupation centres, NCCOP having been set up as a linked charity that disbursed monies for such worthwhile and necessary ventures. Over the years a number of publications were produced (about 45 NCCOP papers are listed between 1947-1980) and a significant library on ageing had been assembled. Staff were housed in premises belonging to the Nuffield Foundation in the highly desirable area of Regent's Park in London but, in the early days, NCCOP did not have its own telephone number or a separate reception for postal deliveries and the like, so its identity may not have seemed very obvious to the outside world.

In 1980 the change in name to CPA was made, simultaneously shifting the emphasis of the reconstituted organization to become effectively a think-tank dedicated to the analysis, development and promulgation of social policy for older people. The Nuffield Foundation continued to underwrite the core funding for the centre but no longer provided funds for disbursement to other bodies, although CPA did still act as a conduit for some funds from another charity because of its accumulated expertise in residential care. Basically, CPA became a separate unit in another part of the grounds, with its own headed notepaper, telephone number and reception, thus providing an identity that was clearly distinct from the parent Nuffield Foundation. Later, in 1986, the CPA offices moved away from Nuffield Lodge altogether and were re-established in newly-planned premises at Ironmonger Row in Islington, London EC1.

As described in the official literature, available from the CPA website, it has a long and distinguished record as an independent charity promoting the interests of older people through research, policy analysis and the dissemination of information. The Centre aims to raise awareness of issues around all aspects of ageing and to support good practice, always trying to focus on what older people themselves want and need. The first half-century of the work of NCCOP and CPA, including the entire period of Eric's directorship, was celebrated in the book *The Social Policy of Old Age: Moving into the 21st Century*, edited by Miriam Bernard and Judith Phillips, which was published in 1998.

Miriam Bernard, who is now Professor of Social Gerontology at Keele University, has written the following affectionate comments about Eric.

> I first got to know Eric when I was a callow young researcher in the early 1980s for the Beth Johnson Foundation here in Stoke-on-Trent. Our then Director, Arthur Creber, and Eric knew each other because they belonged to some national association of Directors

of Charities/Charitable institutions. The values and aspirations of both organisations and their Directors were also very much in tune – especially their belief that older people had much to continue to offer to society and to each other.

I was in the throes of finishing my PhD and, at the Foundation, I was able to apply my then interests in leisure activity and young couples to the other end of the life-course and begin to look at the leisure lifestyles of older people. It was in that connection that I think I attended an event on this topic at the CPA and was first introduced to Eric. I'd also met the then Librarian, Gilly Crosby, at my first ever British Society of Gerontology Annual Conference in Exeter in 1982 and we struck up a friendship too. I used to travel to and from Stoke to London to visit the CPA library, which was the very best resource for those of us working in this field.

Eric invited me to join CPA's Advisory Council in 1987; in 1990 I was a member of the Editorial Advisory Panel for the CPA/Longman *Directory of Services for Elderly People*; and, in the same year Eric invited me to give the 1990 CPA/Niccol Lecture in Cirencester. It was entitled *'Beyond Our Present Imagination': Leisure and Lifestyle in Later Life*.

I had moved to an academic post at Keele in 1988 and my good colleague and mentor there, the late Frank Glendenning, was also a close colleague of Eric's through their mutual interests in education and older people. Eric was always available if advice or support was needed and, as it came up to CPA's 50th anniversary in 1997/98, my colleague Judith Phillips and I were invited to edit an anniversary collection for CPA on *The Social Policy of Old Age*. At the evening celebrations in the City of London, Eric made one of his fabulous after-dinner speeches about CPA, its work and its role, but I will forever recall with acute embarrassment how, when speaking about the publication, he likened Judith and me to two of the

'Spice Girls' and invited the audience to consider which two exactly! (For the record, he had Judith pegged as 'Baby Spice' and me as 'Posh Spice' – which couldn't be further from the truth!).

In 2005, we were able to entice him up to Keele to be our after-dinner speaker at the Annual Conference of the British Society of Gerontology, which we were hosting in the July. I knew Eric didn't much like travelling away from home and staying overnight, so it was a great honour for us that he agreed – and a mark of the man. Again, he had the audience in stitches as he spoke about his time as Director of CPA.

Eric was a huge influence on me and to my career: he was, and is, supportive, generous, encouraging and, above all, great fun! A truly Renaissance man, he is also one of the most genuinely nice people it has been my pleasure to know over the years.

Eric as Director of the Centre for Policy on Ageing

The CPA library was built up as an increasingly important reference collection during Eric's time as director and it is now a magnificent research resource for those interested in the social policy of ageing. As mentioned above by Miriam Bernard, the current Director of CPA, Gilly Crosby, started there as a librarian, later becoming one of Eric's two Assistant Directors, alongside Deidre Wynne-Harley. Eric and his colleagues produced a steady stream of their own publications about different aspects of social policy of relevance to older people. These consisted of books, papers and reports, many of them with Midwinter as sole or first author, including an important new series of CPA Policy Studies in Ageing and another series of Special Reports on selected topics. A list of publications on ageing written or co-authored by Eric Midwinter, produced in February 2013 by the CPA Information Service, reveals an impressive collection of over 80 contributions to the literature on ageing that Eric made between 1980 and 2011.

Itemised below are a few of the particularly notable publications written and produced by Eric whilst he was Director of CPA. Several of these are much quoted in other important books, such as *Older People in Modern Society* by Anthea Tinker (4th Edition, 1997) and the aforementioned book edited by Miriam Bernard and Judith Phillips (1998).

Age is Opportunity: education and older people (1982): a report in which it was demonstrated that older people can be highly proficient as learners and that a more imaginative approach is required towards education in retirement.

The Wage of Retirement: the case for a new pensions policy (1985): A critique of current pension levels and the case for a radical overhaul of the social security system and introduction of a social wage.

Caring for Cash: the issue of private domiciliary care (1986): A report on the commercial provision of personal social services, including the potential role of private agencies in the future.

Redefining Old Age: a review of CPA's recent contributions to social policy (1987): An introductory essay by Eric to celebrate the fortieth anniversary of CPA, followed by ten chapters on different themes by various authors.

New Designs for Old: function, style and older people (1988): a consideration of the way design affects every aspect of living and how it should be improved to help people cope with the impairments associated with old age.

The Old Order: crime and elderly people (1990): this paper, produced by CPA in association with the charity *Help the Aged*, examines the relationship between old age and the law, focusing on older people as both victims and perpetrators of crime.

Creating Chances: arts and older people (1990): here the participation of older people in the arts is discussed, and the reasons why so much talent may be hidden and unused are examined, complete with examples of good practice and recommendations.

Out of Focus: old age, the press and broadcasting (1991): in this CPA Report Eric examines the portrayal of old age and ageism in the British media.

The British Gas Report on Attitudes to Ageing (1991): the findings of the British Gas Survey on attitudes to ageing in Britain, based on interviews carried out in May/June 1991. It includes many informative and useful statistical tables, and the report opens with a Foreword from Diana, HRH The Princess of Wales, who was Patron of *Help the Aged* at that time.

To summarise in a single phrase the main thrust of the work of the CPA, it was, in Eric's words, to view 'the older person as a positive, active citizen, not as a negative, passive social casualty.'

Needless to say, Eric continued to write on other subjects during the eleven years he was at CPA, and he produced other publications relevant to ageing long after he had moved on to other things. Eric was always much in demand as a speaker, both for serious lectures around the country on various topics and, in more light-hearted mode, for after-dinner speeches and entertainments.

In addition to his many contributions to the literature, Eric was also called upon as an adviser to various organisations concerned with ageing and older people. He made a number of radio broadcasts and television appearances, including, in 1983, a five episode series for the BBC2 entitled *Ten Million People,* which Eric devised and presented himself. These programmes were concerned with the position of older people in society in the 1980s, covering aspects such as:

1. Their numbers and demographic significance
2. Their financial situation and the cost of being old
3. Their circumstances, including the environment in which they lived and material resources available to them
4. The character and the self-perception of the older people
5. The image of older people in the mind of the public at large.

A series of essays, published by CPA under the same title, came out to accompany these television programmes in 1983.

A good friend and colleague of Eric, Robin Webster, Founder Director of Age Action Ireland, first got to know him during the early 1970s when Eric was working with the Liverpool

EPA. Like many people contacted during the preparation of this book, Robin is a great admirer of Eric's work in education, social policy and in other fields. He writes warmly:

> Our work on ageing began in 1980, when Eric became Director of the Centre for Policy on Ageing, just after I started as Director of Age Concern Scotland and then joined the Advisory Council of the CPA. He was an extraordinarily successful leader and in 11 years he turned it into one of the leading institutes on ageing in the UK. He and his colleagues produced well written reports on a wide range of ageing issues, many of which are still relevant today, including Eric's own papers on income in retirement and private sector care. He integrated ageing with other topics such as the rights of consumers and travellers based on his time at the National Consumer Council or with the London Regional Passenger Committee or several committees for people with disabilities.
>
> I salute Eric as a gifted and generous gentleman, who has always shared his talents with others to the considerable benefit of many more people.

Another person who remembers Eric well from his days at CPA, who was put in touch with the author via a mutual friend from the world of cricket (Nigel Hancock), is Stephen Shaw. He was at the time director of another charity, the Prison Reform Trust, which was also a tenant of the Nuffield Foundation in what was then called Nuffield Lodge. Stephen points out that this Grade 1 listed building, formerly known as Grove Lodge and designed in 1822-24 by Decimus Burton, was ideally situated at the edge of Regent's Park on the St John's Wood roundabout, directly opposite Lord's Cricket Ground. This location seemed peculiarly appropriate for a cricket lover like Eric. The CPA team evidently inhabited outbuildings directly facing the lodge itself. Stephen Shaw writes:

NCCOP, funded by Nuffield, had basically been a grant-giving body until re-constituted and renamed under Eric's leadership as a think-tank on the social issues associated with old age. Eric already had a reputation as a polymath, but he proved to be an energetic leader of CPA's predominantly young staff. During his time as director, the Centre poured out a succession of reports and tracts: all of them well-argued and concise, all of them un-stuffy and 'un-academic' despite the rigour of the research on which they were based, all of them representing genuine contributions to the public good. I remember it as a happy organisation with a real sense of purpose. Indeed, it is worth remembering that 30 years ago there was virtually no other public policy focus on the issues that arise from an ageing population (quite unlike the situation today). In that regard, Eric's work (and that of his colleagues) really was at the cutting edge.

Gilly Crosby has commented that Eric's appointment to CPA was a very interesting one, bearing in mind his slightly unusual background and extraordinary range of talents and interests. She felt that he had a special view of the world and of people, and describes him as being very inclusive as a leader. He clearly valued individuals, whom he enabled to find their own way whenever possible, but he was also extremely good at guiding people and making constructive suggestions, when necessary. After a few necessary changes of staff and some adjustment of management structure when Eric first arrived on the scene, they ended up with a good, happy and vibrant team.

As had occurred in other places where Eric had worked, he initiated a variety of social gatherings which the staff enjoyed. These did not include regular Christmas shows, such as Eric had organised in previous situations, but there were various other events, around which socialising of one kind or another was nourished. For example, the official business of the Annual General Meeting was reduced to a minimum length of time

– usually about ten minutes – and was regularly followed by some theatrical or other form of entertainment, often with an agreeable 'age' flavour. If a new book or report was to be launched, it was frequently attended by suitable music or other festive activities. On one occasion, HMS Belfast was hired for such a launch and the report in question was powered on its way by balloons. When CPA moved to new premises, a string quartet was in attendance for the official opening by the Minister of State for Health, Norman Fowler. A programme of jolly events was organised during 1987, to celebrate the 40th anniversary of CPA, including the commissioning of a special piece of music to mark the occasion. This evidently turned out to be rather 'modern' and 'atonal' in character and was somewhat baffling to the ears of some of those present – one journalist apparently confided that he thought the musicians were still tuning up when the performance came to its conclusion. Leaving parties were invariably accompanied by lots of fun, including amusing speeches, and special cakes were produced for these and all sorts of other events. Splendid meals were laid on for meetings of both the governors and the advisory council, members of which often thanked Eric for the excellent 'party' at the end of the evening. As at NCC in previous years, there were lots of informal charades and other forms of game-playing at social events, all aimed at keeping everybody happy and working well together as a contented team.

When asked about his own attitude to teamwork and his experience of this at CPA, Eric provided the following revealing self-analysis:

> On moving to CPA, just as it changed its name and function to become a think-tank rather than a grant-maker, I determined to regulate along such lines, but this was not without controversy and a barney with two staff, who eventually left. I sheared the staff at both ends – there were too many chiefs and a longish tail of Indians, so I came up with a directorate of three – me, Gilly

Crosby and Deirdre Wynne-Harley – and about a dozen others all of similar ranking and pay scale.

We ran it as a kind of commune or module, with a weekly staff meeting chaired in turn by staff members and minuted likewise. There were no low-tech posts – for example, the receptionist was also cashier and in charge of orders and some other administrative duties. Having computers helped of course; most people did their own typing. We had quite a lot of social interaction as well, so that coffee breaks were normally taken together, and we took it in turns to relieve the receptionist. This led the editor of one professional journal who phoned when I was on duty to describe this in his columns as the equivalent of intellectuals working in the paddy fields in Maoist China.

It wasn't wholly communistic. The three directors had to manage within the rules of charity law but it was as inclusive as we could make it in normal practice. Certainly we were well within the egalitarian norms proposed by some social reformers, of the top pay being no more than ten times that of the bottom pay. It was hardly more than twice as much, although it was a small group.

One of the attractions of running a small team without a great genealogical table of departments and the like is that it is more 'hands on'. The job specification when I applied for the job said the director would be too occupied in administration and running the place to become involved in his own work. I simply ignored that and, in eleven years wrote and published eleven books and reports under the CPA label as well as lots of articles and other publications.

I do believe that modular or small team working is highly fruitful. For me, this is better than working alone or in a huge outfit. It may be a personal preference, but I recommend it, being after Michael Young, a great de-centraliser. Work with a human face.

Of necessity, working in the field of social policy on ageing required close interaction with other charities concerned with older people, such as Help the Aged and Age Concern, as well as with politicians and relevant government departments. Baroness Sally Greengross, who was at one time Director of Age Concern England and is to this day much involved with many aspects of ageing and the concerns of older people, recalls that she first got to know Eric in the 1980s because, like her, he ran one of the three main age-related charities. They soon became great friends as well as colleagues, and she greatly appreciated Eric's mixture of compassion and energy. Sally Greengross said that she enjoyed his wonderful sense of humour and found their occasional informal talks about social policy in the local pub extremely useful. She also observed that he had to cope with many difficult situations during his time at CPA, to which he had come as a breath of fresh air, bringing a valuable new perspective on the issues which surround the social policies of ageing. At the time of Eric's retirement from CPA she wrote to Gilly Crosby saying that she hoped to be able to get to the party because the occasion would be very important to her '... as it will give me an opportunity to say thank you for the support and collaboration of a very good friend as well as to acknowledge his immense contribution to the field of work in which we are both involved.'

Incidentally, it was Baroness Greengross's husband, Sir Alan Greengross, who succeeded Eric as chairman of LRPC when he relinquished that position in 1996.

The patron of CPA in the 1980s was the Queen Mother. When Eric and his team at CPA were invited to participate in her 90th birthday celebrations in 1990, there was the chance for them to take part in a huge procession in London and this was too good an opportunity to be missed, even for a paid-up republican. Making good use of his transport contacts, Eric was able to obtain, free of charge, the use of a horse-drawn bus from the London Transport Museum that had been on the streets of London when HRH was born in 1900. Via other influential connections, he also secured the services of the Whitbread shire-horse team, complete with attendants, to propel the bus, again without charge. Finally, with the help of one of Eric's theatrical contacts, an appropriate set of period theatrical costumes was borrowed for the day and a number of nonagenarian residents from a residential home were invited to join them for a lovely bus ride around London and to enjoy the day's fun. With everyone thus decked out in appropriate period finery, Eric walked in front of the bus dressed as Sherlock Holmes and carrying a CPA sign. This display attracted the attention of the BBC's David Dimbleby, who made particular mention of it during his broadcast commentary. Eric also produced a special brochure for the occasion, in which he described some of the significant demographic differences between 1900 and 1990, pointing out the striking divergence of population levels, death and survival rates between the two years.

Continuing for a moment the royal theme, Eric served from 1990-95 on the Prince of Wales Advisory Group on Disability as the 'old age adviser'. On one occasion he was deputed to write a speech for Prince Charles to deliver when six major 'old age' charities got together for a big function at the Queen Elizabeth Conference Centre. According to some of the CPA staff, the resulting presentation was so redolent of Eric's characteristic style and phraseology that they half expected the Prince to adopt a Mancunian accent at any moment. Although Eric and others had for some time prior to this been talking publically about the 'third age' concept, it was mentioned for the first time ever on the front page of *The Times* in their report of the Prince's speech.

Princess Diana was also at this function, in her capacity as patron of Help the Aged, and Eric got to speak to her briefly after the Prince had delivered his address. Apparently she was more used to rather shorter speeches, 'fifteen minutes max' was the normal guide, although she was admiring of her husband being able to speak for forty minutes on this particular occasion.

Eric Midwinter and Sally Greengross meeting the Prince and Princess of Wales at an Older Age charity event

OPEN UNIVERSITY DOCTORATE

During Eric's time at CPA, on 22nd April, 1989, he was awarded an honorary doctorate by the Open University. The Chancellor of the OU at the time was Lord Asa Briggs, who had previously examined Eric's DPhil degree from the University of York and who remarked that it was the first time he had ever given anyone two doctorates. The erudite and eloquent orator who presented Eric for this distinguished award was Professor Malcolm Johnson, at that time Professor of Health and Social

Welfare and first Dean of the School of Health and Social Welfare at the Open University. The ceremony was held at the Conference Centre in Brighton. After a succinct review of Eric's life and many achievements, the orator concluded his presentation thus: 'Had he not shone as a schoolboy, Eric Midwinter would inevitably have been an Open University student. Instead he has been an ardent supporter and constructive critic for most of its existence. For the past four years he has also

chaired the Health and Social Welfare Sector Programme Board'. So, along with his continuing chairmanship of LRPC, this revealed yet another example of the several significant outside responsibilities that Eric undertook in addition to his 'day-job' at CPA and to his varied writing exploits.

One of the issues that Eric pursued actively during the 1980s was that of the upper age limit

Eric at the Open University honorary degree ceremony in 1989, with Professor Malcolm Johnson, the orator

for jury service, this being a blatant example of what he has referred to as 'official ageism'. He pointed out that people over the age of 65 were banned from participating in one of the longest running Magna Carta-like freedoms available to the British population, and that age should not be regarded as a sufficient reason for exclusion; only physical or mental infirmity should be used as the defining criterion. Initially, perhaps predictably, the authorities seemed unsympathetic to Eric's arguments, stating that his suggestion to raise or remove the upper age limit for eligibility would be impractical and expensive, as well as illegal. Later, rather to his surprise, Eric received an official letter asking him to re-state the case, which he duly did, and the result was that age limit for jury service was raised from 65 to 70 in the 1988 Criminal Justice Act. In a letter from the Criminal Justice Bill Unit of the Home Office, dated 4th March, 1987, S.C Wells writes in typical civil service style:

'I am writing to thank you for your most helpful letter and information of 20 January. The relevant clause of the Criminal Justice Bill was voted through Commons Standing Committee yesterday without discussion. One feels, therefore, that the measure is justified and that, although there are a number of Parliamentary stages yet to come, we can with reasonable confidence look forward to seeing the upper age limit raised in due course.' The writer goes on to state 'We will draw upon your memorandum frequently, I suspect, during the next few months', and to thank Eric for his assistance.

Eric recalls that there was a hint that Mrs Thatcher, the Prime Minister at the time, quite liked the idea of getting some sensible, 'right-thinking' oldies on to juries as a buffer against the young 'pinkoes' and 'yobos', who were always letting people off when they came to trial. Whatever the truth in that particular rumour, this was one of the few impacts that Eric managed to make on actual legislation.

Ironically, this success did not go down well with everyone for whom Eric had campaigned so hard. When Eric's views were published, or when he spoke about them at meetings, he received objections from a number of over-65s who did not wish to be eligible for jury service, including one who claimed that he had served four times on juries before he reached retirement age. One woman wrote to say that she had lost 3.5 stones in weight through the stress of doing jury service, prompting Eric to consider sending her letter to *Weight-Watchers* and to entertain thoughts of obese jurors in a film entitled 'Twelve Hungry Men'.

Retirement from CPA

The splendid party arranged by Gilly Crosby to mark Eric's retirement from CPA, to which Sally Greengross had referred in her letter quoted earlier, was evidently a very special two-stage event, held on 20th December, 1991. It started in the morning at the offices of CPA, with champagne and presentations from the staff, including a couple of first editions of books about Dickens, Eric's favourite author, and then proceeded by taxi to a mystery destination for lunch in order to continue the celebrations. Details of what was planned had successfully been kept as a secret until the last moment. It transpired that the event was to be held in the Banqueting Suite at Lord's, where a large number of Eric's family, friends and colleagues had gathered to see him off and wish him well. In his thank you speech, Eric confessed that on the way he thought they might have been heading for London Zoo, or even the headquarters of the Nuffield Foundation in Regent's Park where he used to work, but Lord's was obviously the ideal location for such a cricket enthusiast. When they finally arrived at Lord's the penny dropped, as Eric kept bumping into people he knew between getting out of the car and walking to the lunch venue. Once they got inside, he found that about 200 people had assembled to wish him well, although a number of others he would like to have seen were unable to come. A Christmas-style lunch was served, followed by four huge iced cakes in the shapes of the letters E, R, I and C, decorated with imagery to represent older age, cricket, trains and other Midwinter interests. Peter Shea, an expert on adult education and country dancing, together with some of his musician friends, provided music for a barn dance during the party, including the *Midwinter's Jig*, which he had devised and dedicated to Eric with appropriate choreography a year or two earlier. Peter Laslett apparently claimed that he had danced for the first time in his life in Eric's honour. Further details of *Midwinter's Jig* are provided in Appendix 1.

An eloquent farewell speech was made by Professor Robert Pinker, Chairman of the Board of Governors of CPA, during which he briefly reviewed Eric's career and described him as an exemplary ambassador, who had put CPA in the forefront of debate about policy for ageing. Michael Young also spoke very warmly and observed that he and Eric had worked closely together during three major phases of his career. Lord Young was evidently amazed that Eric had turned down his recent invitation to take on another job – heading up his latest new foundation – in order to concentrate on the many other things he wished to do during his forthcoming so-called 'retirement'. Drawing an analogy from an old *Punch* cartoon of 1898 featured in Eric's biography on W.G. Grace, Michael Young declared that Eric may have been leaving CPA and moving on to pastures new, but he was definitely 'Not Out'.

Eric began his response to the kind words from Robert Pinker and Michael Young by saying that he been carrying around the draft for such a speech in his pocket for about the last ten days, just in case the occasion arose, in order to avoid being caught off guard. He paid particular tribute to the sterling and invaluable support he had been fortunate to have from Gilly Crosby who, in the later years, had, as his deputy director, played a vastly significant role in the CPA's success story. With the help of the musicians present, he was able to recite one of his favourite party pieces called the 'Miners Dream of Home', complete with actions, and he also performed a short playlet, taking all the parts himself, about Bob Crachitt's retirement, no doubt to the great amusement of one and all.

Letters of appreciation were received from a number of eminent people at the time of Eric's retirement from CPA, including Queen Elizabeth the Queen Mother, Neil Kinnock MP, Leader of the Opposition, the comedian Ken Dodd, the broadcaster Jimmy Young, and several other friends and colleagues, who were unable to attend the leaving party at Lord's because of other commitments. By all accounts it was a tremendous occasion and greatly appreciated by Eric himself.

So, at the tender age of sixty and with his mortgage paid off, Eric had relinquished his final full-time professional appointment and, technically, entered the Third Age. However, as will become obvious over the remaining pages of this book, his active working life was far from over and this so-called 'retirement' was to be far from leisurely or uneventful. Eric had deliberately decided to concentrate on writing more books, perhaps taking on the odd consultancy, and to play a bigger part in the affairs of the Savage Club in London, which would become his main 'social hub'. At the same time, he maintained in a number of ways his continuing interests in social history, education, U3A and social policy for older people. Some of these more work-related activities with which Eric was involved after ceasing full-time employment are described briefly below.

LIFE AFTER CPA

After relinquishing his Directorship at CPA, and apart from his sustained activities with U3A, Eric was offered several consultancies in the field of ageing, most of them associated with Sally Greengross. Among the more prominent products of these was his supervision of a major cross-national European Community investigation into the concept of a Senior Euro-Pass, a passport to all discounts throughout the EC, which led to the publication of a lengthy report written by Eric entitled *Towards a Senior Euro Pass: The final report 1997*. Another was his role as independent reviewer for the Department of Health of the UK's part in the European Year of Old Age, leading to another report written by Eric, *European Year of Older people and Solidarity Between Generations, 1993*, with a Foreword by the Secretary of State for Health at the time, Virginia Bottomley. In addition, there was also his mainstream contribution to the Age Concern England engendered 'The Debate of the Age' at the time of the Millennium, which resulted in his well-received *Towards a Balanced Society; a Contextual Commentary on the Debate of the Age*, published by Age Concern in 2000.

Not being one to rest on his laurels, needless to say, Eric was also involved in several other activities during his post-CPA days.

CARNEGIE INQUIRY INTO THE THIRD AGE (1990-93)

In 1989 the Carnegie Trust had organized a conference on 'Life, Work and Livelihood in the Third Age', after which it set up the Carnegie Inquiry into the Third Age in order to examine issues such as employment, pensions, education and training, volunteering and leisure activities. Whilst he was still at CPA, Eric was appointed as a member of the prestigious Advisory Committee to this inquiry, which was chaired by Sir Kenneth Stowe, and he continued to serve on the committee after retirement until its work was completed in 1993. Nine research papers were produced and published during the inquiry, the two on 'Leisure' and 'Citizenship' being written by Eric, and the final report 'Life, Work, and Livelihood in the Third Age' was published in 1993. Helpfully, all the reports from this inquiry are still available on-line from the Carnegie Trust website.

OTHER SENIOR ADVISORY POSITIONS

As mentioned previously, Eric served from 1990 to 1995 on the Prince of Wales' Trust Committee on Disability, an appointment that started whilst he was still in charge at CPA and continued for several years after he had retired from that post. In addition, he was a member of the Advisory Committee on Telecommunications for Disabled and Elderly People, a Trustee of Education Extra, and a Vice-President of Counsel and Care. He was also Chairman of CPA for six years from 2002-2008.

UNIVERSITY OF EXETER (1993-2002)

One source of frustration that became evident to Eric soon after his retirement was his lack of affiliation to any particular place or institution, which meant that he no longer had an identifiable operating base. This proved to be something of a problem when he was participating in a conference or writing a learned paper, since he had no wish to be labeled permanently as 'lately of CPA'. On one typical occasion, Eric was asked where he came from by a conference organizer. When he gave her his home address she replied 'No, where are you **from**?' After lamenting this inconvenient state of detachment to his friend Ted Wragg, the well-known educationalist and broadcaster who was Professor of Education at Exeter University, Ted asked him if he would like to become a Visiting Fellow there. Eric was enthusiastic about this suggestion and, to his great surprise and pleasure, he was invited a few weeks later to accept a position as Visiting Professor of Education at the University of Exeter. Apparently the senate of the university had been very keen on the proposal from Ted Wragg, no doubt impressed by Eric's many notable academic achievements, and this professorial appointment helpfully provided a title and academic base that Eric could thereafter use as his 'strapline' when giving talks and in his writings.

There were no particularly onerous duties attached to Eric's visiting professorship, although he did deliver a few lectures and seminars in Exeter, including a paper on 'Mirror Images: the Contrasting Educational Views of W.E.Forster and Matthew Arnold' and a staff seminar on 'the History of Old Age'. It was during his tenure at Exeter that Eric produced two of his most significant books about education, *State Educator: The Life and Enduring Influence of W.E Forster* (1995) and *The Billy Bunter Syndrome; or why Britain failed to create a relevant secondary school system* (1998), both published by the Community Education Development Centre (CEDC) in Coventry. Although his appointment at Exeter was unpaid and mainly ceremonial, it was also a considerable honour that was bestowed on Eric in recognition of his many contributions in the field of education, and he was rightly very proud of it. The visiting professorship was renewed three times for three year periods, and it was doubtless of considerable benefit to the university as well as to the incumbent, since it became possible for them to list Eric's numerous books and papers when making statistical returns to various official higher education review and funding bodies, who always were, and still are, keen to assess the number and quality of publications produced by the staff of university departments. So, all in all, this was a happy and mutually beneficial association.

COMMUNITY EDUCATION DEVELOPMENT CENTRE (1995 - 2001)

The Community Education Development Centre (CEDC), based in Coventry, was started in 1980 by its founder-director, and Eric's great friend and ally, John Rennie. The work of the centre was supported financially by Coventry City Council, and with additional funds from two educational and child-related charities, The Charles Mott Foundation in the USA, and the Bernard van Leer Foundation in The Netherlands. CEDC was established as a charitable trust that worked towards improving access to learning, especially for those who had previously benefited least from learning opportunities. John Rennie had been invited to Coventry, he thought initially for a meeting rather than an interview, by the Director of Education, Bob Aitken, whilst he was working in Nottingham. As a result of this unexpected interview, he was offered a job and his role was to establish Coventry as a strong centre for Community Education.

Eric served as founder Trustee from 1980 and as Chairman of CEDC from 1995 until 2001. In order to identify and develop effective ways of extending learning opportunities, CEDC worked with a wide range of organisations in the fields of health, education and economic and community development.

Phil Street, OBE was John Rennie's successor as Director of CEDC and he has kindly sent this account of his time working under Eric's chairmanship:

> When I joined the Community Education Development Centre (CEDC) in 1985, Eric was already a trustee of CEDC. I didn't see much of Eric during my early years at CEDC as John Rennie preferred not having other staff members at Board meetings, a tradition I carried on when I eventually become Director.
>
> However, as John and I became increasingly interdependent I was invited to trustees meetings and began to see more of Eric in action. In many ways Eric and John shared a number of similarities. They were both Mancunians, both loved sport (although Eric was a red and John a blue), they were both Renaissance men with a wide knowledge of literature, politics, art and much more.
>
> Both men were addictive, at least to me, I craved their company and delighted in their tales and listening to them recounting experiences and incidents, often feeding off one another. They were both fun to be with, extremely humorous and real raconteurs. I think they embodied what I had come to know as the aristocracy of the working class. They were inclusive, encouraging and free from arrogance,
>
> Eric was chairman when I became Director in 1996. He was to be chairman as CEDC experienced enormous

growth. Thanks largely to the benign and supportive Labour Government of 1997, CEDC grew from a £600,000 a year Coventry-based charity to a several million pounds a year national educational organisation punching well and truly over its weight.

Executive officers do not always enjoy or welcome the fact they have a chairman to report to and sometimes have to obey, but with Eric I never felt an atom of tension. He was clearly a great man, he knew exactly how to fulfil the role of chairman, and it was a pleasure to be able to boast of him as my chairman. I regarded him as a trophy chairman. He oozed wisdom and possessed characteristics that made his leadership style special.

He was always calm and calming. It appeared he could always see the light at the end of a troubled tunnel, even if he could not always map the journey to that light. He generated a sense of security, probably because of the faith and loyalty he seemed unerringly to project. He made you feel important as though you were the most important person he had ever met, but maybe his greatest ability as a chairman was to encourage the magician in me. For a working class youngish man full of all the insecurity and self-doubt that is often inherent in those that come from such a background, he enabled me to compensate for these traits.

They say all good leaders are magicians. They do things that seem impossible, defying the laws of organisational physics. I am not sure if Eric was ever an organisational magician himself, I was never privy to his operational activities. However, like some supreme football manager who may never have been able to run the full length of the pitch, beat five defenders and place the finishing shot past the goalie and into the top corner of the net himself, he certainly could inspire others to do so. He might have believed in the art of the possible, but he empowered me to push the possible to the very margins.

CEDC went through some difficult periods before we experienced the good times, but I can only ever remember Eric being the steady hand, a source of constancy whatever the weather. I was privileged to be the most senior officer at CEDC, but being senior officer on Eric's watch was living the dream.

JOHN RENNIE (1937-2013)

John Rennie, whom Eric has described as 'my best friend and closest colleague' was born in 1937 in North Manchester and made his career in teaching and education, beginning with teaching PE and English at a Manchester school, where he was soon promoted to deputy head at the very early age of 28. From there he moved on to Nottingham University to organize a pioneering and influential Schools Council programme on social education in secondary schools and this subsequently propelled him to his post as education officer for the Home Office Community Development Project in Coventry. It was from here that John conducted his high-level work in community education in that city and far beyond. In his very active retirement, John went on to become chairman of the Warwickshire police authority and he was appointed Deputy

Lieutenant of Warwickshire, an office from which he, quite rightly, derived great pride.

The author interviewed John Rennie at his home in February, 2013, by which time, sadly, he was already very unwell with the severe respiratory problems that would eventually lead to his demise a few months later. A highlight of that particular occasion was the delicious lunch generously provided by John's wife, Cynthia Rennie, who cared for him so lovingly during his long illness. John recalled that it was whilst he was a lecturer at Nottingham in 1968 or 1969 that he first got to know Eric, who was at that time working with the Liverpool EPA. He received a telephone one day from a colleague, John Mitchell, who reported that he had just been to an inspiring talk in Manchester given by Eric Midwinter, and had met him there. John Mitchell advised 'You'd love him, you must get him to come and give a talk to your students'. John Rennie thought that this might be a bit risky, since mature graduate students could be rather stroppy at times, but he invited him anyway. Eric duly came and delivered a talk to the students in Nottingham and, according to John, 'knocked them out', helpfully underlining during his lecture many of the same points that John normally made when teaching. It was clear from the outset that John and Eric had similar ideas about education and that they were on the same wavelength about many things; they hit it off immediately and remained good friends and colleagues from that time onwards.

This first meeting was to be the start of a long and productive working relationship ranging over a variety of activities over the years. John used to visit Eric in Liverpool quite frequently and was asked to evaluate some of the work of the LEPA. Both men strongly believed that education should be based on the community.

In John's opinion, 'Eric is brilliant with teachers. He is first and foremost a community educator, as well as being a talented speaker, writer, mover and shaker, with an ability to influence people'. He also made the point that, like a good actor, Eric always gives a proper performance when making any sort of verbal presentation, whatever the subject or circumstances of the particular talk.

Like Eric, John Rennie met, and came to know and like, Michael Young, whom he also regarded a something of a mentor. It is not hard to imagine John and Eric as a formidable double-act when they went on the road to meetings and conferences together, beating the drum for community education and equality of opportunities for education.

During his talk at John Rennie's funeral in August 2013, Eric recalled with affection how, when he and John shared a platform at numerous courses, conferences, seminars and workshops around the British Isles, John would say 'you can always tell the difference between Eric and me; he speaks with a South Manchester accent and I speak with a North Manchester one'. In fact, they had many other things in common in addition to their birthplace and shared views on education, including political outlook, affection for Lancashire County Cricket Club, love of theatre and entertainers, and much more besides; the only serious divergence of opinion was in their choice of which Manchester football team to support, with John being a 'paid-up' Manchester City fan, whilst Eric is of a contrary persuasion. Needless to say, this footballing disparity provided endless opportunities for jokes and good-natured sniping over the many years of their long friendship.

In his latter years John became a member of the Savage Club in London, which he much enjoyed, and where his lively conversation and abundant good humour were greatly appreciated by other members. A moving tribute to John Rennie, written by Eric, appeared in *Drumbeat*, the club's newsletter, in its edition (No. 123) of Autumn, 2013.

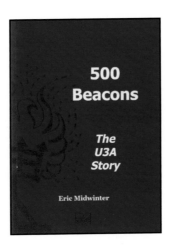

THE WORLD OF U3A:
THE CO-FOUNDER AND ACTIVIST

Perhaps the most widespread and lasting testament to Eric Midwinter's many contributions to education, consumer affairs and the well-being of older people can be witnessed all over the country in the continuing success and vitality of the University of the Third Age (U3A). This organization, now with hundreds of branches and many thousands of members, provides opportunities for continuing education, both academic and intellecual, as well as participation in practical and leisure activities of a staggering variety, and enjoyable social interchange with other older people.

Eric is rightly celebrated as one of the three founding fathers of U3A, alongside his mentors Michael Young and Peter Laslett, although the latter two individuals might almost be regarded as the movement's grandfathers in view of their relative seniority. Eric has written a detailed account of the origins and early history of the U3A in his 318-page book *500 Beacons: The U3A Story*, published by Third Age Press in 2004 (with a short update to 2014 for the electronic version published that year). From that excellent first-hand description of the U3A's history, it is evident that many other individuals also played – and continue to play – a crucial part in the story as a whole, in addition to the essential contributions of the founding trio.

It would seem very remiss of anyone trying to give a fair and balanced account of Eric's working life to pass over this important innovation without at least picking out some of the highlights of such an inspirational and instructive story.

Eric readily acknowledges that U3A came into being as a result of the coming together of several streams of thought and analysis. The first of these was the recognition that, with the well-documented demographic changes in Britain and other countries over the last century, leading to a larger proportion of older people in the population, the issue of older age had come to play an increasingly important part in the affairs of society. Moreover, with this growth in what came to be known as the Third Age, there also developed a belief that this later phase of life should be viewed more positively, since it could provide ample opportunities for creative self-fulfilment and enjoyment for older individuals, rather than the steady decline into inactivity and decrepitude that is so often depicted. The second thread was the concept of social mutuality or co-operation, meaning that older people could and should do more to help and encourage one another, without the need for everything to be determined and organized for them by younger, Second Age people. The third idea was that of recurrent education, whereby older people could continue to learn and develop their interests and skills, or acquire new ones, long after their years of formal education during childhood and early adulthood, and the experience gained later during their working careers, were over. The clear conclusion from these intertwined ideas was that there is no necessity for older people to stop thinking and learning just because they have reached a particular age or have retired from paid employment, or are no longer responsible for childcare.

There was an important precedent for the creation of the British U3A in the form of the 'Universités du Troisième Age (UTA)', which had first been set up in France in 1972, under the leadership of Pierre Vella. However, these were largely university-sponsored enterprises and, despite providing enormous intellectual and emotional inspiration to the founding trio, the question of creating a direct British equivalent was never seriously considered by them. But, as Eric has observed in retrospect, without the inspiration of the French model, the British version would probably not have been contemplated.

The coming together of the social entrepreneur, Michael Young, who, like the other two, was a utopian socialist and a dedicated egalitarian, the demographer Peter Laslett, who drew together the disciplines of history and sociology, and the educationalist and social historian, Eric Midwinter, provided a dynamic and effective intellectual powerhouse for the development of the U3A idea. Each of these individuals brought a vast amount of knowledge and experience to the communal table and was able, in different and unique ways, to contribute to the project as a whole. Eric chiefly recalls the harmony of thought that prevailed amongst them, notwithstanding occasional arguments about tactics, during their early discussions. There were no divisions on overall strategy, all three being united in the view that older people deserved decent access to educational facilities and that, ideally, they should manage these facilities themselves.

According to Eric, Michael Young was the key thinker in terms of new social organization, seeing mutual aid as an important supplement to, and potential humaniser of, the collective provision of the state. Young was generally against the tendency for institutions to become too large, what he referred to as 'giantism', he preferred instead the idea of more local provision of services, which were better able to retain a human countenance and allow users to maintain some degree of control. All three had already had a major involvement in education and had been particularly concerned with continuing and adult education, so the concept of creating an educational facility designed specifically for older people, as U3A was to become, fell naturally within their combined spheres of expertise and interest.

A significant step forward was taken at the beginning of 1981 when representatives of various 'older age' charities and academics with an interest in adult education came together to form the Forum on the Rights of Elderly People to Education (FREE). The Co-ordinator of this group was the Canadian-born social scientist, Dianne Norton, who has provided the following recollections of those early days.

> I first met Eric Midwinter (although I had previously been aware of his writings on community education) at a meeting held at North London Polytechnic on January 22nd 1981, to discuss setting up a forum to coordinate developments in, and disseminate information about, education and elderly people. Even at that time Eric was supporting the term 'Third Age' and was disappointed when the new body was given the rather cumbersom name of the Forum on the Rights of Education for Elderly People mainly because it translated into the reasonably meaningful acronym of 'FREE'. At that meeting Eric offered the support of the Centre for Policy on Ageing - specifically through their library and information centre. Having been appointed as Co-ordinator of FREE, one of my first tasks was to prepare a bibliography on 'education and elderly people' using the CPA library.

> Eric became a part of the Advisory Group for FREE, whose office was housed at Age Concern England (ACE). It produced regular Newsletters (which I edited), organised seminars and lobbied for older people's access to education programmes. Over the years - when no independent funding, as had been envisaged, was found - I was gradually subsumed into ACE and became their

Information and Policy Officer, but continuing my basic stewardship of FREE on a part-time basis. Peter Laslett had also attended that inaugural meeting of FREE.

A few months after the founding of FREE in April 1981, Eric approached me - as a result of discussions he had been having with Peter Laslett - and asked if I would be interested in taking on the (also part-time) administrative work involved in trying to launch U3A in the UK. For the next 8 years the national HQ of U3A was in my 'spare room'.

Before Dianne Norton joined the team, discussions had continued with other people interested in the U3A concept at the higher education level, including Frank Glendenning in Keele, David James at the University of Surrey, and Brian Groombridge and Peter Shea in London, and, in Eric's words, 'sparks began to fly'. A potential problem emerged because of worries about the prospect of U3As not paying fees to their tutors, raising the spectre in some people's minds of possible future unemployment amongst university lecturers. Needless to say, this point was not lost on their union representatives, who were initially wary about the whole idea. Fortunately, the U3A pioneers were not to be deterred by this potential source of resistance to their project.

Peter Laslett was always keen on moving towards more complete self-determination for Third Agers in Britain, unlike the situation in France where the universities were in control. He spoke of 'a self-generated governing body of elderly and retired people' as the key to U3A structure. Eric's wide experience of community education in Liverpool and elsewhere allowed him to draw on parallels between the potential for self-help within U3As and the successful co-option of parents to help in running play-groups for pre-school children. Michael Young was also a staunch supporter of the idea of community education and self-help. So, by 1981, all the pieces of the intellectual jigsaw had more or less fallen into place for the launch of the U3A, and the small team of committed enthusiasts was ready for action.

Incidentally, with regard to the terminology used to describe older people, Peter Laslett wrote in his book *A Fresh Map of Life: The Emergence of the Third Age* (1991):

> The Third Age is a phrase of French origin, and was used in the title of *Les Universités du Troisième Age* when they began to be instituted in France in the 1970s. It seems to have entered Anglo-Saxon vocabulary when the first of the British Universities of the Third Age was founded in Cambridge in the summer of 1981. Because of the spread of these societies in the UK, and perhaps because of the perennial need for a term to describe older people, a term not already tarnished, the expression is now in fairly common use.

Another important U3A stalwart, Keith Richards, who came on to the scene more recently, has commented: 'Peter Laslett's book *The Fresh Map of Life* was like the bible; it set out everything'. Some years after publication of this book, in response to a request from Peter Laslett shortly before he died in 2000, Eric was to write a piece for the journal *Age & Society*, entitled 'How many people are there in the third age?' In this article he developed and updated some of Laslett's concepts – originally intended for another book that he did not have time to complete – about the different stages of life and underlined the importance of getting away from the idea of using chronological age as the principal means of determining older people's capabilities.

In February 1981, Peter Laslett hosted a meeting in Cambridge to discuss the notion of bringing the U3A to Britain and this was soon followed by a Spring Workshop on the same theme at the Nuffield Foundation in London, then the base of the CPA, organized by Eric. These meetings led directly to two important follow-up actions, an application to the Nuffield Foundation for financial assistance drawn up my Michael Young, an old hand at such matters, and a public meeting in Cambridge, held on 20th July, to demonstrate and advertise the concept of the U3A in the UK. The Cambridge meeting, which was held in the Guildhall, included addresses by Peter Laslett and Eric Midwinter, and these were followed by an inspirational speech from Michel Philibert from Grenoble, one of the leading lights of the French U3A movement.

Publicity for this meeting was accompanied by a press release to the national newspapers and other media, but unfortunately this elicited no immediate response and none of them actually attended. However, shortly after the Cambridge meeting had closed came a request for an interview from the BBC Radio 4's 'You and Yours' consumer programme and Eric was thus able to make the first broadcast petition on behalf of the U3A at noon on Tuesday, 21st July, 1981. The reaction to this interview was quite staggering, with almost 400 letters received in the first few days after the broadcast. It was clear that the new U3A concept had touched a chord with the public, or at least with those who habitually listened to Radio 4. Unfortunately, no recording of this programme appears to be available, either from the BBC or from the British Library sound archives, but it was obviously very effective as a recruiting mechanism.

Stimulated by this mounting evidence of interest from the general public, Peter Laslett duly set about composing *The Objects, Principals and Institutional Forms of the U3A*, a document that was first published in August, 1981. This soon became the national basis for all subsequent statements about the new movement. The original version laid out twenty objects and eight aims, but this was subsequently summarized in a shorter document prepared by Eric and Dianne Norton, under the title *All Our Futures*, with just eight objects and five guiding principals.

As well as creating the 'word' (or rule book), progress was also made with raising money for the new project, with Eric and

Michael Young taking the lead in the fund-raising efforts. In October 1981 the Nuffield Foundation agreed a grant of £9000 for the nascent British U3A, with the CPA acting as a conduit for the money until such time as the U3A's position as a charity could be regularized.

At about the same time, funds from elsewhere were obtained for the proposed London U3A, this time channeled through the Department of Extra-Mural Studies at the University of London, where Brian Groombridge and Peter Shea were keeping an eye on things.

An Easter School was held at St John's College, Cambridge in March 1982, attended by about 75 people (50 of them from Cambridge), with a programme designed to foreshadow the future pattern of U3A activities. This generated substantial enthusiasm and optimism amongst those present and it seemed certain that a Cambridge U3A would soon be established. Delegates also learned that an embryonic London U3A had convened a steering group, with Brian Groombridge in the chair. Several other attendees wished to initiate similar activities in their own areas and, as a result, it was thought that about six U3As would soon be up and running around the country.

One immediate and important administrative result of this Easter School was the formation of a four-person National Committee (in later years to become the National Executive Committee or NEC). This consisted of Michael Young (Chair), Eric Midwinter (General Secretary), Peter Laslett, and Dianne Norton (Executive Secretary). The now legendary first meeting of this National Committee was held in Michael Young's car on the drive back to London from Cambridge.

Dianne Norton recalls specifically:

> With regards to the meeting in Michael Young's car, Eric has mentioned in *500 Beacons* an unofficial meeting of the newly formed national U3A committee (he implied

Peter Laslett was also present but it was only Eric and I with Michael in his car driving back to London). I do remember, for what it's worth, Michael talking about employing a professional journalist to edit the newsletter. To me this seemed the most interesting part of the job and, as I had considerable editing experience, I'd been looking forward to doing it. I was at this point receiving a fairly risible stipend for what I recall was meant to be one day a week but was invariably much more. When Michael stopped for petrol and went to pay, I said to Eric that I didn't mind doing interesting work for nothing but I did object to doing boring work for nothing. I don't know if this message got through to Michael but I was allowed to take on the task of editing what eventually became the national U3A newspaper.

The three senior members of the new National Committee all had considerable previous experience of helping to start up voluntary bodies. They enthusiastically seized this opportunity to establish an effective bipartite system that might enjoy the best of both worlds (i.e. local and national), by achieving an appropriate balance between local groups, operating freely and independently, and a national framework, working support-ively and innovatively. All three were avid 'decentralisers' and from the outset they realized the need to have good models of what could be achieved, strategically located, that could be used as 'windows' on the new project, through which others could view the potential benefits. There was clearly a need to proselytize the idea and start to propagate new U3As all over the country, and this was to be a task that would particularly involve Eric over the succeeding years.

Flexibility and independence was their motto. There were only three articles of doctrine to which all would-be supplicants were expected to subscribe to when establishing a new U3A:

1. The group must be open to all Third Agers

2. The purpose must be educational (although a broad definition of the term was allowed, so that it encompassed suitable non-academic activities)

3. The group must be run democratically, with members being the sole arbiters of content, approach and style.

True to their guiding philosophical principles, after defraying the costs of the Easter School, the money received from the initial Nuffield grant was divided equally, down to the last penny, between the national base and the emerging Cambridge U3A group, which, it was assumed, would become a model for use in other areas.

The national headquarters in Dianne Norton's spare room provided a small propagandist machine, intent on trying to persuade others to start their own U3A groups, and it acted as hub for keeping the growing number of groups in some form of meaningful contact. Communication between the centre and the periphery of the organisation was considered from the beginning to be an important factor in the potential success of the whole operation, and as early as August 1982 a newsletter was sent to all known groups with a progress report. Quoting from Dianne's recollections once again:

As Eric was most readily available 'on the ground' in London, some decisions were left with us – one being what to call the new U3A Newspaper. We mulled over many possible names – given his talents as a 'wordsmith' – some, as you can imagine, had an unusual twist. When he suggested 'The Last Post', we both thought it was very clever but neither of us expected the reaction of some of our readers. So we did a quick re-think and came up with 'Late Extra' only to be told, after the 2nd edition had gone out under that title, that it was already in use by a College in Yorkshire so we had to content ourselves with what seemed to us to be the very safe *Third Age News*.

In September 1982 the National Committee published a practical manual, *U3A DIY*, outlining the 'what, how and where' of setting up a new U3A group. In his role as Director of CPA, Eric had a wide-ranging brief to speak and write about the positive aspects of Third Age life, of which U3A was rapidly becoming a fine illustration. He embarked upon a series of talks up and down the country, both to professional educators and 'older age' specialists, as well as to new or incipient U3A groups. Meanwhile, Peter Laslett continued to watch over the development of the Cambridge model and generally did all he could to keep alive the issues of older age and education, hailing U3A, whenever possible, as a living example of how older people were capable of organizing their own affairs. Michael Young was committed to legitimizing the national U3A by negotiating its legal status, as he had done successfully for the many other agencies with which he was associated. This work came to fruition in October, 1883, when *The Third Age Trust* was registered as a Company Limited by Guarantee, and as a Charity in the same month. Whilst all this was going on, Dianne Norton continued networking and was much in demand, like Eric, to speak at public rallies and initial U3A steering group meetings.

With the birth of the British U3A in 1982, there began a unique trial of an intricate web of hypotheses of a social, political, cultural and demographic nature, as well as ideas directly related to education. Only time would tell if this was the right moment for such an enterprise to be launched and the four original members of the National Committee all understood, albeit tacitly, that the experiment might fail. It was to be a giant leap of faith.

U3A groups gradually began to be formed in different parts of the country. In the early days, wherever possible, Eric or Dianne Norton would attend the opening public meetings when each new group was initiated. Prominent amongst the first groups to be formed were Cambridge, London and

Huddersfield, but several smaller places were soon added to the list. Fifteen of the first tranche of U3As registered by the end of 1984 were still going strong twenty years later in 2004. These were, in chronological sequence, Yeovil, Nottingham, Oxford, Barnstaple, London, Wakefield, Tynedale, Merton, Bradford, Harpenden, Bristol, Stevenage, Saffron Walden and Abergavenny, plus West Midlands, which later was subdivided and registered under various separate districts. Predictably, perhaps, there were to be some failures and disappointments. Two of the larger original U3As, Cambridge and Huddersfield, so prominent and successful in the early days, eventually decided to go their own separate ways, and were not affiliated to the national organization.

Eric's home U3A was started in Harpenden in 1982. Here, he persuaded a neighbour, Reg Davis, to form the group, which met weekly in the local Trust Hall. Eric attended many of these meetings and was able to try out different ideas, thus using the group as a kind of communal guinea pig for testing different educational approaches that might be effective in the U3A context. In general, it soon emerged nationally that smaller interest groups were to become the essential units for the U3A experience rather than larger, plenary sessions involving the whole membership, although such larger-scale activities, often involving invited speakers, still constitute an important feature of many U3A programmes.

Someone who became involved a few years later with the Harpenden U3A, eventually becoming its Chairman, was Roy Evans. He had been a lecturer in Management Studies and still gives lectures from time to time to older age groups, as well as being involved with various action groups concerned with education, culture and senior citizens. Roy recalled how he had first come across Eric when he joined the U3A in 1992, by which time the Harpenden branch had already been in existence for ten years. He understood that Harpenden U3A was one of the oldest active U3As in the country, having been initiated by Eric, with the late Les as Founder and Chairman. He knew that Eric was very instrumental in setting up activities and was later elected as President. Roy clearly views Eric as a man of wide interests, with many literary and other achievements. He also regards him as an excellent performer who relishes giving his own version of various monologues, an aspect of Eric's many accomplishments that will be elaborated upon in later chapters.

The Bath U3A was established in 1986 and it soon became a large and highly successful example of the U3A in action. One of its two co-founders was Audrey Cloet, who later went on to become the U3A's National Organiser. This came about after Eric had managed to arrange for the Rank Foundation, who had been anxious to make some grants in the field of older age, to fund a Rank Fellowship. Audrey was duly appointed to start work in January 1990 and her brief was 'to promote and develop localized and autonomous U3A groups throughout Great Britain, within the framework of reference provided by the constitution of the U3A movement nationally'. By the end of 1992, Audrey was able to report that the agreed target of another hundred groups had been added to the list of U3As in the country.

Audrey Cloet has added her own personal commentary about later events, when she and Eric went on the road to further promote U3A activities:

> After the Rank Foundation Fellowship, it became clear that further help was needed in the generation of group activities, so Eric obtained some funding from the insurance company Frizzell to inspire the co-ordinators. We devised the U3A Roadshow, which entailed getting the key people from U3As around a region to a morning workshop that he and I ran, followed by an open meeting for U3A members in the afternoon. These took the

form of an inspirational talk by Eric, followed by lots of opportunity for the audience to discuss their problems and ideas. Eric and I fielded these – he always claimed that we were like a couple of comedians – and I have to admit I look back on the Roadshow with great memories of the fun we had together. Twelve years later, at a conference, I met a woman from Sheffield who said she'd never forgotten it – or my enthusiastic response to the idea of starting a whippet-training group!

Eric with Audrey Cloet

Continuing the theme of comments from Eric's many U3A friends and colleagues, Norman Richards, founder of the Swindon U3A, has written:

> I used to be a regular reader of *New Society* throughout the 1960s and 70s, in which I read with interest of Eric Midwinter's work on the priority educational project in Liverpool. Therefore, when on my retirement I became interested in the University of the Third Age, and saw his name as one of the founders in the UK of this organization, which aims to involve older people in continuing education, I immediately felt I was in good company.
>
> After launching my local U3A in Swindon in 1987, I was elected to the NEC of the central coordinating body in

1991, and was grateful to Eric for his inspiration and creative thinking in relation to my role in developing new U3As throughout the UK. He is a real visionary and a brilliant communicator whose ability to convey his ideas to either a large meeting, or individually, energises his listeners to pursue the objectives of U3A with enthusiasm, offering new ways of learning and sharing knowledge in an informal setting.

Over the years I invited Eric to speak to U3A members both in Swindon and Christchurch, usually about the early origins of U3A, but sometimes he surprised everyone by sharing his enjoyment of music hall and stand up humour particularly that of Ken Dodd. Eric Midwinter is a person of wide interests and great integrity, and he must be very proud of his role in establishing the U3A in the United Kingdom.

There are a number of references to Norman Richards in *500 Beacons*. Not content with starting the Swindon U3A, he later transferred his attentions to Christchurch, after a move of house, where subsequently he became Chairman. Norman was also elected as Vice Chairman of the NEC, and went on to undertake important work as chair of the Development Sub-committee.

Keith Richards (no relation to Norman), like Eric, was a sergeant instructor or 'Schoolie' during his National Service in the 1950s, in his case in Berlin. He later became a secondary school teacher in London, then went on to undertake fifteen years of teacher training, before becoming Head of Continuing Education at the Polytechnic of Central London (now the University of Westminster). Whilst working there on the development of experimental modular courses, he was invited to meet Peter Laslett at Trinity College, Cambridge and, as a result, was introduced to the U3A ideal. Some time later, Keith became Chairman of the Third Age Trust, serving with distinction in this capacity from 2003-2006. He came to know

Eric well through U3A activities and also had some contact with him over CPA business, to which Eric had returned for a while as Chairman.

According to Keith Richards, one of Eric's main contributions was to hammer home the idea that everyone can teach. Following on from principles expressed many years earlier in the Plowden Report, where 'child-centredness' was such an important theme, he advocated a combination of appropriate academic content and, most importantly, enjoyment, regardless of the age of those involved. Keith recalls that there was a constant plea from some individuals to stop using the word 'university' in the U3A title. He also comments that, of the three founders, that Michael Young was a highly original thinker but far less directly involved than either Eric Midwinter or Peter Laslett in the practical details of getting individual U3A groups off the ground.

Like many others who have communicated with the author, Keith Richards has an extremely high opinion of Eric and of his contributions to the U3A movement, saying of him:

> Eric has 'no vein of nastiness'. Although ceaselessly bothered by people who complain that U3A is predominantly white and middle class, Eric's (somewhat tautological) reply is always that 'The U3A is the answer for those for whom the U3A is the answer' (one might also add, as an aside, 'horses for courses').

> Eric's name carries tremendous weight; he writes regularly and speaks all over the place. Of the three founders, he was always the popular favourite, being the most flexible, approachable and friendly. He is also a boundless idealist; he thinks the whole educational establishment will have to listen to the example set by the U3A.

The story as outlined so far has been mainly about the origins and early days of the U3A, and of Eric's close involvement in it at every stage. Since then, the organisation has gone on from strength to strength, continuing to expand and attract new members. At the end of 1989 there were a hundred U3As registered around the country and by the time Eric came to collate statistical information in order to write the U3A story, this number had risen to an impressive five hundred, with a membership of over 140,000 by 2004. This constant expansion has continued steadily to the present day.

The contributions made by Michael Young, Peter Laslett and Eric Midwinter in the creation of the U3A in the UK were formally acknowledged by the Third Age Trust in 1999, less than a year before the deaths of the two most senior members of this illustrious trio. In a letter to Eric dated 1st November of that year, the Chairman, Len Street, wrote: 'At the Annual General Meeting of the Trust held in London in September, the meeting unanimously passed a resolution expressing the desire of the delegates to honour the three key founder members whose initiatives have led to so many men and women enjoying the pleasure of U3A membership. Accordingly, I have great pleasure in asking you, on behalf of the many delegates and the 85,000 plus members throughout the UK, to accept the title of 'Founder Member Emeritus'.

Dianne Norton, who contributed so much to the successful launch of U3A, had also received much deserved recognition and was honoured in 1995 by the award of an Honorary Associate Life Membership of the National U3A. In the words of the Annual Report of that year 'Dianne Norton, without whose efforts since the early days of 1982 there would be no U3A today ...'

No doubt there are interesting stories to tell about each and every U3A group, and many of these, from the first twenty-two years or so, are related in *500 Beacons*. There are also many individual enthusiasts who have played a key role in the development of the U3A over the years, only a few of whom have been mentioned by name here. Of course there have been problems and crises at various stages along the way, but despite various obstacles that somehow had to be overcome, U3A has survived and triumphed.

Eric has given many talks about U3A over the years, and also written extensively on the subject. In 1996 he published, on behalf of the Third Age Trust, the results of a independent evaluation for the Calouste Gulbenkian Foundation in a 66-page document entitled *'Thriving People': The Growth and Prospects of the U3A in the UK*. In this paper, as the title indicates, Eric covers in considerable detail the origins, growth, incidence, character, structure, potential and future prospects of the U3A, as seen thirteen years after its inception.

On 23rd March, 2007, Eric delivered the Frank Glendenning Memorial Lecture at the University of Keele, the text of which was published the following year by the National Institute of Adult Continuing Education (NIACE). This annual lecture series was instituted in 2003 in memory of Frank Glendenning, who was the prime mover in the development of the Association for Education and Ageing and one of Eric's old friends and allies. The title of this presentation was *U3Alogy: The thinking behind the U3A in the UK*. Here, in a rather more succinct format, Eric was able to outline some of the background to the formation of the U3A as viewed twenty-five years after the great experiment had begun. In this lecture he recalled with affection the many occasions over about 30 years that he had been at meetings with Michael Young, during which he had been attacked on the grounds of being idealistic. 'Oh, I do hope so,' he would murmur quietly, 'I do hope so.' No doubt much of this 'Youngian' idealism was shared Eric.

Eric delivered another big set-piece lecture in 2011 at the U3A 30th Anniversary Conference in Nottingham. On this occasion, the title he took was *Look Back in Wonder* and during it he marveled at the amazing growth of the U3A from its humble beginnings thirty years earlier to the thriving organization of the present day. He said towards the end of this lecture:

> As I look back in wonder at the success of this crusade, with enormous gratitude to all those pioneers, dedicated people like yourselves who have striven to make that misty dream of thirty years ago a stunning reality, I also sometimes look forward pondering whether we have reached maturity and should be looking another 30 years ahead or whether we are still in our infancy and should be looking 300 years ahead.

> What I am completely sure of, and I can confirm to you from my last conversations with both Peter Laslett and Michael Young that they were of the same opinion, both of them inordinately proud, as I am, of your thrilling realization of our hope, is this:

> Each time one of your members attends a weekly interest-group, be it local history or play-reading or whatever, he or she is also a part of the larger U3A group, which is part of a regional network, both of which are part of an immense national body, with, indeed, international ramifications as well, each time that happens your local member is raising the standard that proclaims 'I am an older citizen, not a social casualty, and, collectively with my friends, I am investing in my own destiny.'

In his letter of thanks to Eric after the Nottingham conference, Ian Searle, Chairman of the Third Age Trust, wrote: 'It was a privilege as always to share a platform with you and be part of that very welcoming audience. I was absolutely delighted at your standing ovation. It was richly deserved and movingly spontaneous. I was left almost without words after that, as I suspect you might have been, too.'

THE U3A LEGACY

And what about the U3A today? According to Lin Jonas, SEO of the Third Age Trust, as of January 2015 there were 953 U3As in the UK with some 341,843 registered members and the average number of interest groups per U3A was 40, usually representing about 30 different subject areas, since some of these require more than one group to accommodate all those members who are interested. Thus, it would appear that at the time of writing, there could be over 36,000 U3A interest groups in operation.

The U3A movement has on occasions been accused of being predominantly white, middle class and female in composition and people are well aware of this criticism, with efforts being made all the time to widen the spectrum of membership where possible. The geographical spread of the U3A across the country is generally broad, although coverage is rather patchy in London and a few other regions. According to Lin Jonas, there has been an average growth in U3A members of about 8% per year and the Third Age Trust is always looking to identify places where a new U3A might be successful, given suitable encouragement, rather than waiting for people from such locations to come forward unprompted.

In addition to kindly providing the above statistics, Lin Jonas has added the following comments about the impact of the U3A over the years since it first started and her personal view of Eric's contribution to it.

> The impact of the U3A movement is huge. For many people it has literally transformed their lives and for some it has been a life saver. U3A members are living life to the full – discovering new talents, learning new skills, making new friends, staying active both mentally and physically. So many members say they cannot imagine life without U3A and it has made their retirement so rewarding and full of purpose.

> As far as Eric is concerned, he is such an inspiring man. I am full of admiration for him and for all he has achieved and he has achieved so much. He is for me the best

speaker I have ever had the pleasure and good fortune to hear. I feel privileged to have been involved for the last 18 years in what I consider to be a truly wonderful organisation and honoured to count Eric Midwinter as a friend.

As you can tell I don't like him very much!!!

Eric with Barbara Lewis at the U3A Founders' Lecture 2013

The current National Chairman of the U3A is Barbara Lewis, who has known Eric for the last twelve years or so. Her husband, who is also a friend of Eric, is, like him, a keen cricket enthusiast and a member of the MCC. Barbara even confesses to liking cricket herself, which, as she says, is quite unusual for an American. Barbara was a U3A activist and gave talks around the country, sometimes sharing a platform with Eric. Some of her abiding memories are of the inspirational talks that Eric gave on such occasions and she always wished that some of his 'magic dust' would touch her too. In Barbara's view, his enthusiasm and vigour produced a kind of aura around him that was hard to forget, and he inspires her to this day. Sitting on the U3A National Executive, Barbara has always felt that Eric's spirit is with her and fellow members.

Barbara commented that Eric's presence is not intrusive; he could be involved in everything they do, but choses not to interfere. With changes of NEC chairs and the like he allows everything to go forward without trying to influence the changes. Barbara herself tries desperately to do things in his image and feel the passion for U3A that Eric conveys. In general, U3A is constantly going forward. Whatever the national and international situation, in her opinion, the flame somehow carries on.

Barbara also noted:

> In the early days, the French U3A was a possible model to follow, based on universities, but the universities here were not interested and shut the door. In my imagination, I can visualize the three co-founders going to the pub and deciding that they could do this thing themselves, with self-funding and self-help. It was such a grand idea and revolutionary to start it all from scratch, as they did.
>
> I sometimes feel like turning to Eric and saying 'Look what you have done'.

Whilst they were preparing for the 30th Anniversary of U3A, the idea of a Founders' Lecture was proposed, with Eric as the obvious choice as lecturer. It seemed astonishing to Barbara Lewis that there was no readily available living record of the man (at least as a presenter of talks to U3A gatherings; there are several recordings of Eric doing other things, including television broadcasts, as noted elsewhere in this book). All past NEC chairs and Trustees were to be invited to the lecture, of which a DVD would be made so as to create a permanent record of the event.

The Founders' Lecture was duly delivered by Eric on 9th April, 2013 at the Central Friends' Meeting House in Euston Road, London. There was a large audience in attendance to hear Eric talk on the intriguing subject *'Ouch Leggo' uttered Bunter: Schooldays Stories, Educational Failure and the U3A Ideal*. As

THE WORLDS OF ERIC MIDWINTER

mentioned above, the whole event was recorded on DVD by the estimable film-maker Winstan Whitter, and it can be viewed on the national U3A website.

U3A audience enjoying one of Eric's stories at the U3A Founders' Lecture 2013

As is usual in Eric's presentations, the lecture started with one of his signature funny stories, before getting into a serious consideration of education as viewed through popular schoolboy and schoolgirl literature, and by selected popular entertainers. This was followed by a detailed and provocative critique of failures in the British educational system, as he saw it. One of the other familiar themes explored was the balance between environmental and genetic factors in determining educational outcomes, with Eric coming down firmly on the side of 'nurture' over 'nature'. In the final part of his lecture, Eric turned to the ideal of the U3A, suggesting that perhaps this could be used a model for much needed improvements to the education system a whole. As Eric concluded 'Is there anywhere in this country a working model of a service rather than a system, where education is for its own sake and for that moment? Yes. It is the University of the Third Age.'

Eric's U3A Founders' Lecture was previewed in the Spring 2013 issue of *Third Age Matters* and a summary of it appeared in the subsequent Summer 2013 issue under the headline 'No true education occurs without enjoyment'. However, the ideas expressed by Eric during his provocative Founders' Lecture were clearly not without controversy and a number of letters from U3A members were published in this and the following Autumn edition of *Third Age Matters*, several of which were critical of his views on education, whilst others were supportive. Perhaps this mixed response is an indication that Eric actually achieved his objective of stimulating thought and discussion about the current state of the British educational system. Even those who disagreed on some of the points made would surely have to agree that the lecture was both informative and entertaining.

As he said in his 2011 *Look Back in Wonder* lecture, which was quoted above, Eric takes great pleasure and pride from the amazing success of the U3A. It brings together those three essential guiding principles of being open to all those in the Third Age, of being devoted to self-help, and of relying on co-operation and mutual aid, all of which were ideas close to the hearts of the three founding fathers. It is a shame that only Eric has lived long enough to witness the continuing progress of the movement into the early 21st century, but there is no doubt that Michael Young and Peter Laslett would have shared his delight in the breadth, scope and vitality of the U3A today.

Eric's involvement with U3A started whilst he was still working as Director of CPA in the 1980s and has continued ever since, in various capacities, so he has clocked up over 30 years of service to the organization he helped to found. However, as we have seen to some extent already, this is not the only kind of activity that has occupied Eric's time and energy in the years since he retired from full-time paid employment and entered the Third Age himself.

THE WORLD OF COMEDY

An important part of the cultural heritage that became mani-
fest in Eric Midwinter from an early age is his great love and
appreciation of popular theatre, comedians and entertainers,
and this sits well with his communitarian philosophy and
general sense of fun. To a considerable extent, this fondness,
along with his passion for Lancashire County Cricket Club and
Manchester United Football Club, came from and was actively
encouraged by his father, Ack, as has been acknowledged by
Eric in several of his writings. As a child growing up in Sale
in the pre-television age, Eric would go regularly to the local
cinemas with his pals or with his family, listen at home to some
of the popular broadcasts of the day on the wireless, and, of
particular significance in the context of this chapter, see the
acts of many of the great music hall and variety entertainers
live. The family lived close to several theatres, to which Eric
went frequently, and he was also taken to see George Lockhart's famous Belle Vue Circus in Manchester for the Christmas
1937 show, Lockhart being the first of his calling to wear the
'pink' hunter tails and top hat and who has been described as
the 'doyen of ringmasters'. Eric first attended a pantomime
at Christmas 1936, at the age of four, in which Albert Modley
appeared in 'Mother Goose' at the Princess Theatre, Manchester (which was later bombed in the blitz). His first experience
of a summer show, a year later in 1937, was at Will Parkin's

concert party on the promenade at Rhyl, with the comedian, Hal Blue, from whose saucy lips Eric heard his first rude joke. All of these theatrical experiences were highly memorable occasions for Eric and, no doubt, had a profound influence on his life-long love of live entertainment and performers.

It became increasingly obvious during the collection of material for this book that Eric has a prodigious memory for almost everything he has ever seen, heard or read throughout his life, and an enviable ability elegantly to encapsulate his recollections, either in his writings and or in verbal presentations. These attributes have enabled him to write extensively about entertainers, both in the form of numerous short articles for various newspapers and magazines, and, more extensively, in several books, always with a strong historical perspective. As of 2014, Eric has published six such books, to great acclaim, and, in addition, has contributed a number of short biographies of actors and entertainers for the *National Dictionary of Biography*, plus innumerable articles, obituaries and book reviews. He has also given many talks, to a variety of different audiences around the country, on the great entertainers about whom he has written. It is hoped that a brief exploration of Eric's major writings about the world of comedians and other popular performers will reveal something of his deep appreciation and understanding of those whose vocation it is to amuse and entertain.

Eric has himself always much enjoyed taking part in amateur entertainments of one kind or another, starting during his schooldays and continuing throughout university and his various jobs until the present day, as revealed by his numerous splendid contributions to the after-dinner entertainments at the Savage Club in London. In his time he has written and produced many amateur pantomimes, including five that he wrote for Sale Nomads, acting in and producing two of them; at the time they were regarded as the premier amateur pantomimes in the North-West. He has also written and performed revue sketches and amusing after-dinner entertainment routines, coupled to which he invariably introduces a touch of humour into his more serious talks and lectures by adding a few well-chosen stories. In another life, perhaps, Eric might well have made a successful career as a stand-up comedian, comic actor and parodist.

Eric's first venture into writing about entertainers happened in 1976 when he wrote an article for the journal *New Society* entitled 'The Geography of Ken Dodd'. Eric had first worked with Ken Dodd during his time as Director of the Liverpool Educational Priority Project and he managed to persuade Ken to take part in an extended interview about comedians and his own unique approach to comedy. Eric's own account of how this came about, as related to the author, is as follows:

> A pal of mine, Richard Bourne, who had been education correspondent for the *Guardian* and was now deputy editor of *New Society*, cottoned on to my connection with Ken Dodd and asked me to do an article on him. When I approached Ken, he was a bit chary about the idea – he didn't want his personal life exposed in print – but I stood on my dignity as an academic and said I was not interested in kiss'n'tell, nor was I. He agreed and promised to ring me when he had a free evening; luckily I happened to be at home quite early one day when the phone rang – having sorted it out it was really him and not my colleague Keith Pulham trying to hoax me – I shot round to his family house at Knotty Ash, with the coal lorries grinding at the back – his father had been a coal merchant – and we talked for four or so hours, until his pianist-cum-chauffeur arrived to take him to do a midnight cabaret at Stratford-on-Avon (I dread to think what time that finished). On hearing about this episode from me some years later, Patrick Newley (former editor of the magazine *The Call Boy*) commented that it was

probably the longest interview Ken Dodd ever gave to anybody.

I did the article - and it was the basis of a commission I subsequently got from John Bright-Holmes (of the publishers George Allen & Unwin) to do *Make 'em laugh'*- and that was how the 'comedy' writing began.

The short (two page) *New Society* article included a brief survey of some forty well-known comic entertainers classified by their place of birth and then went into an account of how Ken Dodd operated by keeping a detailed written record of audience reactions to his jokes. From his logbooks, collected over many years of performing all over the British Isles, Ken had been able to build up a comprehensive picture of which gags went down best with different audiences and in different places. As a result, he was – and still is – able to tailor his performance specifically for each location and type of audience, not only from the point of view of content, but also style and speed of delivery. As Eric remarked in this article, 'His talent and technique give him a sway over massed assemblies.' He concluded the piece with the words 'Ken Dodd traces his professional ancestry back to the court jester – he is the people's jester.'

Eric was especially struck by Ken Dodd's attention to detail, such as the weather and how the audience was dressed, for example in dinner jackets as opposed to holiday attire, which led to different types of expectation. When Eric, loftily playing the academic, quoted P.G. Wodehouse's comment 'Humour is the kindly contemplation of the incongruous', he replied, quick as a flash, 'P.G. Wodehouse never played the Golden Garter Club in Wythenshaw', going on to explain that heavily boozed audiences need what Ken called 'release' gags.

In *Make 'em Laugh*, published in 1979, Eric gives a fascinating account of the work of a selection of his favourite comedians, each one a representative of a particular era, from the days of the music hall up to more modern times. There are chapters dedicated to Billy Bennett ('The Raucous Parodist'), George Formby ('The Troubadour of Voyeurism'), Will Hay ('Tutor to the Thirties'), Robb Wilton ('The People's War Correspondent'), Jimmy James ('Pilgrim of Comedy'), Max Miller ('Cock of the Comic Midden'), Tony Hancock ('Cultural Casualty of the Fifties'), Frankie Howerd ('A Gossip for the Sixties'), Morecambe and Wise ('Twins of Mirth'), Les Dawson ('The Doom-laden Dumpling') and, as might be expected, Ken Dodd ('Comedy's Evangelist'). Although these are the major players discussed, Eric also refers in passing to many of their contemporary entertainers, often with pictorial illustrations, and gives interesting insights into the historical and social context in which they operated.

Eric wrote in his introduction to the book, 'As I have tried to study these comedians, my warm affection and admiration for them has grown beyond bounds. Of course, it is a self-indulgent list, introducing the entertainers who have brought me most comic pleasure over the years. Yet, at the same time, I have become increasingly aware of their value as

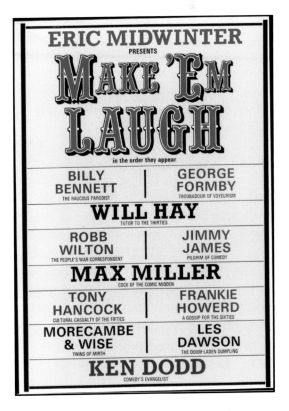

ERIC MIDWINTER PRESENTS

MAKE 'EM LAUGH

in the order they appear

BILLY BENNETT	GEORGE FORMBY
THE RAUCOUS PARODIST	TROUBADOUR OF VOYEURISM
WILL HAY	
TUTOR TO THE THIRTIES	
ROBB WILTON	JIMMY JAMES
THE PEOPLE'S WAR CORRESPONDENT	PILGRIM OF COMEDY
MAX MILLER	
COCK OF THE COMIC MIDDEN	
TONY HANCOCK	FRANKIE HOWERD
CULTURAL CASUALTY OF THE FIFTIES	A GOSSIP FOR THE SIXTIES
MORECAMBE & WISE	LES DAWSON
TWINS OF MIRTH	THE DOOM-LADEN DUMPLING
KEN DODD	
COMEDY'S EVANGELIST	

lightning conductors as I have endeavoured to locate them in their social context.' He concludes 'This book, part theatre criticism, part social analysis, tries to pick up this tale as, in the aftermath of the Great War, along with much else the old music-hall tradition was giving way to newer approaches.'

Jimmy James

As mentioned earlier, Eric's personal favourite amongst the various comedians featured in *Make 'em Laugh* is Jimmy James. In that book he describes with considerable glee an occasion at about the turn of the 1950s when he enjoyed perhaps his happiest evening of light entertainment, on the Central Pier in Blackpool. The two main acts were Morecambe and Wise, then just on the verge of national fame, and

the very well-established comedian Jimmy James, with his two regular side-kicks Hutton Conyers and Bretton Woods, each act performing twice during the show, giving altogether about ninety minutes of wonderful comedy. As Jimmy James was doing his stuff on stage, one of Eric's companions, Billy

Ack

Day, leaned over and whispered 'Christ, he's the spitting image of Ack (Eric's father)', since when Eric has never been able to think of them apart.

For many years, one of the two stooges in Jimmy James's act was his son James Casey, later to become a scriptwriter and a senior BBC Radio Light Entertainment producer, who helped Eric with both *Make 'em Laugh* and the notice about Jimmy James that he wrote for the *Oxford National Dictionary of Biography*. Referring to the chapter that Eric wrote about Jimmy James in *Make 'em Laugh*, James Casey said 'It is the best thing ever written about my father', a comment in which he takes considerable (and justifiable) pride.

Eric ends *Make 'em Laugh* by quoting an exchange between W.S. Gilbert, of Gilbert and Sullivan fame, and the great impresario Richard d'Oyly Carte. When the latter remonstrated with Gilbert that he earned more than the prime minister, he apparently replied curtly: 'I give more pleasure'. The comedians portrayed so vividly portrayed by Eric certainly gave more pleasure to the British public over the years than generations of prime ministers. Whether the same Gilbertian argument can be applied as appropriately to the relative earnings of modern Premier League footballers and our current prime minister is perhaps more open to debate, even if some of them do happen to play for Manchester United.

Some time before *Make 'em Laugh* was actually published, Eric received a delightful hand-written letter from Ken Dodd, with whom he had been in touch about choosing a suitable photograph to include in the book, in which he says 'Thank you for "starring" me in your book'. The letter ends "Kindest regards, hope you are fit and full of "plumptiousness", Ken'.

There was a highly favourable review of the book in the *Manchester Evening News* edition of April 19th, 1979, under the headline 'Go on, have a laugh'. The reviewer, Keith Macdonald, wrote: 'Setting each comedian clearly in the social context of his time, Eric Midwinter has written not only an entertaining book but also a masterly analysis of what 'Makes 'em Laugh'. And along the way he recalls a half forgotten world of favourite entertainers who included George Formby, Tessie O'Shea, Wee Georgie Wood, Albert Modley, Frank Randle, Sandy Powell, Arthur Tracy and stuttering Tubby Turner'.

On the same date, a somewhat fuller and more searching review was published in *New Society*, written by the flamboyant critic, writer and jazz singer George Melly. The review starts 'Eric Midwinter, who seems to be an honorable old-fashioned socialist, has written this book to illustrate a thesis: namely, that from Billy Bennett in the twenties – booming out surrealistic parodies of jingoistic ballads which echoed the general disillusion with that spirit of patriotism which had led to the great war – right through to Les Dawson, whose habitual pessimism could be said to personify the grim uncertainties of the seventies, the great comics reflect their times.' After commenting that this was a perfectly feasible theory, albeit scarcely an original one, the reviewer goes on to remark, '. . . and to substantiate it the author seems to feel the need to insert rather turgid passages of social history every now and then.' Had he known more about Eric's background and been familiar with some of his other writings, George Melly might well have acknowledged that putting people and events in their social and historical context was one of the great strengths of his literary output and was a good illustration of his grasp of the wider picture of the times in question. Notwithstanding this slight criticism, Melly went on immediately to add: 'I must hasten, however, to eradicate any impression that this is a dull book. Midwinter's love and understanding of his subject overcomes his didactic purpose.' After discussing in more detail – and in generally complimentary fashion – some of the subject matter of the book and referring to a few examples of the same genre written by other authors, the *New Society* review concludes 'Midwinter's book is a useful and heartwarming contribution to this growing canon.'

One of Eric's friends, John Raynor, a former colleague from Edge Hill College days, had read *Make 'em Laugh* soon after it was published and had also come across George Melly's review of it in *New Society*. He wrote in a letter of 30th April, 1979:

> *Make 'em Laugh* did the trick for me. I came home from work last week feeling decidedly ropey and took to my sick bed. Before doing so, I dropped into the bookshop and bought your book. I must say how much I enjoyed it - it was a most happy read, recapturing for me old favourites and past performances. But more than that, I marvelled at the way you interweaved the social and social history into the accounts - I wish I had such skill in writing and in understanding as you have. When George Melly described you as an old-fashioned socialist he got it right - it's a description to be proud of. Certainly the book is one you should feel most pleased with. It is a book that you feel was written and will be read with great affection. Thanks.'

It is clear from this letter that not everyone shared George Melly's critical opinion on the elements of social history incorporated by Eric into his book. Regrettably, John Raynor is no longer available for further consultation about his recollections of working and watching cricket with Eric. Another late friend of Eric's, the great cricket enthusiast Charles Oliver, used to say that of all his books, *Make 'em Laugh* had 'more of you in it than any other'. Dave Allsop, yet another of Eric's many pals with cricketing connections, sums up his feelings this way: 'For my money, his best book is *Make 'Em Laugh* in which he takes a comedian from each decade of the twentieth century and puts them into their historical and social context. Interesting; funny; perceptive.'

In his review of *Make 'em Laugh* for *The Guardian* of 19th April, 1979, Stephen Dixon confesses that Jimmy James, revered in the business as 'the comedian's comedian' was the funniest man he had ever seen, and he congratulates the author for 'returning to modest prominence a neglected master'. He concludes 'Although Mr Midwinter's book is beautifully illustrated and often acutely perceptive, what we laugh at is personal and doesn't really bear too profound an analysis. What our fathers and grandfathers found funny is another matter, however, and that is why the chapters on James, Wilton and Bennett work best.'

Eric was also involved in a number of radio interviews about the book and a half hour illustrated discussion programme for Piccadilly Radio, so it clearly made quite an impression.

Although Eric continued to write occasional articles and give talks about comedians and entertainers, there was a gap of over twenty years after *Make 'em Laugh* before the next book on the subject appeared. This was *Best Remembered: A Hundred Stars of Yesteryear*, published in 2002 by Third Age Press. In this book, which includes illustrations by Rufus Segar rather than photographs of the various characters, there are brief profiles of ten well-known performers in each of ten different categories. As the 'blurb' on the back of the cover explains, '*Best Remembered* presents a galaxy of 100 stars from the days before television ruled our lives'. One of the purposes of the book is to act as a trigger for personal or group reminiscence, particularly for 'third agers', as Eric explains in the introduction.

The ten areas from which the stars in the book are drawn are American Films, British Films, BBC Radio, Band Leaders, Theatre, Popular Vocalists, Comedians, Famous Imaginary Characters, British Sportsmen, and Overseas Sportspersons. The time period covered is from about 1927 to 1953, so that people who might actually recall seeing or hearing live performances by these individuals, all of whom were famous in their time, would by now be well over sixty years old, apart from any younger folk who may have had the good fortune to catch more recent appearances of the amazingly well-preserved Ken Dodd. In order to keep readers alert and attentive, this highly readable and nostalgic book ends with a 'Best Remembered Quiz', with ten questions relating to each chapter. 'Wake up at the back there!' as Jimmy Edwards might have shouted.

In his review of the book for the April 2007 edition of *Drumbeat* (The Quarterly Newsletter of the Savage Club), David Howe wrote affectionately: *'Best Remembered* is an excellent read. Somehow, when Eric writes about one of my particular favourites, his memories are my memories, his thoughts are my thoughts, and with his distinguished record as a social historian, he is able to explain why

I remember what I remember and its significance in the greatness of the character's performance.' David Howe's one complaint, no doubt shared by others, was that the book has no index, making it difficult to locate references to the individual performers mentioned in the text. It is important to mention here that David Howe, himself an expert on theatrical matters with an amazing personal archive of material, has often been a willing and able help to Eric in his work in this field.

Other reviews appeared in an eclectic variety of publications, including *Encore* (by John Wade), *Evergreen, Third Age News* (by Francis Beckett), *Best of British, Mercury Lane, Plus* (Newsletter of the Christian Council on Ageing, written by

Major Angela Irving of the Salvation Army), *Options* (Civil Service Retirement Fellowship), the *Newsletter of the Max Miller Appreciation Society*, and *Pensioners' Voice*, all of them encouragingly complimentary. The anonymous *Best of British* reviewer wrote, 'This is an invaluable trigger for reminiscence purposes and reflects a mountain of social and cultural history in a lively and enjoyable style.' Francis Beckett comments that it is Eric's erudite explanations that distinguish his work from 'the usual products of the nostalgia industry' and these make it 'illuminating and enlightening as well as a joy to read.' In addition, there was even a kind and friendly review of *Best Remembered* in *Focus*, the Parish Magazine of John Keble Church in Mill Hill, written by Charles Oliver, who admits that nearly all of the artists described by Eric in the book brought back happy memories.

From all these reviews, it is clear that *Best Remembered* struck a chord with many readers, for whom, like Charles Oliver, it conjured up fond recollections of performers they had seen or heard and enjoyed in the past.

In the same year as *Best Remembered* (2002), another book appeared, also published by Third Age Press, but this time it was about one remarkable entertainer. The title of this work is *As One Stage Door Closes . . . : The Story of John Wade, Jobbing Conjuror*. John Wade and Eric Midwinter are both members of the Savage Club in London and it is through this, as is the case with the present author and Eric, that they became even greater friends. John Wade had for some time been considering putting together some memoir of his intriguing career, whilst Eric himself was contemplating writing a new piece on the social background of entertainment in the post-war period. After a couple of preliminary lunchtime conversations, no doubt accompanied, in the inimitable words of Brother Savage Stanley Unwin, by an element of 'tilty elbow', they decided to embark upon a collaboration and produce a kind of 'bio-documentary' of John's life.

Following a series of discussions between author and subject, Eric rapidly sketched out the fascinating story of John's life from his suburban childhood in London and his early ventures into the world of magic, then through the development of his professional career in show business, decade by decade, from the 1940s up to the present time. John's great ability to charm, mystify and amuse audiences – large

and small – in different locations and settings around the world are movingly described, as are the cruel changes in circumstances brought about by the onset of arthritis in mid-career. Clearly such physical problems created enormous difficulty for a performer whose act is so dependent on manual dexterity, but they inevitably led John to seek new directions and outlets for his talents as an entertainer. The book was rounded off by a very effective 'Afterword' by the subject himself, in which he reveals some of his personal reflections on a long and successful life dedicated to magic and entertainment.

As might be expected, considering the allegiance of both author and subject, this book was also reviewed in *Drumbeat* (in the issue of December, 2002), on this occasion by Professor Vincent Porter. His perceptive article begins: 'At the centre of *As One Stage Door Closes* lies an age-old epistemological dilemma that most biographers seek to avoid: how should your narrative balance the personal qualities of the man whose life you are telling with the economic and political forces that shape all our lives? Where does biography end and social history begin? Eric Midwinter has embraced the epistemological challenge with gusto, offering us a history of John Wade's life as jobbing conjuror that is firmly set within the changing economic fortunes of the post-war entertainment business. What he gives us is not a fully-fledged Marxist dialectic, but instead a meditation on the manner in which John Wade, a man with talent to amaze, has adapted to the changing demands for entertainment during the second half of the Twentieth Century.'

Perhaps uniquely, publication of *As One Stage Door Closes* was accompanied by two well-attended book launches, one at the Savage Club and the other at the London headquarters of the Magic Circle, much to the enjoyment of those lucky enough to be there on either or both occasions. The presence of both Eric and John, as well as a number of other members of the Magic Circle and of the Savage Club, together with family and friends, made for two most joyous and convivial events, as might be imagined.

In *The People's Jesters: Twentieth Century British Comedians*, published by Third Age Press in 2006, Eric revisits, updates and widens the material used in his earlier book *Make 'em Laugh*. In this 229-page book, complete with comprehensive index (David Howe take a bow) and photographic illustrations (kindly provided by Patrick Newley), Eric traces the world of British comedy from the nineteenth century, via the early stars of Music Hall and Variety, through the twentieth century and up to modern times. There are informative and evocative chapters about Christmas Pantomimes, Summer Seaside Shows, the Advent of Radio, The Influence of Cinema, Comic Groups, Comedy Playlets, Comedy Double Acts, Specialist 'Funny Turns', Women in Comedy, Regional Variations in Humour, and Metropolitan Icons from London. In order to mention the fifty or so other comedians not already included in these chapters, Eric also compiled a helpful Comedy Alphabet, with short descriptions of other, less well-known performers.

In the penultimate chapter, entitled 'Television: Box of Delights', Eric examines further some of the changes consequent upon the closure of the old music halls and variety theatres, and the growth of television viewing. He also discusses performers who have appeared in cabaret and stage revues, using *Beyond the Fringe* as one example of a particular kind of British humour, as well as considering influential radio and TV programmes such as *The Goon Show* and *Monty Python*, and examples of the comic sit-coms and popular dramas like *Hancock's Half Hour, Dad's Army, Only Fools and Horses* and many others. As Eric remarks towards the end of this chapter 'There can be little doubt that comic actors have largely replaced comedians on television over wide stretches of the comedy shows on offer.' As he goes on to point out, in the past the title of 'comedian' was then more broadly bestowed on those who did stand-up or sketches in variety and later on radio. He speculates that perhaps distinguished comic actors like Sir David Jason, star of so many popular television series, should be re-styled as 'comedians' of the old Victorian dispensation, that is, the complement of the 'tragedians'.

In the final chapter, Eric draws up a list of his fifty 'Tops of the Bill', revealing his personal favourite performers out of over 800 comedians and comic actors who are mentioned in the text. Unsurprisingly, the number one spot is taken by Jimmy James, closely followed by Robb Wilton and Ken Dodd, but there are also places for the two George Formbys (Senior and Junior), Albert Modley, Tommy Handley (and the entire ITMA cast), Billy Bennett, Stanley Holloway (some of whose famous monologues Eric has been known to reproduce at social gatherings), Max Miller, Morecambe and Wise, and many other great characters. Although male performers inevitably

constitute the majority of Eric's nominations to this list of favourites, the female of the species is not altogether overlooked, being represented by such different characters as Victoria Wood, Gracie Fields, Hylda Baker and Marie Lloyd, together with a handful of female impersonators, including Mrs. Shufflewick (Rex Jamieson), Old Mother Riley (Arthur Lucan), and Danny La Rue. The relative paucity of female performers amongst the long list of male counterparts is an issue that Eric had visited earlier in 1985, in an article for *New Society* entitled 'Where are the women comedians?' Here he refutes the argument that women are basically non-humorous and goes on to ponder: 'Why the naughty nineties should throw up Marie Lloyd in London, and the fidgety fifties Marilyn Monroe in Hollywood is an unanswerable show-business riddle', and he wonders what female comedy stars the future might bring. With the more recent popularity of artistes like Dawn French, Jennifer Saunders, Joanna Lumley, Miranda Hart and many others, it is evident that the present comedy scene can offer plenty of fine examples of female entertainers.

Aware that his particular selection might not accord with everyone's preferences, Eric concludes by inviting his readers to make up their own list of favourite 'People's Jesters'. Finally, at the end of this nostalgic and entertaining account of the world of British comedy, he allows Jimmy James to have the final words with a characteristic quotation from one of his classic sketches.

Reviewing *People's Jesters* for *The Stage*, Patrick Newley wrote, his piece appearing under a splendid colour photograph of Ken Dodd, 'Midwinter traces the history of British comedians, beginning with the decline of music hall around the end of the First World war, when comics were the dominant factor in entertainment. As well as analyzing some of the great comedians' unique styles – including Sandy Powell, Arthur Askey, Harry Tate and Will Hay – Midwinter delves deeper into the history of the comic tradition in both music hall songs and the literature of writers such as Charles Dickens.' Newley concludes: 'Meticulously researched and vastly entertaining, *The People's Jesters* is a worthy addition to any theatre buff's bookshelf.'

Wyn Calvin, writing in *The Call Boy*, comments that 'This is a fascinating review of a cavalcade of comedy stars, as well as many smaller names, who have helped to make Britain arguably the world's richest nation of laughter-makers.' He ends his review with the words 'A splendid reference book – and an excellent read.' A similarly enthusiastic review, was written by John Wade for *Encore Theatre Magazine*, who concludes 'It works as a social history, showing how the prevailing circumstances of war, economic slumps and happier times often affected the style of comedy, but above all it is a book to make you laugh and recall fondly performers who have been part of our lives since childhood.'

I Say, I Say, I Say: The Double Act Story is the title of the next book in the series about comedians, again published by Third Age Press, in 2009. Although he had already referred to a number of comic double acts in his earlier books, with the result that some of the better-known characters take a well earned encore here, in this work Eric explores the whole phenomenon of comedy partnerships in considerably more detail. The book is divided into three main parts, in the first of which Eric considers 'Why Were There So Few Double Acts Before 1918?' with the two chapters giving a brief outline of the origins of such acts and certain barriers to them. In Part Two he addresses, over the course of four chapters, the question 'Why Were There So Many Double Acts Between 1918 and 1953?', illustrating the narrative with many fascinating examples of different types and styles of performers who worked together in partnerships, often somewhat uneasily. The third part comprises a consideration of yet another potentially difficult question, 'Why Were There So Few Double Acts After 1953?'

In this slim volume, the whole history of comedy double acts is explained in the context of their times, and scores of performers, some of them household names whilst others are somewhat less familiar, are fondly described. As Eric writes in the Valediction at the end of the book 'The standard double act, scarcely known before the 1920s, had more or less vanished by the 1960s'. He concludes : 'The wireless and the variety stage were choice arenas for the double act. Thus there were few before and few thereafter. The old-style double acts had finally obeyed the classic command of the offended and irked straight man. They had kindly left the stage.' As the reviewer in the Winter 2009 issue of *Drumbeat* put it 'This is a book that can be enjoyed either as a sit-down and read from cover to cover or as one where dipping in always comes up with a fascinating fact.'

In a highly thoughtful and analytical review for *Wallpaper, the Max Wall Society Journal*, Michael Pointon draws attention to the absence of several other double acts, including some of his own personal favourites, such as 'The Two Ronnies' and writing in *U3A News*, Francis Beckett bemoans the omission of Flanders and Swann and others but hails *I Say, I Say, I Say* as 'a delightful read, clear, accessible and entertaining, and written with the knowledge and affection that he brings to his favourite subjects, of which the history of comedy is one. At 150 pages, in reasonably large type, it's a quick and enjoyable read.'

In both *I Say, I Say, I Say* and *The People's Jesters* Eric warmly acknowledges the help and advice of Patrick Newley, not least for the provision of some of the material used as illustrations, in addition to his expertise on all things theatrical and for his general support and encouragement. Patrick worked at various times as an actor, agent, publicist, entertainment manager, and comedian, but in more recent times was best known as an author, editor of the journal *The Call Boy*, and as an obituary writer for *The Times* and *The Stage*. Like Eric and the present author, he was also an active member of the Savage Club, where he was greatly respected and his company was much appreciated by all who knew him. Tragically, Patrick died of oesophageal cancer in May 2009, at the far too early age of 54, and is sadly missed by his many friends. Only a few weeks before he died, Patrick wrote a short review of *I Say, I Say, I Say* for *The Stage*, in which he comments 'Highly readable, the book shows how the dictates of fashion, coupled with the demands of variety and the wireless created a boom time for cross-talk comics'. Newley goes on to recommend the book, 'not least for the picture on page 125 of a certain seventies clubland double act, Ruck and Newley. Now I wonder what happened to them?'

The most recent of Eric's books on comedians and entertainers is *Best Remembered Two: Cinema and Radio*, once again published by Third Age Press in 2013. After an introductory prelude in which Eric surveys what forms of entertainment were available to the general public before the advent of cinema and radio, Eric provides evocative profiles of forty films, and their stars. These start with 'The Good Companions' of 1933 and proceed chronologically to 'Father Brown', released in 1954, by way of 'The Thirty Nine Steps', 'Oh Mr Porter', 'Goodbye Mr Chips', 'Henry V', 'Brief Encounter', 'The Third Man', 'Passport to Pimlico', 'The Blue Lamp', 'The Cruel Sea', and many other classic movies. Because so many thousands of films were made between 1930 and the mid-fifties, the selection of examples inevitably had to be limited to a reasonable number, and it was sensibly decided to include only British films for the purposes of this particular book.

What is amazing from today's perspective is the huge popularity of the cinema, or the 'flicks' as they were commonly known during this period, before virtually every household succumbed to the insidious temptations of television and the subsequent dramatic decline in the number of cinemas around the country began. For example, as Eric points out, by the 1940s about 30 million cinema tickets were sold each week and 75% of the adult population in Britain were regular filmgoers.

After the films comes a selection of the most popular radio programmes, eighteen of which are featured in a series of short essays. These include a wide variety of types of broadcast, from children's programmes such as *Children's Hour*, a medley of Music Hall and Music Programmes, Magazine Programmes like *In Town Tonight* and *Monday Night at Eight*, examples of 'Shows Within Shows' such as *Garrison Theatre* and *Happidrome*, and, for more serious listening, *The Brains Trust*. Needless to say, comedy offerings are also prominent, with affectionate coverage of popular shows like *Bandwaggon, Mr Muddlecombe JP, ITMA, Waterlogged Spa, Stand Easy, Much Binding in the Marsh*, and *Take It From Here*. Following some interesting further insights into the world of radio under the headings of 'School For Laughs' and 'Late Flowerings and Evergreens', the radio section concludes with a description of 'The Phenomenon of Wilfred Pickles'.

A number of these programmes were compulsory listening in the homes of many families, and their highly popular stars, particularly of the comedy shows, often became household names. Generations of youngsters memorised large chunks of these broadcasts and attempted to imitate their favourite comedians for the benefit of friends and family. Catch phrases from *ITMA, Much Binding in the Marsh, Take It From Here* and other shows are still widely recognized today, stirring up fond memories for those of a certain age who can joyfully recall listening to them in their younger days.

Altogether, almost 600 film and radio personalities are mentioned during the course of this fascinating and nostalgic survey of two of the major sources of mass entertainment in the middle part of the twentieth century. As is very aptly stated on the back cover of the book, 'It is a feast of memory-tugging delights for the older reader and a mine of historical treasures for the young'.

Under the heading 'A bran tub of treats', Tony Russell's review of *Best Remembered Two* for *Third Age Matters* (the successor to *U3A News*) opens: 'Eric Midwinter's investigations of all our yesteryears should be prized by nostalgics and students of popular culture. He recalls the manifestations of what he terms "collective leisure": the entertainment Britons shared, sometimes physically united, in music hall, cinema or dancehall, sometimes remotely when people "stayed in" by the million to listen to a single radio programme.' After commenting that 'The descriptions of films, programmes and actors are encased in social and historical commentary' and mentioning some of the characters portrayed in the book, Russell concludes that *Best Remembered Two* is 'a mighty feat of recollection and interpretation'. Although mildly critical of the low number and quality of the illustrations used, and of the book cover, he advises potential readers that '. . . you will find yourself digging delightedly into a bran tub brimming with old-fashioned treats.'

Perhaps inevitably, in the course of writing several books about the world of popular entertainment, there is a certain degree of overlap as some of the colourful characters make more than one appearance within these surveys of the many comedians and entertainers who were plying their trade in the theatres, dance halls, radio and television studios, and on the cinema sets, during much of the twentieth century. Eric's obvious appreciation and love of these entertainers, as well as his inimitable ability not only to encapsulate their performances but also to set their achievements within the social and cultural conditions of their times, makes these enjoyable and informative books to read. They also represent a significant contribution to the social history of the British people during that turbulent and war-torn century.

In addition to the books summarized above, Eric has also contributed many articles about entertainers to various newspapers and journals, including *The Call Boy* and *Drumbeat*. The current editor of *The Call Boy*, Geoff Bowden, wrote in January, 2013:

> When I took over as Editor in the spring of 2009, because of Patrick Newley's illness, I contacted all the regular writers to ask them if they would stay on during my 'reign'. They all agreed and although one or two have now stopped their regular contributions, Eric still continues to be a regular and highly valued member of the team. He has become, over the last year or so, my book reviewer-in-chief. He is the first person I go to if I want a book reviewed. His reviews are always incisive, sympathetic and well written. In addition, Eric contributes the occasional article. He is especially interested in comedians and comedy programmes, from what would be known to many as the 'golden age of radio'. He wrote a fascinating piece on the radio show *Take It From Here* and excellent pieces on *Happidrome*, *Garrison Theatre*, Jimmy Clitheroe and Wee Georgie Wood and an article looking at taboos in variety. I also have an, as yet unpublished, article of his, on *Band Waggon*, the Arthur Askey/Richard Murdoch success. His knowledge and love of these comedians and comedy

shows are evident in every article he writes and in addition Eric's work is eminently readable.

The National Dictionary of Biography (2004) contains no less than 25 entries written by Eric Midwinter, of which a 'baker's dozen' are about comedians and actors. This varied and distinguished list of performers includes Hylda Baker, Billy Bennett, Jimmy Clitheroe, Tony Hancock, Robertson Hare, Will Hay, Stanley Holloway, Jimmy James, Fred Karno, Stan Laurel, Ted Ray, Max Wall, and Robb Wilton. Between them, these artistes represent the worlds of music hall, variety theatre, film, radio and, to a far lesser extent, television. It appears that Eric's affection and regard for those whose main mission in life is to amuse and make us laugh has no bounds, and in recording so faithfully the history of many of the entertainers of the twentieth century he has done a great service, both to those older individuals who enjoy being reminded of some of the wonderful comic acts of the past, and to future students and historians of the world of comedy.

Eric's particular knowledge of Fred Karno was put to good use when one of the contestants selected this famous theatre impresario and comedian as his specialist subject for the BBC's *Mastermind* programme, back in the days when Magnus Magnusson was the quizmaster. The researcher who telephoned Eric asked him to set thirty questions about Fred Karno (Frederick John Westcott) and when challenged as to what she would do if he were unable or unwilling to assist in this way, she replied, succinctly, 'Panic!'

Another of Eric's interests and enthusiasms is in the work of Gilbert and Sullivan, and he seems to have an almost encyclopedic memory of the songs that form the substance of their many light operas. He did at one time plan to write a book about W.S. Gilbert and had actually started working on it, but then he discovered that the distinguished American opera and theatre scholar, Jane W. Stedman, was already preparing what is now the standard biography of the great man. Jane Stedman was Professor of English at Roosevelt University in Chicago, and a regular contributor to *Opera News*, who died in 2003 at the age of 83, and her book is *W.S. Gilbert: a classic Victorian and his theatre*, published in 1996 by Oxford University Press. Eric did meet Jane Stedman on one occasion and corresponded with her frequently and was privileged to have his work acknowledged in a couple of footnote references in her book.

So, having been 'pipped at the post' in the race to produce the definitive Gilbert biography, Eric had to content himself with writing an article for the *New Theatre Quarterly* entitled 'W.S. Gilbert: Victorian Entertainer', which was published in July, 1987. In Eric's view the 'musical plays' of Gilbert and Sullivan were the originators of the light entertainment industry, as it is known today, and he has used this idea as the basis for talks at the Savage Club and elsewhere.

For a final comment on Eric's contributions to the world of comedy and entertainers, with a propitious link back to his favourite comic, Jimmy James, the writer and broadcaster Michael Pointon has added:

> I first learned of Eric Midwinter's devotion to the variety theatre when I was working in radio for the BBC in 1979 and Jimmy James's son, Jim Casey, then a producer based in Manchester, told me how much he had enjoyed *Make 'em Laugh*. Eric's perceptive study of comedians had included an insightful piece on Casey's late father. Several years later I was invited to contribute to the *New Dictionary of National Biography* and write about variety entertainers. Eric had already written several detailed entries in this category so I was in the best of company. What I find appealing about Eric's approach is that he writes with a clear and informed love of his subject rather than with an overly analytical academic style, which can often make the humour in a subject

evaporate. He brought the same light touch to his more recent book on double acts, *I Say, I Say, I Say.*

For many people the achievement of writing so many excellent books about entertainers might have been sufficient, but that would be to overlook Eric's great love of sport where, once again he has been able to cast his social historian's keen analytical gaze to good effect.

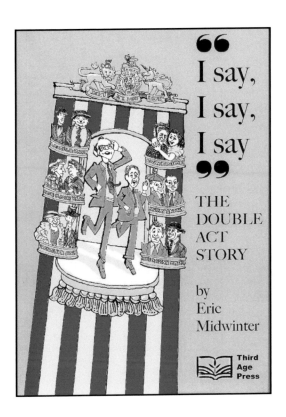

Eric wins the Cricket Book of the Year Award for 2005 with
Red Shirts and Roses

THE WORLD OF SPORT

Without doubt, sport is one of the most popular, avidly followed, and commercially significant of human activities in the modern world. As a result of widespread television coverage, worldwide audiences for major events, such as the football World Cup, are vast and the money spent on and generated by popular sports is mind-blowing. At grass roots level, participation in sports is an enjoyable pastime for many, with important advantages for health, physical and social development of young people, and for those with conspicuous talent may even offer opportunities to become professional sportsmen and women. For many, following sport, either by attending games in person or via TV, radio and internet coverage, is a lifelong source of pleasure and enjoyment, and spectators often become very passionate about the teams or individuals they support.

Eric's lifelong interest in sport started at an early age and at Sale Grammar School he played both cricket and rugby with some success. He recalls rushing home on his twelfth birthday to pick up his boots as he was called upon at the last minute to represent Blue House in a junior house match, his first taste of truly competitive sport. Thereafter, he continued to play both sports throughout his schooldays, as well as amateur soccer for Sale Oakfield at weekends.

Whilst still at school, Eric sometimes played for Sale Cricket Club, where his father was scorer, usually appearing for the 3rd XI and Sunday XI, but with occasional outings for the 2nds. There were further sporting opportunities during his time doing National Service and at Cambridge, after which he continued to play some sport at the various places where he worked until moving South in 1975, at the age of 43, never to play cricket, rugby or football again. The high point of Eric's cricketing achievements was his best ever score of 86, triumphantly attained whilst opening the batting for Ponteland 2nd XI against Ashington in the summer of 1966, possibly motivated by the fact this was the sole occasion he played in a match for which spectators had to pay for admission, and he reached half centuries on a dozen or so other occasions during his playing career. By his own admission, he rarely, if ever, went to net practice or team training sessions, which he found tedious, but always loved the society and collective spirit of team sports. In contrast to this strong affection for team activities, he was never much drawn to participation in individual games such as tennis, squash, golf or snooker, being particularly unimpressed by games that involved hitting a static ball, and he never learnt to swim.

As is described in his book *Red Shirts and Roses: The Tale of Two Old Traffords* (2006), Eric was born and bred a minute's walk from Sale Station, within easy travelling distance of the 'Twin Temples' of the home grounds of Manchester United Football Club and Lancashire County Cricket Club at Old Trafford. As he wrote at the beginning of that book: 'The two Old Traffords were quickly in my sights and proximity was an important issue. Even more significant, my father was a keen sports follower, with "Lanky" and "the Reds" his rooted preference, so that there was about as much chance of my becoming, say, a Manchester City and Yorkshire fan as a child born in Kabul has of becoming a Particular Baptist. Let us assume that nature and nurture brought about this dispensation.' Such was the strength and significance of his life-long attachment to his two favourite clubs that, years later, Eric came to realize that 'Lancashire County Cricket Club and Manchester United played the role and satisfied the niche in my life that religion does for others'.

As a youngster, Eric had many opportunities to watch his sporting heroes in action, although for a number of years, due to air-raid war damage at Old Trafford, Manchester United had to play their home matches at the Maine Road ground of their local rivals, Manchester City. Some of his memories of these occasions are lovingly recounted in *Red Shirts and Roses*, including the ritual awarding of a Mars bar by his father when he attended his first home football match, a tradition that was subsequently carried on into the next generation of Midwinters.

Since moving South in later years, Eric has frequently enjoyed watching cricket at Lord's, where he is a much respected life member of the Marylebone Cricket Club (MCC) and is able to meet and chat with other cricket-loving friends. Apart from the youthful joys of participating in sports, and the continuing pleasure of being a spectator, Eric has been able to indulge his interest in his favourite sports by writing about them, both in the form of books and in numerous articles for papers, magazines and newsletters. He has also given many talks on sporting topics and is greatly in demand as an after-dinner speaker at cricket and rugby clubs.

Eric's first book about sport was *W.G. Grace: His Life and Times*, published by George Allen & Unwin in 1981, two years after the same firm had brought out *Make 'em Laugh*. It carries the dedication 'For John Rennie, Brian Walsh, John Raynor and other nostalgic and talkative watchers', each of whom is mentioned elsewhere in this book, although, regrettably, the two Johns are no longer with us to continue their talking and watching. When Eric first discussed the possibility of writing a sports book with the editor, John Bright-Holmes, he was strongly advised to opt for cricket rather than football as his chosen subject, mainly on the grounds that a hardback book on cricket would be far more likely to appeal to people over the age of 45, the age group that generally tends to purchase and read such books. Eric's initial idea of writing about the Victorian transformation of cricket into a major entertainment business was also turned round by John, so that the well-known character W.G. Grace became the hook for the book. According to some, the resulting work was the first cricket book to put the game in its broad historical perspective and to treat WG as an important historical figure rather than, simply, another – albeit rather special – cricketer.

W. G. GRACE
His Life and Times

Eric Midwinter

The distinguished Australian cricket historian and writer Bernard Whimpress has written about his one and only meeting with Eric at a lunch at the Cricketers Club in Marylebone in 1999, during which, with black pudding on the menu, he evidently offered to tell Bernard which Lancashire village produced the 'blackest' black pudding. Bernard went on to add:

I had first come across his work in his biography of W.G. Grace a decade earlier when I was writing an honours thesis on Australian crowd responses to WG on his two tours down under. What originally impressed me about

Eric's analysis was his depiction of WG as the 'eternal boy' and a mischievous figure caught between the ages of the professional travelling elevens and the amateurism of the new public schools. This made his subject's 'shamateurism' and gamesmanship understandable as well as forgivable.

Bernard Whimpress is just one of a number of eminent cricket enthusiasts who have kindly corresponded with the author about Eric's many contributions to the literature and history of the game. With regards to the W.G. Grace biography, Stephen de Winton has written:

> My first acquaintance with Eric Midwinter was when I read his *W.G. Grace: His Life and Times*, published in 1981, and acquired by me in the same year. I enjoyed the book very much, as it placed Grace firmly in the context of Victorian society and explained his significance as a seminal figure in the development of cricket. I was also intrigued with Eric Midwinter's connection with W.G.'s contemporary of the same name, Billy Midwinter.

On the same theme, Dave Allsop, one time Chairman of the Cricket Society, writes:

> My first knowledge of Eric Midwinter came when living in Northumberland in the late 1970s/early 1980s. I was an avid cricket book reader, and my eye was caught by Eric's book about W.G. Grace. I had heard of Billy Midwinter, of the same era as WG, so bought it – for money! I really enjoyed it. Some cricket books are full of statistics. This one set the great man in his social and historical context.

The W.G. Grace biography attracted considerable interest amongst cricket lovers and a number of favourable reviews were published, including one by the inestimable John Arlott in the *Guardian* newspaper. The reviewer in *Wisden*, the cricketers' 'bible', wrote that the book: '... is, unexpected as it may seem, a genuine addition to knowledge about "The Old Man". It admits modern values – especially on financial matters – to ground where it had hitherto been banned, or at least ignored; and, simultaneously, sets the great cricketer in the perspective of his time. More strikingly it deals also with the short, but striking and tragic career of the author's ancestor, that William Midwinter who played Test cricket for both England and Australia. Less a biography than an historic study, this is indeed a most impressive chronicle of cricket.'

Billy Midwinter

William ('Billy') Evans Midwinter, referred to several times above, was born at St Briavels in the Forest of Dean, Gloucestershire, in 1851 and died in 1890 in Melbourne, Australia. According to family tradition, as related to him by his grandfather, Billy Midwinter was Eric's great grandfather's cousin. Billy's family had emigrated to Australia in 1861, when he was just ten years old, whilst the Mancunian branch of the Midwinter clan had moved North from Gloucestershire some years earlier in 1835, as the wool trade dwindled and the cotton business expanded in Lancashire. As is recorded in some detail in Eric's study of W.G. Grace, Billy was an accomplished all-round cricketer who became the first transoceanic commuter amongst professional sportsmen, dividing his playing career between England and Australia. He played in eight Test Matches for Australia against England, and in four matches for England against Australia, becoming the only cricketer to have achieved this unique double. In Australia he represented Victoria, whilst in England he played for W.G. Grace's Gloucestershire. It is said that Billy visited his northern kinsfolk during one of his cricketing sojourns in that part of the country; ever the romantic, Eric has speculated if that could well have been during the famous occasion in 1878 when Lancashire and Gloucestershire met for the first time, a match in which W.E. Midwinter scored 22 and 25 in a low-scoring draw. This was the very match that haunted Francis Thompson for the rest of his life and led him in 1907 to write his famous poem *At Lord's*, with its ghostly refrain 'my Hornby and my Barlow'.

Following the successful publication of the W.G. Grace book in 1981, Eric has gone on to produce – so far – a further eleven books on sport, most of them about cricket. The latter include *The Lost Seasons: Cricket in Wartime* (1987), *Red Roses Crest the Caps; Story of Lancashire Cricket Club* (1989), *Brylcreem Summer: 1947 Cricket Season* (1991), *The Illustrated History of County Cricket* (1992), *First Knock; Cricket's Opening Pairs* (1994), *Surrey CCC: 150 Years – A Celebration* (Ed, 1995), *Darling Old Oval: Surrey Cricket at the Oval* (1995), *From Meadowland to Multinational: a Review of Cricket's Social History* (2000), *Quill on Willow: Cricket in Literature* (2001), *George Duckworth: Warrington's Ambassador at Large* (2008), and *The Cricketer's Progress: Meadowland to Mumbai* (2010). In addition, he has contributed eleven brief biographies of distinguished former cricketers for the Oxford Dictionary of National Biography.

Readers will no doubt be pleased to learn that it is not the intention here to attempt a detailed critical analysis of all these books, but rather to pick out a few examples for discussion in order to illustrate the range and variety of Eric's contributions to the field, and to amplify these with selected comments from reviewers and cricketing friends. As can be seen from a quick perusal of the above titles, these cover the histories of particular cricket clubs and grounds, reminiscences on the summer of 1947, including the wonderful exploits of the author's personal schoolboy heroes, Denis Compton and Bill Edrich, and the biographies of individual cricketers. Two of the books represent serious and scholarly treatment of the social history of cricket as it developed over the centuries, although, as noted previously in other contexts, social history forms a significant feature of all Eric's writings, whatever the subject.

The second sporting book to appear, also published by Allen & Unwin, was *Fair Game: Myth and Reality in Sport*, which came out in 1986. As the publicity material on the dust jacket proclaims '*Fair Game* looks at modern sport in its social context and concludes that it is a mess, beset with greedy and over-commercialised motives, damaged by dangerous political alignments, and marred by wrongheaded personal and social values.' This brief descriptive statement concludes '… he properly utilizes his grasp of social and political trends to illustrate the perils into which sport – for which he has a most genuine attachment – has fallen.'

Unlike many books about sport, which often tend to idolise the star participants and idealise the games themselves, this is a radical and stimulating critical account of the world of sport, amateur and professional, national and international, warts and all.

The highly readable and entertaining *Red Shirts and Roses: The Tale of Two Old Traffords*, published in 2006, is one of the most autobiographical of Eric's books, with many references drawn from personal experience. As the title reveals, it is an account of the history of the homes of his two favourite sports teams, Manchester United Football Club and Lancashire County Cricket Club, both of which he started to support in early childhood, and it is obviously of particular significance to followers of the 'red shirts' and the 'red roses'. As one enthusiastic reviewer has written: 'Eric has a unique and engaging style of writing, bringing past famous events and household names back to life. Full of humorous anecdotes and detailed stages of development, it is a mammoth entertainment from start to finish.' This view is fully endorsed by the Australian writer, critic and cricket enthusiast J. Neville Turner who starts his review with the words 'This is a remarkable book by a remarkable man' and, whilst confessing that he himself is no great lover of Manchester United, concludes it by writing: 'But I venture to suggest that any lover of cricket would find delight in every page of *Red Shirts and Roses*. On the evidence of this and his other writings, I unhesitatingly rate Midwinter the finest writer on cricket since Neville Cardus (who he copiously and generously cites and praises throughout the book)'. High praise indeed!

Further evidence of the high regard in which this book is held can be deduced from the fact that it was selected for the Cricket Society's Book of the Year Award in 2005. As the acting chairman of the panel of judges for that year, Stephen de Winton, recalls:

> Eric's *Red Shirts and Roses*, a history of his twin enthusiasms, Lancashire C.C.C and Manchester United F.C. was nominated for the Book of the Year Award in 2005. Eric had therefore to step down as Chairman of the award panel and it fell to me, on the 'Buggins Turn' or longevity of service principle, to chair the award panel that year. It was no surprise to me at least that Eric's book proved far superior to the others and I had the pleasure of officiating at the award ceremony at which Christopher Martin-Jenkins presented the award to Eric.

The citation which accompanied this award read 'For a book distinguished by the writer's erudition, passion, wit, and thorough understanding of cricket in particular and sport in general, in history and society, the Book of the Year Prize is awarded to Eric Midwinter for his *Red Shirts and Roses*'.

Eric had previously published, in 1989, a whole book dedicated to the story of Lancashire County Cricket Club, under the title *Red Roses Crest the Caps*, which is taken from a line in the aforementioned poem by Francis Thompson's 'At Lords'. As described in *Wisden* (1990), 'This is a good, friendly book with humour as well as accuracy. Above all, it is extremely readable.' Reflecting further on Eric's writing about cricket in general, and about Lancashire County Cricket Club in particular, one of Eric's Lancastrian friends, Keith Hayhurst, has written:

> Eric's writing was unique having a style of its own rather like the distinctive Sir Neville Cardus. Its original metaphors and similes hinted the influence of a brilliant Cardus who reported on Lancashire cricket and the Hallé Orchestra's performances for the Manchester Guardian. One example, not specially picked from a hundred examples, was a description of the rather heavily built Dick Tyldesley's bowling. "Protesting, plaintive, perspiring, he trundled painfully up to the wicket and, with an exaggerated demonstration of creaking arm and revolving wrist, the ball would present itself for examination. As the batsman pondered on the likely outcome of this contorted wizardry, the ball going straight on, might rap on the pads. The reedier tenor of Duckworth would combine with the anxious baritone of Tyldesley after the fashion of Flotsam and Jetsam, the premier male duet of the age". Taken at random from *Red Roses Crest the Caps*, Eric's story of Lancashire County Cricket Club, one can perceive a sense of influence from Sir Neville which must be high praise indeed, being linked to such a distinguished writer.

The 'reedy tenor' referred to above by Keith Hayhurst was the famous Lancashire and England wicket keeper of the 1920-30s, about whom Eric has also written a delightful short biography under the title *George Duckworth: Warrington's Ambassador at Large*, which was published in 2008.

Another highly acclaimed and rather unusual cricket book is *Quill on Willow: Cricket in Literature* which came out in 2001, most effectively combining Eric's love for cricket and his deep appreciation and knowledge of English literature, particularly of the 19th and early 20th centuries. A number of favourable – indeed, almost rapturous – reviews in the cricketing and national press accompanied its publication, with comments such as the following:

'To this immense assembly of literary and cricketing allusion the author brings his own discernable drift. . . and quirky humour . . . I hope it is the sell-out that it deserves to be . . .'

Robin Marlar in *The Cricketer*

'Professor Midwinter is a splendid example of a type that has long adorned our game: the cricketing polymath . . .'

Matthew Engel in *Wisden Cricket Monthly*

'. . . this rambling but absorbing study . . . this gentle, scholarly book'.

Murray Hedgecock in *Cricket Lore*

'. . . a fascinating book, as highly entertaining as it is wonderfully informative . . . from this most adroit of cricket writers . . .'

Anthony Burgess in *Bodyline Books*

'Anything written by Eric Midwinter is special . . . a quality of writing which expresses ideas and observations that leave the mind with extended thoughts . . .'

Keith Hayhurst in *Cricket Memorabilia Society Bulletin*

'Dr Midwinter wears his knowledge lightly, with engaging shafts of humour punctuating his writings . . . His encyclopaedic knowledge never ceases to fascinate . . .'

Roy Burgess in *Journal of the Cricket Society*

'Eric Midwinter's scholarly and enjoyable new collection of essays . . .'

Francis Wheen in *Wisden Cricketers' Almanac 2002.*

Frank Keating, that much-lamented doyen of cricket journalists, wrote in *The Guardian*, 'Eric Midwinter – this light touch scholar – is a distinguished social historian, eminent writer and cricket historian.'

The only serious note of criticism that may be offered to counter-balance slightly the paeans of praise heaped upon *Quill on Willow* is the absence of an index. In retrospect, this seems an unfortunate omission, since it is the sort of book to which readers might well return repeatedly in order to look up particular literary references.

The Cricketer's Progress: Meadowland to Mumbai was published by Third Age Press in 2010 and was something of a departure for this particular publisher, since it is not normally associated with books about sport but recognized its potential appeal to older readers. The book traces the development of cricket from its earliest days up to the early 21st century, placing each event in the social, political and economic

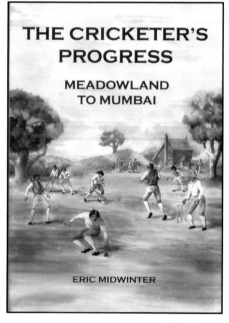

THE CRICKETER'S PROGRESS

MEADOWLAND TO MUMBAI

ERIC MIDWINTER

context of the time. One reviewer has written: '. . . here, in a rich and multi-layered text, he creates an interpretation of the evolution of both English and global cricket that is refreshingly insightful and often controversial. He stylishly guides the reader from a thoughtful and sometimes amusing discussion of theorizing about the origins of the game to a shrewd analysis of the power of finance and television with much of today's focus on the subcontinent'. He concludes ' . . . it is essential – and immensely enjoyable – reading for the genuine student and lover of cricket'.

Even more lavish praise is offered by J. Neville Turner in his review for *The Yorker*, the magazine produced by Melbourne Cricket Club, in which he ends with the words 'By virtue of its wit, scholarship, mastery of language, vision, modesty and wisdom, Eric Midwinter's *The Cricketer's Progress* has persuaded me that it is the finest book on cricket of all time. It is unquestionably my favourite.'

The success of this particular book and its widespread recognition by Eric's peers in the world of cricket is illustrated by the fact that it was short-listed for both the Cricket Writers' Club Book of the Year and the Cricket Society and MCC Book of the Year in 2011. Going one step further, it was actually selected as the Wisden Book of the Year, for which the judge was the well-known Australian author on cricketing subjects, Gideon Haigh, who has summarized his high opinion about Eric's work as follows:

Eric is that rarest of figures in the ranks of its writers: the serious scholar. He is not a scholar in the sense of cordoning off a tiny area and making it his own; on the contrary, his aims are wide, his spirit generous and his probing relentless. His biography of WG opened up whole fields of inquiry. Books such as *The Lost Seasons*, *Brylcreem Summer* and *Quill on Willow* filled gaps in cricket literature so tightly it was as though they had always existed. The *Cricketer's Progress* reminds me of a remark by a character in Anatole France, who describes a great historian as having 'enriched his subject with a new uncertainty.' I'd read anything Eric wrote on cricket – and that's not a compliment I bestow lightly.

Clearly *The Cricketer's Progress* made a great impression on those who read and review books about cricket, like many of his other books on the subject. In fact, it was originally commissioned as a kind of sequel to *Parish to Planet*, described briefly below, before the originally intended publisher went bankrupt. Fortunately, Third Age Press came to the rescue at the eleventh hour and Eric's highly successful and well-received book was salvaged.

Some years before the appearance of *The Cricketer's Progress*, Eric produced his main contribution to the literature of football, *Parish to Planet: How Football Came to Rule the World*, which was published to considerable acclaim in 2007. Here, in some eighteen chapters, he traces the pre-history of football from the towns and schools of old England to the game's consequent spread across the globe to become an unprecedented international phenomenon.

J. Neville Turner, who had previously written highly complimentary comments about several of Eric's other books, wrote him a letter in June, 2011 in which he expressed the view that '*Parish to Planet* is the greatest book that I have ever read on any sport'. This is high praise indeed from a man who has extensive knowledge of sporting literature, to which he himself has made significant contributions.

The Cricket Society has organized a prestigious literary prize for books about cricket since 1970, and Eric was Chairman of the Panel of Judges for the Cricket Society's Book of the Year Award for eight years from 2002-2009 with the exception of 2005 when, having been nominated himself, he handed over his chairman's duties to Stephen de Winton. During his tenure in office, Eric worked very amicably with two different administrators (Jeremy Hardie, 2002-5, and Nigel Hancock, from 2006), a distinguished group of fellow judges and two Cricket Society Chairmen (Dave Allsop and Bill Allen). Whilst Eric was chairman, this important literary prize was sponsored by several different organisations, including – at different times – *The Times* and the *Daily Telegraph* newspapers, but securing reliable continuity of funding was always something of a problem. Since 2009, which was Eric's last year as chairman, the award has been run by the Cricket Society in association with the MCC, and the panel of judges is currently chaired by the distinguished former international cricketer, commentator and journalist, Victor Marks.

One of the panel of judges for this award was Stephen Eley, who writes warmly:

My association with Eric began when he took over the Chairmanship of the Cricket Society Book of the Year Award. I had already been on the panel for a number of years under the Chairmanship of Clive Porter and David Rayvern Allen. Before then I was aware of Eric through his cricket writing, most notably his biography of W.G.Grace, his book on cricket during the war, *The Lost Seasons* and his book on the 1947 cricket season, *Brylcreem Summer*.

I treasured those lengthy discussions in the warm ambience of the Savage Club and particularly admired Eric's holistic approach to cricket, a lesson for all those cricket followers – statisticians especially - who become too obsessed with the minutiae of the game.

He was very kind to me and gave me the opportunity to do some reviewing for the ACS Journal when he was in charge of the Book Reviews. We had a number of chats about cricket and literature – he was especially interested in the Victorians – and also his love of comedy, theatre and music hall.

Fellow member of the panel of judges, Stephen de Winton, has added his own fond memories of Eric's term of office as chairman of the panel:

I did not meet Eric until he joined the Cricket Society Literary Award Panel and became its Chairman in succession to David Rayvern Allen. I immediately recognised Eric's expertise, in cricket history certainly, but in all aspects of modern history, sport and popular culture. Above all, I recognised his warm, friendly and engaging disposition, a sensitive understanding of other people and his expertise in running the committee. He introduced me to the delights of the Savage Club, approached through the imposing and formidable portals of the National Liberal Club, but itself an informal friendly location for our committee meetings. I have had the pleasure of dining in the grand National Liberal Club restaurant, either with committee members and occasionally just with Eric. Eric was the ideal host, business-like and efficient when needed, and then relaxed and genial. I very much enjoyed and appreciated his company and he was kind enough to express his appreciation of what I attempted to bring to the committee's deliberations about the variety of books which we considered. I noted also his relaxed and ever present good humour when he chaired the award ceremonies.

The Association of Cricket Statisticians and Historians (ACS) was founded in 1973, for the purpose of researching and collating information about cricket, and currently has over 1000 members. Originally referring only to statisticians in the title (hence the ACS abbreviation), the words 'and Historians' were added later in 1993. Eric Midwinter, always more drawn to the history of the game than its bare statistics, was subsequently invited to become its President, a post he held with distinction for seven years, from 1997 to 2004. The ACS produces a quarterly journal for members, *The Cricket Statistician*, and has published a number of short paperback books about different aspects of cricket over the years, including Eric's biography of George Duckworth. The Association also has a very useful and informative website for cricket enthusiasts.

Eric has contributed numerous articles about different aspects of cricket to a number of magazines and periodicals over the years. In addition, he edited the influential MCC Annual for ten years, from 1997-2006.

One of the magazines to which Eric became a frequent contributor was *Cricket Lore*. The editor was Richard Hill and he has kindly sent the author the following affectionate thoughts about working with Eric.

When I had the idea of launching a new magazine called *'Cricket Lore'*, Eric was one of only two target writers I hoped to recruit. His cricket writing I admired, not simply for its cricket content but for the wider scope and perspective he brought to his subjects. It was this broader view that I hoped *Cricket Lore* would also contain and reflect. I was also aware Eric's writing on other subjects, which confirmed my belief that of all the other cricket authors, he would perfectly embody the idea I had for the magazine.

My first meeting with Eric was in fact accidental. I was researching some articles in the Lord's library, for the still pipedream of my magazine. Eric came into the library to do some work himself. I recognized him from dustcovers and was preparing to introduce myself when a third party came in and asked the Lord's curator, the inimitable Stephen Green, perhaps the most naïve question he could ever had been asked . . . Did the library have any books on W.G. Grace?! Stephen introduced the questioner to Eric who had published a biography of Grace. When that conversation was complete and the questioner left, I had a simple opportunity to open a conversation with Eric. My opening remark being along the lines that the Grace enquiry must have been the silliest question ever asked in the Lord's library.

From this point it was an easy step to tell Eric of my plans for a new magazine and my keenness to recruit him as a contributor. He readily agreed. This introductory conversation illustrated immediately what an easy, relaxed and naturally friendly person Eric was.

Eric rapidly became a source of encouragement and support for *Cricket Lore* as well as a regular and prolific contributor. His advice and enthusiasm was one of the inspirations to get the magazine off the ground and his contributions helped shape and develop its progress and ethos. There were others, of course, who helped greatly in the development of *Cricket Lore* – Peter Hartland, Roderick Easdale, Bill Lewis, Richard Parry and Peter Wynne Thomas – and the magazine soon evolved into something of a 'friendly society'. Eric's work for the magazine was tireless and without him I am certain that the magazine would not have lasted so long nor have achieved the respect that it gained.

We shared very many interests besides cricket – Music Hall (Variety), comedians, football, education, politics, – and our conversations, face to face, through correspondence and by phone, were always wide-ranging and extremely convivial. As our acquaintance and friendship developed, my admiration and true affection for him grew.

Eric is a man who shares his knowledge and opinions gladly and freely and is as ready to listen as to speak. That I can call him a friend is one of the happiest statements I can make.

Another of Eric's many cricketing friends, Peter Hartland, also with connections to *Cricket Lore,* has added the following comments:

I first met Eric in the early 1990s. We were both regular contributors to the new *Cricket Lore* magazine, founded by editor Richard Hill in 1991. Eric's first article appeared in the second edition of the magazine (January 1992) and was entitled *1962 – The End of Innocence.* He subsequently contributed more pieces than anyone else, including a ten-part *Review of Cricket's Social History,* and a further series *The Anxious Century* which also ran to ten parts and linked twentieth century cricket to developments in the wider world. Some of this material featured in his excellent book *The Cricketer's Progress: From Meadowland to Mumbai*.

A formidable social historian and educationalist, Eric brought erudition, new angles and academic rigour, which were a tremendous boost to the fledgling *Cricket Lore* magazine and helped lend it authority. One of the key points he made was that, after both world wars, cricket was irreparably damaged by the backward-looking nostalgia of old, conservative decision-makers.

'The effect of World War 1 on cricket – the yearning for the lost past it engendered – meant that from 1919 to about 1961, cricket played out a reverie of late Victorian and Edwardian spaciousness.'

Unlike most other critics, Eric also saw the balmy summer of 1947, when Compton and Edrich made hay in front of large ecstatic crowds, as less of a triumph than an unfortunate illusion that convinced the old guard that all was well, when in fact the game desperately needed modernising. This became clearer as crowds dwindled during the attritional 1950s, leading to the drastic changes of the following decade, which Eric saw as too much too late. He noted the inability of the pessimists of the time to foresee the massive potential of television, advertising and sponsorship.

Another interesting theme he developed in impressive detail was that the game is not as old as Victorian cricket historians would have us believe. They invented an idyllic pre-history to try and convince their contemporaries that cricket was a virtuous, respectable pastime worth supporting, rather than just another outlet for skullduggery and corruption.

Eric is very much of the view that cricket writers, as a small but important, often voluntary, group, ought to support each other, rather than waste energy competing and picking holes in others' work. He made this point on more than one occasion during his presidency of the Association of Cricket Statisticians and Historians.

'In that cricket is as much a cult as a sport, then cricket scholarship may well be indispensable to its continuance.'

Eric's parallel study of football, *Parish to Planet*, was another original, fascinating work, cleverly linking the people's game to underlying trends in society, other leisure activity and popular culture. He has watched Manchester United since the war, and from many conversations with him it is clear that he has a profound understanding of football and its place in the world.

Bernard Whimpress also commented about other aspects of Eric's output.

Eric's wide range of articles for *Cricket Lore* – some collected in book form – provided evidence of the brilliant social historian. So impressed was I by his work that when I convened the national biennial conference of the Australian Society for Sports History in Adelaide in 2001, and had invited Gideon Haigh as one of the guest speakers, I nevertheless made reference to Eric as cricket's finest historian.

It is arguable whether it is wise to discriminate in this way. For instance, I have since labelled Haigh as cricket's finest writer (as have a number of other people) but journalist Haigh is also a historian. Likewise, journalist Duncan Hamilton is a marvellous writer with a great feel for history as he has shown in a succession of cricket and football books over the past few years. But Eric Midwinter, trained as a historian, is also a writer with a deft touch across various modes of history. These three have reached the pinnacle of their varied professions and we are fortunate that they each turn a considerable part of their energy to cricket writing.

For instance, Eric opens the first chapter of *The Cricketer's Progress: Meadowland to Mumbai* (2010),

'Just as according to Jane Austen, 'a single man of good fortune must be in want of a wife', then an institution that evokes reverence must be in need of a heritage. Cricket is such an institution.'

In my view, this thesis is as powerful as C.L.R. James' 'What do they know of cricket who only cricket know' from *Beyond the Boundary*. In *The Cricketer's Progress*, as in much of his other work, Eric wears his erudition lightly. Yet the reader is charmed by his references to literary sources – The Bible, Shakespeare, Dr Johnson, Fielding, Tennyson, Hardy, Orwell and so on; is left to marvel at his familiarity with Carlyle, Darwin, Gilbert and Sullivan, and Freud; and totally gob-smacked by forays into popular culture from 'Anything Goes' to 'Rock Around the Clock'.

If Eric, the consummate all-rounder, displays a full range of skills in *The Cricketer's Progress*, the same must be said for *Red Shirts and Roses* (2005) which mixes his loves for the Manchester United Football Club and the Lancashire County Cricket Club; and *Parish to Planet: How Football came to Rule the World* (2007), his social history of football. It is a rare writer who can combine memoir, family history, cultural history, economic history and social history, as well as drawing on wider influences from the social sciences and humanities to produce such brilliant analyses in gracefully written books.

In the last year I have become aware of Eric's wider writing in short booklets for Third Age Press, particularly his guides to memoir and family history. These are excellent tools for the beginner and it is easy to see how well he has mined his own life experiences and reading to create his impressive oeuvre.

It is noticeable that amongst the many admirers of Eric's cricket writings is a significant number of distinguished and erudite Australian cricket enthusiasts – in fact, almost constituting an antipodean fan club.

Eric has edited a fond tribute to the late lamented *Cricket Lore* magazine, which was published in 2014 under the title *Cricket Lore: the guide*. Much of this short book is taken up by a full listing of all the articles published from Issue 1 of the first volume, which came out in November 1993, until the final Issue 7 of Volume Five (July 2005). In the section headed 'Thank you from Eric Midwinter', Eric notes that he had compiled the remarkable total of 86 articles for the journal during its twelve year existence.

As noted throughout this chapter, Eric's writings about cricket have generally been very well received and his dealings with other cricket historians, editors and enthusiasts, almost invariably, have been entirely harmonious and good-natured. However, one notorious exception to this comfortable pattern of relationships and exchanges occurred in 1997, when the cricket statistician and author, Irving Rosenwater, reacted adversely to an article by Eric in the *Cricketer* magazine. Rosenwater, who died in 2006 at the age of 73, was a dedicated cricket researcher whose outstanding achievement was, perhaps, a biography of Sir Donald Bradman, published in 1978. According to one obituary writer, Irving Rosenwater contributed much to the understanding of the game's history, concentrating on facts and figures. He was apparently 'enthusiastic and amiable in his early years, but his pedantic approach irritated many and cost him much of the recognition that was his due . . .' Later in the same obituary, the writer notes: 'Rosenwater's search for cricketing truth found an apparently ideal outlet in *The Cricket Quarterly* (1963-1970), where he contributed to the game's most erudite periodical, until he fell out with the proprietor . . .'

In Eric's offending article in the April 1997 issue of *The Cricketer*, entitled 'Contrary End to Victoria's Century', he referred to the occasion in 1897 when a drunken county cricketer allegedly passed water on the field of play. The exact words used by Eric in this piece were:

This was the year that the Yorkshire left-arm spinner, Bobby Peel, was led inebriated from the field at Bramhall Lane by Lord Hawke, never to play for Yorkshire again. (The jury is still out on the famous allegation that he urinated in front of his lordship: if so, the slope at Bramhall Lane may have contributed to his dismissal.)

Rosenwater's extraordinarily intemperate and defamatory letter in response to the paragraph printed above was published in the May issue of *The Cricketer* under the well-chosen heading 'Pissed Again!', although this might well have been modified slightly by the addition of the word 'Off' in the middle of the phrase. Apart from stating his view that 'There is not, and has never been, a scintilla of evidence to link Peel and the urination canard', he goes on to say in a later paragraph that 'Mr Midwinter has no credentials whatever to be writing on this subject' and opines that 'This is nothing less than ignorance triumphing in print'. He concludes 'Any writers who henceforth choose to propagate the myth deserve only contempt, not letters to the press. Let Mr Midwinter stick to J.K. Starley and Rudyard Kipling, and leave matters of cricket history to others.' The editor, Peter Perchard, added at the end of this letter '*The article clearly stated that the jury is out on whether the incident occurred. Ed'.*

In a private letter to Eric following the publication of Irving Rosenwater's outburst, E.W. (Jim) Swanton, who was Editor in Chief of *The Cricketer* magazine at the time and had received a separate communication from IR, wrote encouragingly: 'Having always regarded you as an exemplary historian I leave the matter to your discretion.'

In the event, Eric reacted in a moderate and balanced way by writing a considered response to Rosenwater's letter, which was published in the June 1997 issue of the same magazine.

After a brief review of the background circumstances that led to the writing of this letter, Eric explained: 'I half-expected to be irritated, but then, not least because of an unexpectedly welcome stream of messages of condolence from other writers and commentators, I found I felt mournful.' One of these correspondents was the distinguished editor of *The Journal of the Cricket Society*, Clive Porter, who expressed the view: 'I feel I must write to you to express my sympathy for you regarding the astonishing outburst from IR. Frankly, I'm amazed the magazine saw fit to print it. Apart from being vicious, offensive, patronizing and arrogant, it is completely unjustified.' Eric's letter concluded as follows: 'At a time when some would criticise cricketers for incivilities on and off the pitch, it is so depressing to find – and I believe it is a rarity among what is a relatively small fellowship of cricket historians and analysts – one who appears loath to conduct himself in public discussion in a seemly, dignified and courteous fashion. Irving Rosenwater has self-revealingly written, in my view, an embarrassingly sad letter. It is a moment, not for annoyance, but for genuine sorrow.'

After his response was published, Clive Porter wrote again to Eric again, saying: 'Having read your letter of admirable restraint and characteristic courtesy in the June *Cricketer*, I respectfully doff my 'titfer' in your direction. I think you struck just the right note. Doubt if I would have been able to keep so calm. Unquestionably, it's the best possible approach.' Similar views were expressed by others who had been equally appalled by the tone of Rosenwater's original letter, some of whom considered that Eric might have had sufficient grounds to start legal proceedings for defamation of character. This opinion was endorsed by two lawyers who subsequently contacted Eric and asked if he wished to sue Irving Rosenwater.

By way of a postscript to this whole unfortunate affair, Eric recalls: 'In the following years it afforded me much pleasure at Lord's when encountering IR, who would never speak or recognise me, to respond with exuberant 'helloes' and lavish opening of doors for him. My daughter said it was curious that a man called Rosenwater could be so obsessed with urine.' It is apparent that Eric was not the only person in the cricket world with whom Irving Rosenwater enjoyed somewhat 'strained' relations. He is reported to have said to one erstwhile friend after an MCC Annual General Meeting 'you did not clap when I made my speech; I shall never speak to you again'.

Eric at Lord's with Charles Oliver, Ken Cranston (former captain of Lancashire and England) and Brian Walsh

On a more cheerful note, one of Eric's good friends, with whom he much enjoyed watching cricket at Lord's and elsewhere, was Charles Oliver. The author also got to know Charles slightly towards the latter part of his life, and a common bond was soon established when it was discovered that they were both Old Gowers (i.e. Old Boys of University College School), albeit of slightly different generations. In fact, this coincidence of a shared school background was rediscovered anew, usually loudly, almost every time they met at Lord's!

From 1989 to his death in 2004, Charles Oliver was a stout friend of Eric on the cricketing front. It was a staunch and close alliance for fifteen years. Charles was a Vice-President and the first official statistician of Lancashire County Cricket Club and one of those 'Walking Wisdens' celebrated in the limerick.

There once was a Hertfordshire Rover
Who bowled seven wides in an over
Which hadn't been done
Since 1901
By a curate in August at Dover.

Royal genealogy and railway timetables being his companion interests to cricket data illustrate his mind-set. Eric would say that if Professor Hudson required models for his theory about divergent and convergent thinkers, Charles and he would pass muster. When Charles died, Philip Talbot, a fellow-Savage who had joined Eric and Charles several times at Lord's, said he had never met a couple who were so much alike and yet so different.

Charles and Eric, both non-drivers, travelled all over the place by rail to watch Lancashire, including hospitable days in the Lancashire committee room, as well as days on end at Lord's. It was in the Lord's pavilion that an incident occurred that told much of Charles' mellow but 'tunnelled' take on life. Eric tells the tale in this wise:

> As usual Charles was chattering away and I soon became aware that the two men sitting in front of us were irked by this. My responses were so non-committal, as I tried to indicate their irritation, that Charles even asked me if I was unwell. He never picked up pointers of that kind; he once said to me, 'they didn't have body language when I was young.' Eventually there was a break and I stood up to stretch my legs. Charles had dropped off to sleep. The

two men in front stood up and collected their belongings and one turned, his face inches from mine, saying in a veritable MCC accent, 'my friend and I are having to move because of your confounded conversation.' It did not help matters that my reaction was to laugh out loud in his face, given the sheer injustice of the accusation. They went elsewhere. Charles awoke, surprised to find two empty seats; with his binoculars, he typically studied the crowded pavilion until he spotted the itinerant couple. 'Fancy them moving there', he said, 'it's a much better view where they were'.

Telling the story at a memorial event for Charles, Eric described how he felt like Max Miller in his tale of promising to commit suicide if his wife became pregnant again, having already had six children. Sure enough, she did become pregnant and Max made a noose and prepared to hang himself; then he paused: 'wait a minute', he said to himself, 'I might be hanging the wrong man.'

Another of Eric's many friends who was also a great cricket enthusiast was the well-known author and comedy scriptwriter, Peter Tinniswood. Peter was an old school pal of Eric's from grammar school days in Sale who became famous for, amongst other things, the delightful television comedy series about the Brandons, a northern family, which was successfully adapted from some of his novels under the title *I Didn't Know You Cared*. This series was first transmitted by the BBC in the 1970s and introduced several wonderful characters to the British public, including Uncle Mort, memorably played by Robin Bailey. Peter wrote several highly amusing books about cricket, including *Tales from a Long Room*, *More Tales from a Long Room*, and other titles featuring 'The Brigadier'. Incidentally, the aforementioned actor also took the part of the Brigadier when that colourful character's exploits were subsequently televised. When Peter died of throat cancer in January, 2003, at the age of 67, Eric wrote an affectionate appreciation that was published in *The Cricketer* in March of that year.

Sport has clearly played a very significant part in Eric's life, through his earlier years as a player and continuously from schooldays to the present as a keen follower and spectator, becoming along the way a serious historian and writer on sporting subjects. His large output of books, articles and reviews, particularly on cricket and, to a lesser extent, football must make him one of the most prolific and highly respected authors in the field.

THE WORLD OF THE SAVAGE CLUB

It might seem rather surprising to find that Eric is a long-standing member of a Gentlemen's Club in London, given his strongly egalitarian political views on life, but such a reaction would fail to take account of the unique character and wide-ranging membership of the Savage Club, and of Eric's strong affiliation with the arts, especially literature and the theatre. On one occasion, he even described the club as 'a bastion of under privilege.' It might also be noted that his other two clubs, Marylebone Cricket Club and Lancashire County Cricket Club, were both men only establishments when he first joined them, although they now admit women members, assisted by Eric's vote in both instances. Certainly membership of a club like this has provided a wonderful outlet for his love of good company, lively conversation and humour.

The Savage Club was founded in October 1857 by the journalist George Augustus Sala, who famously invited a number of friends to a convivial gathering at the Crown Tavern in Drury Lane. As Eric has written in his biography of John Wade 'It was formed as a Bohemian resort for impoverished penny-a-liners in the writing trade and those similarly struggling to make a crust in the artistic world.' The club has always been peripatetic, occupying a number of different premises during its over 150-year history, and has had a number of very famous and distinguished members. The Savage Club is currently housed in its own small clubroom on the ground floor of the splendid National Liberal Club at 1 Whitehall Place, London, where it has been, for its second period of residency there, since 1990. Further details about the history of the club can be found in several books, including *The Gentlemen's Clubs of London* by Anthony Lejeune, a new and lavishly illustrated edition of which was published in 2012, and from the club's own website.

New members of the Savage Club are admitted under one of six disciplines, which are art, music, theatre, literature, science and law, although many individuals have more than one string to their bow and could easily be classified under at least two of these categories. Candidates are proposed and seconded by existing members, and all applications are considered by the club's Qualifications Committee to determine their suit-ability for membership. It is fair to say that the six categories of membership are interpreted quite broadly, thus allowing a wide range of professional occupations within each definition.

In Eric's case, his proposer was the eminent clarinet, organ and tennis-playing ophthalmic surgeon, Kin Wang, who lives near the Midwinters in Harpenden, where their two families are friends. Like Eric, Kin is a graduate of Cambridge University, where he read medicine at Selwyn College. As Kin has written 'I became a member of the Savage in 1981 and realised what a great asset Eric would be as a member.' Kin duly proposed Eric, under the discipline of Literature, with the late Ralph Barker, another distinguished writer about cricket and other subjects, as his seconder, and he was elected as a member in 1985.

One of the main activities run by the Savage Club, greatly enjoyed by members and their guests, is the series of regular House Dinners, these days usually held on a Friday evening in the David Lloyd George Room at the National Liberal Club. Most of these dinners are men-only events, but several times a year – including at Christmas – they are also open to lady guests. Brother Savages take it in turn to act as chairman at these functions, a role always considered to be a great honour, but the making of speeches is strictly prohibited. The only times when this rule is relaxed are when a distinguished Guest of Honour has been invited by the club, on which occasions 'a few words' from him or her are always welcome.

The most important distinguishing feature of all Savage Club dinners is the excellent entertainment provided at the end of the meal, very much in the tradition of the Victorian or Edwardian 'smoking concert'. This entertainment always starts with the lusty communal singing of several choruses from the club's own chorus book, the contents of which have been edited by Eric and David Howe, accompanied by the highly skilled club pianist, Alan Gout. This collection of 60 popular songs from the past is largely drawn from the world of the music hall and musical theatre, each selection traditionally ending with 'If you were the only girl in the world.' The instrument played on these occasions to accompany the singing is a fine Steinway grand piano, originally selected for the club in 1957 by the famous concert pianist and club member, Benno Moiseiwitch, who died in 1963.

After the choruses comes a series of short 'turns' by members or guests, mostly of a musical nature, but usually including at least one spoken word act. Because the club is fortunate to have so many excellent professional musicians, actors and entertainers amongst its membership, as well as a number of talented amateurs, and since some highly accomplished guest performers are invited to attend from time to time, the standard of the after dinner entertainment is invariably extremely high. The type of music on offer varies enormously; it may include, for example, a solo pianist, a solo singer or duet accompanied on the piano or by other instruments, a small vocal ensemble, a solo or accompanied instrumentalist, a variety of instrumental ensembles of one kind or another (up to and including a full brass or military band, or a large group of French horn players), and a wide range of different jazz ensembles. Non-musical acts may feature magicians, poetry readings, humorous monologues and anecdotes, recreations of popular comedy sketches from the past, or stand-up comedy. The repertoire selected by most entertainers is usually aimed towards the lighter end of the spectrum, although many moving performances of more serious pieces have also been enjoyed at times. There are even occasions when the audience is treated to a joke or story-telling instrumentalist, thus combining two of the staple forms of entertainment in one performer.

One of the most popular and frequently invited spoken word entertainers is Eric Midwinter. His after-dinner speaking skills were noted at an early age whilst he was still an undergraduate at Cambridge, and throughout his life he has practiced and developed his talent for entertaining and amusing audiences in all sorts of situations. Dave Allsop CBE, retired civil servant and fellow Brother Savage and cricket enthusiast, recalls one particular example:

> A friend of mine, who was then the President of the Chartered Institute of Legal Executives, was looking for a speaker at their annual dinner. This was an event attended by all the big wigs (pun intended) in the legal profession, including the Lord Chief Justice and the Solicitor-General. I suggested Eric, who readily agreed. I was unable to be there, but I know that he was a huge success. The toastmaster asked for his details because he said that he could get him work as an after dinner speaker every day!

> His stand-up turns at the Savage are always extremely popular, and he bases some of his material on his knowledge of music hall and variety stars. He can do accents and mimicry; and he even sings a bit.

Savage Club House Dinner menu in April 1992 by Pat Adams

Stephen Henderson (usually known as Hendo), himself a brilliant orchestral percussionist and a popular toastmaster, is the Chairman of the Savage Club Entertainments Committee, the talented group of members responsible for all the after dinner shows put on at club functions. His succinct reaction to be being asked about Eric's contributions was: 'I would comment that, with his extensive knowledge of the social history of showbiz, he never fails to answer the call and delight us with some long forgotten nugget from yesteryear when asked to perform.'

For every Savage dinner one of the club's members – or occasionally a guest artist – is called upon to draw a suitable menu card, almost invariably featuring a likeness of the person who will be in the chair on that occasion. Over the years many hundreds of such menus have been prepared by a variety of different artists and, as well as being significant works of art, they provide a fascinating visual record of an important part of the club's history. Interesting collections of such menu cards have been published in book format, the most recent being *Dining with Savages*, compiled by John Wade, which came out in 2000. This book includes one example that features Eric, from the first house dinner that he chaired, on 10th April 1992. The artist was Pat Adams, who was the first of several club artists to have captured Eric's likeness for this purpose. In fact, many years earlier in 1950, he had drawn a sports cartoon for the *Manchester Evening News* that featured Eric's father, Ack.

Other artists who have created menu cards featuring Eric over the years include Robin Mackervoy, Gathorne Butler, Joshua Mowll, and Bo Drašar.

Club artists are also regularly called into action to provide suitable menu cards for the monthly Savage Wednesday Lunches. At these functions, one of the members, or occasionally an invited guest, gives a talk after the meal. Ideally, these are relatively short and not too heavy going, but, nevertheless, it has been known for the odd member to 'rest his eyes' for a few moments when his attention inexplicably flags. The range of subject material covered by these after lunch talks is enormous; they are often amusing and usually stimulate some lively and good humoured discussion at the end of proceedings, not to mention the occasional interjection and exchange of banter when the speaker is in full flow.

Needless to say, Eric has been a regular speaker at these lunches for many years, contributing something at least once a year on one of the many subjects about which he is knowledgeable and has written so much; by March 2014 he had clocked up sixteen of these ever popular annual presentations. For a period of about ten years, Gathorne Butler both organized the lunches and prepared the menu cards, so he has had the opportunity to draw Eric's likeness on several occasions.

In somewhat contrasting style is the interesting menu card for another Club Lunch that was created quite recently by Joshua Mowll. This was the occasion, around the time of Eric's 80th birthday in 2012, when he rather foolishly offered to buy everyone a drink in the bar beforehand, resulting in a sharp pain in the wallet.

Whilst the normal activities of the Savage Club, such as the dinners and lunches, are all highly enjoyable events, there are occasions when members fall on hard times, either because of ill health or for a variety of other reasons. The Benevolent Fund Committee (Ben Fund), chaired for many years by Eric, exists to offer comfort and assistance to troubled Brother Savages wherever possible, and also to keep in touch with the widows of deceased members who are referred to as Rosemarys (for remembrance). Eric and his committee, together with two watchmen, keep their eyes and ears open for news of any members, or Rosemarys, who may be in need of support.

John Carpenter, who is a former chairman of the Savage Club and is also the current secretary of the Ben Fund Committee, has kindly provided the following notes about Eric's role as chairman of that committee.

> Eric joined the Ben Fund committee on 7th March, 1994 and was elected chairman on 27th February, 1996. Under his chairmanship, it is a pleasure to attend the committee, which, while considering serious and sometimes tragic matters, has a pleasant, efficient

and effective method of working. This situation is due to the way he, as chairman, manages the committee. He has also made a number of improvements in the administration of the Ben Fund.

The Ben Fund is, of course, a separate legal entity from the Club but it can only work effectively if Club members know of its existence and its method of working. Throughout his chairmanship he has taken every opportunity to ensure they do, in *Drumbeat* and at lunches, dinners and the AGM. He has also introduced the bi-annual Awareness Evening, which is cost effective and great fun and well-attended by younger members. He generally plays an active and entertaining role in the evening. He has cultivated a mutually beneficial relationship with the Club Honorary Secretary and the Chairman of the Club Entertainments Committee, ensuring their support and also a line of communication with potential clients of the Fund.

He is a champion of the Rosemarys' involvement in the life of the club. He initiated the Rosemary lunch in September, which is attended by a high proportion of active Rosemarys, and invited them to the club annual Carol Service and to the club afterwards. He has also strongly supported the practice for two or three Rosemarys to attend Club distaff events at the Fund's expense.

The Deputy Watchman, Stephen Henderson, has added:

As Chairman of the Ben Fund, Eric is skilled in keeping his committee happy by behaving with strict observance of its constitution, whilst never allowing due process to interfere with the need for immediate action or making an emergency grant. As one of the Ben Fund's two Watchmen, I am privileged to work very closely and in confidence with Eric and together we try to look after Brother Savages who suffer misfortune. He IS the Ben Fund and I hope will continue to be so for many more years to come. He will be a very hard act to follow where doing good by stealth is concerned.

The bi-annual Ben Fund Awareness Evenings referred to by John Carpenter usually take the form of a 'themed' dinner, together with more than usually lavish entertainment. These are always 'distaff' nights with lady guests, including a few invited Rosemarys, and are always great fun, with Eric normally taking the lead as Master of Ceremonies. Examples of themes for these events, often cooked up by Eric, John Wade and Stephen Henderson, by any measure

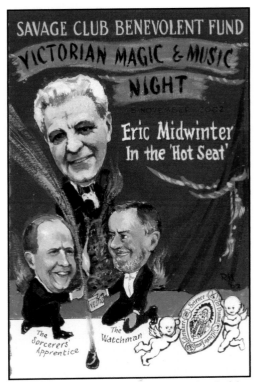

Ben Fund Event menu in 2002, by Robin Mackervoy

a deadly trio of entertainment managers, include a Victorian Magic and Music Night, SS Benevolence, Robin Hood and his Merry Men, Benfuns Holiday Camp, Bun Fight at the OK Chorale, and St Savages Academy for Backward Boys and Forward Girls. Needless to say, these evenings require a special menu card to mark the occasion, always provided by Robin Mackervoy, to great effect.

One particularly special event organized by the Ben Fund Committee, and chaired by Eric, is the annual Rosemary Lunch, to which reasonably fit and ambulant Rosemarys are invited, accompanied by his committee colleagues, who act as hosts. So far, fifteen of these special lunches have been held. After an amusing after lunch talk, invariably given by Eric as chairman, the ladies are presented with a suitable gift, quite often a book or a CD produced by one of the club members, who may be on hand to sign the offering. The ladies clearly appreciate this hospitality, as well as the invitations to other Savage Club events, such as Ladies Night Dinners, that they might receive from time to time. Susan Bradbury, doyenne of the Rosemarys, has written:

> I have sat next to Eric for years at the Rosemary annual lunch and rejoiced in the occasion – he's the perfect Chairman, a dependable rock. We know he's there for us if ever we need his support in that role. These thoughts about Eric are random. We are the same age, share impressions of life but know nothing of each other's backgrounds. He digs out the unsung, transforming them fervently into new, shining lights, astonishing me at least in the process and I suspect all Rosemarys and others, who have like hearts and minds.

> He is the wittiest after-lunch or dinner speaker, a raconteur *par excellence*, not a note to hand. He unfolds a thought, lets it loose all over the place, finally perching it on another thought, transmuting the whole, usually amid laughter. A master of dialect and the English language, he reflects rather than sets in stone. I'd be surprised were he to be a signed up member of a religious following – his stories themselves exude mankind's majesties and messes, enriching his listeners the while.

Susan Bradbury is by no means alone amongst the Savage Rosemarys in her great admiration of Eric. Jean Jaffa is the widow of the distinguished violinist Brother Savage Max Jaffa (1911-1991) – so well known for the enormous pleasure that the famous Max Jaffa Palm Court Orchestra and Trio gave to audiences for many years. As the singer Jean Grayston, she

Top left:Luncheon
menu 2008 by
Gathorne Butler

Top right:
Luncheon menu by
Joshua Mowll

Bottom: Ben
Fund event menu
2008 by Robin
Mackervoy

joined Max in concerts and recitals all over the world for 35 years, including 27 summer seasons at the Spa Grand Hotel, Scarborough. Jean has added her own personal thoughts about Eric.

> Eric Midwinter is a wonderful man. He contributes so much to us Rosemarys by making us feel very welcome. He is always finding delightful and very amusing stories that make us laugh a lot, I am sure that there is no other club in the city that so generously gives such delicious lunches annually, together with beautiful roses, and other gifts, for the widows of its members. We Rosemarys greatly appreciate what Eric does for us – and of course this applies to all the Savages – but Eric is the Master-in-Chief of the proceedings. It is most touching that our late partners are remembered every year. Eric is a real treasure.

Eric has many good friends at the Savage Club, all of whom hold him in high regard. One of the services he has generously offered from time to time to some of these friends, always quietly and discreetly, is advice and editorial guidance when they have first ventured – often tentatively – into the field of writing books. One such beneficiary of Eric's literary expertise is a former Honorary Secretary of the Savage Club, and former Chaplain-in-Chief of the Royal Air Force, The Venerable Brian Lucas CB. Brian has written:

> When it dawned on me that the scribbling which I was engaged in was going to grow into a much larger exercise than my desire to record the early years of my life for my children to enjoy, I sat still to discern the way ahead. It took only a few minutes before the name of Eric Midwinter came to my silent lips.

> Eric is a friend for whom I have enormous respect. This has developed from my knowledge of him as a brother member of the Savage Club. When I was thrust into the position of the Club Secretary I found that I was in a

totally unfamiliar milieu; I discovered a host of tasks that required urgent attention and set about them as best I could. It was Eric Midwinter who saw what I was up against and quietly encouraged me to persevere. He is a rock which blunts the darts and arrows of daily life, while at the same time possessing a compassionate understanding of human nature. As a social historian, he understands better than most the vicissitudes of life in modern Britain. As an educationist he co-founded the University of the Third Age, encouraging folk to learn about the world about them, and to write their story for future generations.

Some years ago I required a 'facilitator' for a study day for a group of Anglican clergy in Lincolnshire, and I asked Eric to consider the role. He was staggered at the thought, considered by him to be like asking a vegetarian to manage a butcher's shop, and we both laughed, but I persuaded him that his agnosticism would be an excellent catalyst to provoke thought and debate about the context of the parish community in the 21st century. He entered into this group in a small Retreat House near Bourne and held it enthralled. There were no holds barred and discussion ranged widely to the benefit of all. Eric enjoyed the day, and the clergy never forgot it.

When I asked for his advice on writing my memoir he offered it with sagacity and humility. At first we spoke of the nuts and bolts of publishing before we moved on to the form and style of writing. It was at this stage that I asked if he would read and comment on the chapters as I wrote them. He agreed, and it was the beginning of the most honest exchange of correspondence I have ever had with anyone. My script would return full of red ink corrections, suggestions and firm opinion. Sometimes I begged to differ, but his sage advice, for it was always such, was usually on the mark. My wife on seeing one of his returned chapters remarked, 'I wish my university dons had been as diligent with some of my essays!'

Brian Lucas goes on to describe Eric's role in another important annual event in the Savage Club calendar, the annual Carol Service, at which Brian officiates in his priestly capacity. During this service, open to Brother Savages, guests and Rosemarys, the carols are always sung and led by the magnificent choir of St Clement Danes Church, in which several club members sing, accompanied by the organ and a splendid ensemble of Savage brass and percussion, specially assembled for the occasion by Stephen Henderson. Readings, both biblical and secular, are delivered by Brother Savages.

> Every year on the first Monday in December the Savage Club holds a Carol Service in the church of St Clement Danes in the Strand. After the first service in 1998 Eric mentioned to me that he would like to take part, and could I insert a secular reading among the Biblical selection, and might he suggest something. Every year since, one or two non-scriptural readings have been included, and Eric had become a firm favourite with the congregation of Savages and their guests. His reading of Dickens, in particular, is welcomed, as are his northern pieces with suitable accent.
>
> This priest and this agnostic, though priests can be partly agnostic too, grew close in respect and admiration for one another. This also arose from Eric's work as Chairman of the Savage Club Benevolent Fund. Eric Midwinter's deep compassion for his fellow men is always apparent, as is his shrewd perception of anyone who thinks the Fund might be a soft touch.
>
> Eric Midwinter is a wise counsel to all his friends, and his integrity with his keen sense of humour ensures that he has a wide circle of them.

The book to which Brian referred, and for which Eric provided his greatly appreciated guidance, was *Reflections in a Chalice: The Memoirs of a Practical Priest* by Brian Lucas, published in 2011 by Adastral Books. Thus encouraged, Brian has continued to write and has recently produced *A Glimpse of Glory in the Gothic Cathedrals of France*, a beautifully illustrated guide to these architectural wonders (Adastral Books, 2014).

Susan Bradbury, who was quoted above, has added her own thoughts about Eric's contribution to the carol service.

> Every Adventide I attend the Savage Club's carol service in St Clement Danes near the Club, for every reason but particularly for Eric's part. Each year he chooses pieces of literature reflecting the essence of Christmas. These texts are always a beautiful way of noting this season, breathtakingly worthy of and chosen by the dearest of so many dear Savages - Eric.

Another Savage friend who has recently written a book, and was greatly assisted in the process by Eric's advice, is David Howe. When asked for his comments about Eric he recalled:

> Coming to the forefront of my mind is Eric's generosity with his time, an example being his proof reading of book manuscripts for the rest of us. This must take many hours, which he happily makes available for us, sacrificing valuable time for the work he himself has in hand. Enhancing this kindness is a gentleness of nature that sees him highlighting the best qualities in his fellow Savages, with a knowing, genial smile.

The delightful book that David produced was *Are You Happy With That?* by David Howe (actor Gerard Hayling), published in 2013 by Third Age Press. David went on to add some more general thoughts on his good friend Eric.

> He is hilariously self-deprecating at times. Last Friday in the Club, he mentioned this project (the Midwinter biography) to me and seemed to know that you would contact me. I confirmed that you had, and that I was writing down all his qualities, dividing them into two categories, good and bad. I told him I had allocated a Post-it note for the good and several sheets of A4 for the bad - he loved it and expressed surprise that the former

SAVAGE CLUB CHRISTMAS DINNER · 9ᵗʰ DECEMBER 2005

ERIC
MIDWINTER
D Phil   M A   OBE
in the chair

*Savage Christmas Dinner menu in 2005,
by Robin Mackervoy*

needed anything as big as a Post-it note!

We went on to avow that one day we would debate the one area where our opinions differ. Eric is of course a social historian, and tends to see everything and everyone through the eyes of a social historian. Fair enough, but I do mean **everything.** Surely, sometimes the happening of a chain of events, is just things happening? I ask, is a social history explanation **always** applicable or appropriate?

Does everything have to have an underlying significance? An example:- take Les Dawson's comedy, variety rather than music hall, it was heady with social history, with its factory women mouthing above the noise of the looms, repressed sexual innuendo and talk of anaglypta wall paper.

Does the same apply to say, Harry Tate? And Tommy Cooper? What about Harry Worth? Surely, they were just being silly to make us laugh. So, here the social history eludes me, but if Eric were to read this he would, in no time, write a script for a Wednesday lunch on the social history behind any of these artists to prove me wrong.

In summary, I think what I am saying is that he often sees underlying social history where I don't.

David Howe concluded his piece about Eric as follows, with particular reference to their shared experiences of frequent appearances as spoken word entertainers at Savage Club functions:

These notes are my thoughts about one of my very special Savage friends, whose friendship I cherish with genuine respect and great Brotherly love. I have laughed more in his company than nearly everyone else's.

His performances at the Savage are always a great delight and few, except those of us who also perform, realise just how much time and rehearsal at home is necessary to make these performances seem so effortless. Time he gives willingly, for the benefit of the Club and its members.

In all the years I have been on that stage, I have never done so without receiving an e-mail from Eric on the Saturday or the Sunday, congratulating me and saying how much he enjoyed my performance – I can't always have been as good as he said, but we all enjoy a little lift, don't we? That's the endearing courtesy of Eric.

Yet let me not portray a man who is precious in any way – he can be mightily quick witted, sharp and as a Northener, earthy. There was a lunch when a member was being a bit tedious and on hearing a name said: "Who is this man XXXX ?" Quick as lightning, Eric interjected with: "He's the chap we take the piss out of when you're not here".

If he were to be cut in half, you would find Savage Club writ large, right through him, I was going to say like Brighton rock, but in his case, Blackpool is nearer to Manchester and more appropriate.

As for amusing anecdotes, our exchanges tend to be more quippish. With both of us being fluent in the 'Lion In The

Box' sketch of Jimmy James, Eli Woods and Roy Castle, our greetings to one another tend to baffle those around. Over the years, we have exchanged many e-mails and post cards and on one occasion, when I was under the weather, there was one get well card that cheered me up above all the others. It was simply a picture post card and on the back was written the Jimmy James comment 'I'll stop you going to those youth clubs!'

Another Savage, Melvyn Crabb, has written fulsomely his own personal thoughts about Eric as a friend and fellow member.

Eric made me feel very welcome when I first joined the Club, and when I have bought guests to the Club has always made them just as welcome and helps them feel at ease.

He has a very sharp wit based on years of observation of the foibles of humanity – always well-drawn, often amusing, sometimes wry or bittersweet, but never cruel; and is a very witty raconteur and can draw on an enormous fund of shaggy dog stories which never fail to delight his audience at Savage house dinners. Eric has an outstanding knowledge of the history of music hall and light entertainment, and draws on this to deliver excellent and very well-attended lunchtime talks.

Eric epitomises what being a Savage is – he is is a first-class conversationalist, is very erudite and enjoys sharing his knowledge and experience without ever imposing himself on others; in short, he is first-class company. If I were ever stuck in a lift, I would hope that Eric was there with me – an hour in his company seemingly passes in the blink of an eye.

He is a keen supporter of Savarail and freely volunteers his time to give a talk on a railway-related subject every May. His subjects have ranged from railways and the industrialisation of warfare in the 19th and 20th centuries, to railways and their impact on leisure and the growth of holidays by the seaside.

If Eric has one flaw, it is perhaps what some might describe as an almost obsessive interest in the fortunes of a small football club based just outside Manchester!

Melvyn mentioned Eric's active support of Savarail, which is one of several informal special interest groups within the Savage Club that have grown up over the years. As the name implies, this group exists for those who take a particular interest in the railways, and, as well arranging regular talks, it also organises occasional excursions for train enthusiasts. Eric's most recent contribution to Savarail, for his regular May spot in 2014, was entitled 'Railway Rhyme and Reason', in which he provided a narrative on the character of railway verse, illustrated by twelve examples of railway poems read by the consummate actor, Brother Savage Nick Murchie. This was Eric's eighth contribution to Savarail's activities.

Other active groups within the Savage Club include Savajazz, for jazz enthusiasts and musicians, and Savacrick, for lovers of cricket. Since many members are interested in both subjects, the two groups often combine forces for a convivial and inexpensive bread, cheese and chutney lunchtime gathering, usually organised by Dave Allsop and the current Savage Club Hon. Secretary, Adrian Mackintosh, who is a well-known jazz drummer and an expert maker of delicious chutneys. Eric invariably enlivens these occasions by arranging a raffle, for which the prizes are usually selected items from his large collection of cricket books. Eric is also a regular participant in the annual Savage quiz, where all the questions are based on the six categories of membership.

In addition to the various regular events at the Savage Club, in many of which Eric has had a hand, a variety of 'one off' entertainments have been produced over the years. Often these special shows take the form of a concert, arranged by one or other of the many highly talented musicians in the club, sometimes involving distinguished guest artists, and there have been some quite remarkable performances. These have included various forms of classical music, vocal recitals, jazz, military bands, show music, and big band music, always of the highest quality.

One excellent example of such special events came about quite recently as a result of a brilliant collaboration between Eric and Max Brittain, the illustrious jazz guitarist and banjo player. As Max has written: 'I was introduced to Eric when I joined the Savage Club in 2005 and soon began to appreciate his talent as a wit, a raconteur and performer at Club dinners and lunches. In September 2011 we started to collaborate on a Wodehouse project which culminated a year later in the first performance of *Wodehouse on Broadway* at the Club.' This show took the form of a combination of words written and spoken by Eric, with music arranged and composed by Max, all performed by two singers and a select group of instrumental musicians. The singers were Riona O'Connor and Dominic Arnal, accompanied by Brother Savages John Elliott, Alan Gout and Max Brittain himself, plus guest saxophonist Peter Ripper.

As Julian Baker wrote in his enthusiastic account of this performance for *Drumbeat*, 'P.G.Wodehouse was described by Brother Savage Eric Midwinter as "the man who built the bridge between the comic operas of Gilbert and Sullivan and the 'musical play' of Rodgers and Hammerstein", and our entertainment used the backdrop of his collaboration with his close friend Guy Bolton and the composer Jerome Kern to illustrate his work as a lyric writer.' He continued 'To sum up the theatrical life and work of such a man in two hours must have seemed an impossible task . . . the success of which depends on a hundred and one things going "right on the night". It did indeed come seamlessly together, thanks to the writing genius of Eric Midwinter and the superb musical arrangements of Max Brittain.'

After describing in some detail the different components of the performance, Julian concluded his review with the words 'Space cannot do justice to the felicities of this wonderful entertainment.'

Another person present on this occasion was Tony Ring, who was a founder member of the P.G.Wodehouse Society and the first editor of the society's quarterly magazine, *Wooster Sauce*. He reports:

I first met Eric on 21 September, 2012, when he scripted and compèred an evening's entertainment at the Savage Club entitled *Wodehouse on Broadway*, with music compiled and arranged by fellow-Savage Max Brittain.

This was an imaginative and enjoyable presentation which was attended by some members of The P G Wodehouse Society (UK). Max's featured songs included some dozen with Wodehouse lyrics and perhaps half a dozen others. Eric's script was informative, providing a good balance between the basics necessary for a Wodehouse musical comedy virgin and some interesting additions for the relatively few who knew the oeuvre well.

As a result of this evening, I contacted Eric through Max Brittain and invited him to assist in helping to provide contextual narrative for a compilation of Wodehouse poetry which I was preparing. His record as a social historian, together with his interest in cricket and musical theatre, both of which were relevant to the book, made him in my view an ideal support to the knotty problem of providing concise yet meaningful explanations as to the relevance of certain verses. I was delighted when Eric agreed, with undue modesty, to help, and I'm pleased to say that the book, *What Goes Around Comes Around*, was published in February this year (2014).

After this triumphant first performance, Max Brittain was invited to contribute an article on *The Making of Wodehouse on Broadway* for *Wooster Sauce,* and this was duly published in the issue of December, 2012. Max had initially discussed the project with Hilary Bruce, who had suggested, after the earlier success of a show called *Jazz and Dr Johnson,* 'Why not *Jazz and P.G. Wodehouse?*' After some time grappling with this idea on his own it had failed to be developed satisfactorily, until Max got together with Eric, who was soon able to suggest a creative and workable way forward. Max also received valuable help and encouragement from members of the P.G.Wodehouse Society, which he joined in 2012. He admits in the article that 'Hilary had set this project in motion, but it was Tony Ring who oiled the wheels by allowing me access to the wonderful Wodehouse Archive. There I discovered song lyrics and scores which long searches on the internet had failed to unearth.'

With regard to the musical arrangements, Max revealed that although he used only four musicians they still managed to wield, between them, the clarinet, flute, saxophone, trombone, piano, guitar, banjo, ukulele banjo, ukulele, double bass and sousaphone – but not all at the same time. As he notes: 'Our first performance at the Savage Club was given a hugely enthusiastic reception.'

One evening in November 2012, not long after the *Wodehouse on Broadway* evening, the Savage Club organised a special in-house version of the popular and long-running radio programme *Desert Island Discs,* during which Martin Hart assumed the role of interviewer originally taken by the late Brother Savage, Roy Plomley. Unusually, there were two castaways on this particular occasion, David Howe and Eric Midwinter, although one assumes they were sent to different island with their own individual selection of five records. As pointed out in the subsequent report in *Drumbeat,* they were following in the illustrious footsteps of three Brother Savages of an earlier vintage who had appeared on the real BBC programme, Arthur Askey, Peter Ustinov and Harry Secombe.

In characteristic fashion, Eric prepared a full script for what he had to say by way of introduction to his selected recordings, giving in some detail his reasons for each of the choices. He also clearly prescribed the questions that he should be asked, in order that the interview might be kept to a reasonable timetable. Eric's first disc, in line with his great admiration and affection for the comic operas of Gilbert and Sullivan, was the 'paradox' song from *The Pirates of Penzance*, which opens with the line *"How quaint the ways of paradox"*.

There followed a discussion about Eric's strong leaning towards the Victorian period, in which he specialised as a historian, and which had provided the basis for most of his beliefs about politics, religion and social policy. When thinking about music from the Victorian era, he recalled a childhood memory of his Aunt Dolly, with her daughter Daphne, woman-handling the piano, screeching a version of Mendelssohn's *Oh for the Wings of a Dove* at some family gathering. Being unable to restrain his giggles at this melodic assassination, he was dragged out of the room by his father and reprimanded with the words 'I know it's bloody awful son, but it's manners.' No doubt this was a salutary lesson in musical appreciation, notwithstanding his grandfather's revelation that Aunt Dolly's top note had castrated the next-door neighbour's cat. The Victorian song selected for Eric's second disc, written by Harry Dacre of *Daisy Bell* fame in 1896, was *While London's Fast Asleep*. This was evidently his father's favourite party piece, sung on family occasions and on the tram with his footballing mates when travelling to away games. The particular performance chosen was from the album *London Pride*, which was recorded in 2003 by the wonderful soprano Catherine Bott, partner of Brother Savage Stephen Henderson, accompanied on the Savage Club's Steinway piano by David Owen Norris, in the splendid David Lloyd George Room of the National Liberal Club, in the presence of an appreciative audience of Brother Savages and their guests.

For his third disc, Eric moved on to the world of the entertainers of his childhood and youth, who included Gracie Fields, Billy Bennett, Stanley Holloway, Max Miller, and many others, and the delights of seaside shows. His choice as a representative of this era was George Formby, that 'Master of the Single Entendre' and 'Troubadour of Voyeurism', as Eric apostrophises him, with his famous song *My Little Stick of Blackpool Rock*, as always, accompanying himself on the ukulele.

Advancing to the inter-war years and the 1950s, and reflecting on his early fondly-remembered experiences of seeing shows from the balcony of the Palace Theatre in Manchester, where his father was the fireman, Eric chose a Flanagan and Allen number as his fourth recording. Rather than going for the very well known *Underneath the Arches* as an example of this genre, he opted instead for *Down Forget-me-not Lane*, which he described as 'that hymn to humdrum niceness.'

Eric's fifth and final disc reflected another of his great loves, the brass or military band. Waxing lyrical about the inspiration he derives from this kind of music, Eric recalled being taken aged four by his grandfather to listen to the Fodens Motor Works Band in Longford Park, Stretford, in the days when Harry Mortimer was a young trumpeter in the band, and how he enjoyed the various bands that played before and during the half-time interval of football matches at Old Trafford. The piece selected was a rousing Sousa march, *King Cotton*, played by the band of the Grenadier Guards, providing a timely and enjoyable reminder of the band that Stephen Henderson and Michael Purton had produced as part of the entertainment at the memorable Christmas Dinner Eric chaired in 2005.

As in the 'official' *Desert Island Discs* programmes on BBC Radio, Eric was offered the choice of a book and a luxury item to take with him to his island. Unsurprisingly, to those who know him, he chose a collection of the works of Dickens as his book, even though he has read all of them several times over already. His preferred luxury was the Savage Club, a laudable choice but one likely to cause some practical difficulties for the organisers to fulfil.

Needless to say, the whole evening was deemed to be a great success by all those present and a full account was later published in the Autumn 2012 issue of the club's magazine.

Hardly an issue of *Drumbeat,* which is currently edited by David Brown, goes by without either some contribution written by Eric or a report on one of his presentations at a club lunch, dinner or other event, or both. For example, in one recent edition there is review by Eric of Brian Lucas's recently published book on French Gothic cathedrals, and a report on his talk at the March, 2014 Club Lunch, which was entitled 'Twiddles and Flicks: The Golden Age of Radio and Cinema', in addition to an appreciation of the late John Braun. He has produced many scores of articles, reports and reviews for *Drumbeat* over the years, perhaps even running into hundreds, and has frequently been mentioned in dispatches about Savage events he has either organised or in which he has taken part. Some of Eric's many books have also been reviewed in this journal, particularly if there has been a book launch at the Savage Club, as has happened on several occasions.

As noted earlier, the youthful Eric used to read his brother's newspaper when Bryan returned home after work, and many years later Eric had an interesting encounter with one of the journalists he recalled from those far-off days. A short while before she died in 2002, he bumped into the politician Barbara Castle around the corner from the Savage Club, in the corridor of the National Liberal Club, who asked him where to find the Ladies. 'Just a minute, don't I know you' he said, 'weren't you the social welfare columnist for the *Daily Mirror* during the war?' She was evidently tickled pink, an apt hue perhaps.

It might be appropriate to draw this chapter to a close with a few more thoughts from Dave Allsop. Some time after Dave had first met Eric and arranged for him to speak at a Cricket Society event, at which Philip Talbot had also read some cricket poems, he continued:

> Eric then invited me along to the Savage Club, where I again met Philip, and after another visit, he asked if I'd like to join. I was a bit wary. I'd always refused to put my name down for the MCC because they did not at that time allow women to be members, and my wife was a keen cricket fan. I did ask Eric how he'd get me past the entrance requirements. His reply; "Lies".
>
> So he proposed me, Philip seconded me; and Eric and I have become ever closer. He always speaks at the March Savage lunch. He has spoken at Savarail. Both involve a serious subject, meticulously researched and presented with humour. It is this mix of scholarship and humour that makes Eric so special, evident both at formal presentations and when tossing ideas and thoughts around in the bar.
>
> We nearly always sit together at House Dinners. He shares with me a dislike of our national anthem, and we both refuse to sing it. He was partly responsible for putting together the Savage book of choruses and he always joins in their singing with relish. At club meals, all the serving wenches know him as the potato man. He loves potatoes and I have made sure that all the waiting staff are aware of this fact. So they come back to him with the remaining stocks.
>
> It says a lot about his standing and popularity that when Bo Drašar. and I organised a lunch to mark his 80th birthday, almost all those invited were keen to be there. Only previous commitments brought forward refusals. At that event, it was again clear how popular he is amongst his many friends. (The artist Robin Mackervoy was one of the guests at this special lunch, held at the Royal Society of Medicine, and he managed to sketch Eric and all his fellow diners on the day).

at:
The Royal Society of Medicine
March 12th 2012

Eric
at
80

Robin Mackervoy

Savage
guests at
Eric's 80th
Birthday
Lunch
in 2012,
sketched
by Robin
Mackervoy

Dave Allsop continues:

I am constantly rubbing up against people who have come across him in one of his many careers. Mention his name and you often get the response, "Do you know him" in a way that shows the respect in which he is held.

I know that Eric loves to write; indeed, he is a compulsive writer and has to write every day. He doesn't really like going on holiday. I have never visited him at home, but I know that he has loads of books and that on one occasion he might have been killed when the bookshelves came away from the wall (fortunately this potentially dangerous bookcase malfunction occurred overnight when Eric was safely tucked up in bed). He himself has produced enough books to have covered him.

Summing up; a top scholar, writer, public speaker who I am proud to count as a friend.

It should be evident from this chapter that the Savage Club means a great deal to Eric and that it has formed an essential part of his social and cultural life over the last thirty years or so. It is equally apparent from the range of his many contributions to club life and the warmth of the comments received from some of his many Savage friends that he has made an important and invaluable impact on the Club. This comes not only through his performances as a speaker or entertainer at various functions, and his writings for *Drumbeat*, but quietly in the background through the unobtrusive but vital work of the Benevolent Fund Committee and by way of his friendship, ready encouragement and constant support for fellow members.

Eric, Robin Mackevoy and John Wade at the Savage Club

THE WORLD OF WRITING AND SPEAKING:
THE GREAT COMMUNICATOR

During his school days, Eric had always fancied the idea of writing for his living, although journalism did not quite seem to be the right avenue for him to pursue. When he was about fifteen, a wise English teacher, Mrs Mead, advised him to embark on a professional career of some kind and continue his writing as a part-time activity. In the event, Eric settled on the notion of teaching as a suitable career and, when called up for National Service, opted for the RAEC, as described earlier. However, he certainly took Mrs Mead's advice very much to heart and has continued writing regularly and very productively ever since he was a schoolboy.

Writing has formed an important element of Eric's life from early days. As he himself told me: 'I think you appreciate I write every day. I treat it rather as some have a round of golf, or do a bit of gardening or play the piano or do some oil painting. I am just very content writing and have never suffered from writing block.' The habit of daily reading and writing started when he was very young and was much influenced by his grandmother, as described previously. Eric recalls:

My grandmother was very much a disciple of all this - encouraging me to read at a time when schools were shocked and dismayed at families helping pupils, especially before starting school - she read the bible daily as well as newspapers - so I followed suit reading the Arthur Ransome/Richmal Crompton/*Wind in the Willows* sort of children's literature and lots besides - I remember having a book of Dickens and children's stories (i.e. excerpts about the young David Copperfield or Jo the crossing sweeper in *Bleak House*) - I had certainly read *Pickwick Papers* and, I think, *A Christmas Carol* before going to Grammar School.

Eric also started writing when he was at school and he has kept several examples of his early efforts. Amongst these are adventure stories, including two about 'fantasy' football teams, a story about an imaginary country called 'Klavia', complete with history, geography and maps, a detailed Order of Service for an Anglican Church Service, and a 108-page notebook entitled 'A Youth Sees Politics', with sections headed the 'History of Politics', 'Parties and Policies', and 'Comparisons and Miscellaneous', plus an Epilogue entitled 'Political Intelligentsia of a Form'. He also wrote pieces for the school magazine. Thus started a serious habit of regular writing that continues to this day.

Whilst he was an undergraduate at Cambridge, Eric had to write a weekly essay for his tutor and, at key stages, examination papers. As he has stressed: 'the weekly essay I had to produce – about four pages of, say, 1500 words – could not have been a better training for the sort of career I have had, both in terms of technique and writing to deadlines.' He also, perhaps rather unusually, enjoyed examinations, as he has described below.

I had worked out that the examination system is, in athletic terms, a sprint (4 essays in 3 hours) whereas most students treat it as a Marathon, that is, they pile up the work, swotting, swotting, swotting, burning the midnight oil right up to the last moment. My technique was, in the last two terms, to reduce and reduce, to simmer down the mix until I had the essentials with what would now be called bullet points and the like which I could use, in the exams, of keys back into all the reading and study. Two or three weeks before my Cambridge Finals I procured nine or ten previous papers for the nine or ten papers I would be sitting and I did, morning and afternoon, three hours papers, to the point where I was able to do a four page/1500 word answer in 40 minutes (viz 180 minute exam/ 3 x 40 = 160 minutes), leaving 10 minutes to sketch out which questions to do and how, and 10 minutes at the end for a corrective read through. Then for a week or ten days before the exam I just rested, watched the cricket, walked on the river bank, went to the cinema, read fiction, messed about, with the aspiration that, come the sitting of the nine or ten papers, I would be absolutely fresh and rarin' to go. The night before the first paper, Doug (Bowler) had a cousin visiting him and, after dinner, we played a madcap game of indoor cricket that we had invented in our set, with a ruler and a ping pong ball – it was hilarious and went on until about 12.30.

I have always enjoyed exams. Mind you, you had to put in the hard mileage beforehand so that you had the confidence to take the holiday. I'm afraid I had one or two colleagues who more or less started their studies at the point I stopped, about three weeks before the exams.

Eric's approach to examinations clearly worked well for him, as we have seen earlier, and he was able to achieve a First in his final examinations in the History Tripos. Significantly, he had also by this time acquired a method, and the necessary accompanying self-discipline, to plan and produce written work more or less to order, as and when required.

When Eric later became a college lecturer and examiner, he sometimes became very irritated by students who failed to complete the required number of questions in examination papers, thereby sacrificing a significant proportion of the available marks on offer. His somewhat caustic response to those who complained was: 'You did have enough time. From the day you entered the college you knew what the time was – four questions in three hours – and the invigilator didn't stop the clock before that.' He was similarly dismayed on later occasions by colleagues who failed to meet deadlines for the completion of research project grant applications within set time limits.

First and foremost Eric is a social historian, both by inclination and by training, and he has made full use of the knowledge and skills associated with that background in his various books and other writings about education, consumer affairs, older people, entertainers and sport, as noted in earlier chapters. However, he has also written quite extensively about British history itself, particularly that of the 19th and 20th centuries. In a way, all of his writings continue the overarching theme of education in its broadest sense, by helping people to teach themselves and learn more about different subjects.

Two of Eric's earliest books, *Victorian Social Reform* (1968) and *Nineteenth Century Education* (1970), were concise but highly informative works in the series *Seminar Studies in History*, edited by Patrick Richardson and published by Longman. At around the same time, whilst he was working in Liverpool, he also produced *Law and Order in Victorian Lancashire* (1968), *Social Administration in Lancashire, 1830-60* (1969), which was based on his University of York DPhil thesis and recommended for publication by Asa Briggs, and a historical study of the city of Liverpool, *Old Liverpool* (1971). In the introduction to the last of this impressive list of titles Eric writes:

> This is not intended as a formal history of Liverpool, either generally or over the last century or so. Indeed, it would be easier to write the history of a country like Norway or Portugal, for no one has yet succeeded in producing a definitive work on this bubbling, fluid,

dynamic city. This is no more than a set of brief sketches that hint, like a series of quickly penciled cartoons, at the profundity beyond. They form an anthology of selected essays on aspects of Liverpool life and society culled mainly from the last one hundred and fifty years.

Notwithstanding the above author's disclaimer, the book provides a fascinating insight into some aspects of the life and history of this great city.

The Development of Social Welfare in Britain, first published in 1994 by the Open University Press (and reprinted in 1994, 1996 and 2000), is a textbook aimed at undergraduate and diploma students across a wide range of the social sciences. As described on the back cover, it covers the story of social provision from medieval times to the present, systematically examining the major themes of the relief of poverty and social care, healthcare and housing, crime and policing, and education.

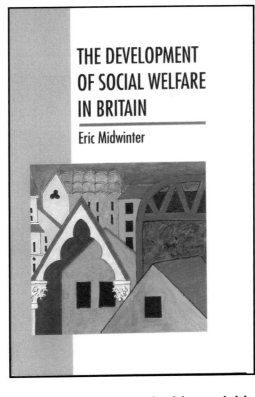

THE DEVELOPMENT OF SOCIAL WELFARE IN BRITAIN

Eric Midwinter

Although intended as a textbook, it is a highly readable account of these subjects, of value as a source of reference to the general reader as well as to students, and the number of reprints provides clear evidence of its well-deserved popularity.

Rather different in nature from most of Eric's literary output are his two largely pictorial accounts of life in Britain in the Twentieth Century. Both *Yesterdays: The Way We Were 1919-1939* (1998) and *Yesterdays: Our Finest Hours 1939-1953* (2001), published by Souvenir Press, are crammed with highly nostalgic black and white photographs, reminding us how things were in earlier days on the street, at home, on the move, at the shops, at school and work, at leisure, and on holidays and outings. In the second book, the effects of war on the population, and how people coped with its various deprivations – and how they celebrated the end of hostilities – are well illustrated. Needless to say, Eric's text accompanying these engaging pictures is full of revealing insights into the times in question.

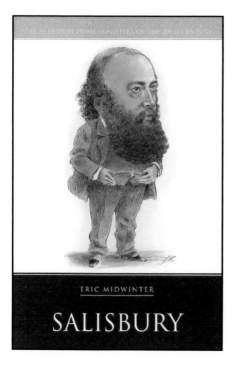

Eric was invited to write the first book in the highly acclaimed series entitled *The 20 British Prime Ministers of the 20th Century*, published by Haus Publishing and edited by Francis Beckett. Eric's contribution was *Salisbury* (2007), covering, in 154 instructive pages, the life of Lord Salisbury (1830-1903), who held the office of Prime Minister for three separate periods, the last being 1895-1902. He was the last person to hold this position from the House of Lords, and his main political interest was in foreign affairs. This is a highly informative and entertaining account of Lord Salisbury's life and work, of particular value to those, like the author, whose education in historical matters is sadly lacking.

Francis Beckett has succinctly summed up Eric as 'basically a professional writer, who gets his copy in on time and whose material meets all the objectives required by an editor (i.e. appropriate content, correct length, well written and constructed).' Francis also edits *Third Age Matters* (previously *U3A News*), which now has a circulation of over 200,000. Unsurprisingly, Eric is a frequent contributor to *Third Age Matters*, and he has described its august and erudite editor as 'that eloquent campaigning writer.'

In *An Outline of Political Thought and Practice* (2009), Eric considers several key themes, namely the precursors of modern state thought and practice, the early modern state, revolution and the civic state, the 19th century state, political theory and action in the 20th century, and political thought and practice in the future. Each chapter of this stimulating 114-page book starts with a brief summary, and the final chapter concludes with an interesting analysis of the interface between the 'ideal' and the 'real' in politics. The back page 'blurb' boldly states that 'This book deserves to become essential reading, not only for undergraduate and postgraduate students, but for the general reader as well, in order to develop our appreciation of the role of the individual and of government in the making of the nation-state, of rights and duties, and of citizenship.' Notwithstanding the publisher's obvious commercial need to publicise and describe the book in glowing terms, the comment about its value to the general reader is very well founded.

Third Age Press has been instrumental in publishing much of Eric Midwinter's writing over the past twenty years. Having been inspired by her work with U3A and Age Concern England and realising the rich vein of experience and talent there was in Britain's older people, Dianne Norton decided to establish an independent publishing company to tap into this reservoir of potential writers and readers. Through her work she had established a valuable network of contacts among whom Eric was the most prolific. The first Third Age Press titles were a trio of booklets under the banner of 'Lifelines', written by Eric and designed to encourage and guide people in the recording of their own life stories and even planning for a 'celebration of their life'. Eric went on to influence the output of the company especially with his work on theatrical popular culture and his introduction to other writers such as Patrick Newley, and then leading into the world of cricket.

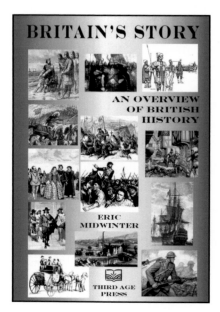

Eric's most recent historical book for Third Age Press is *Britain's Story: An Overview of British History*, published in 2012 by Third Age Press. In this highly condensed 59-page account of a huge amount of material, the intention is to provide 'more of an overview, looking down rather than back and seeing events against a more natural time pattern, trying to judge the relative significance of happenings over the same temporal perspective.' The six concise and very readable chapters cover The Rise and Fall of Roman Britain (55 BC– 40 AD), The Anglo-Saxon and Danish Settlement (440-1066), The Middle Ages from Conquest to Magna Carta (1066-1215), The Later Medieval Age (1216-1485), The Making of a Nation (1485-1742), and The Rise and Fall of the British Empire (1742-2012). Apart from its brevity, this approach is also unusual in the proportion of space devoted to each of these time periods, or, as Eric writes, 'the decision to take a more equitable view of the time frame', which may make the coverage of the 20th century look particularly squashed. Perhaps this succinct style of history writing for adults will one day become a rival to the popular 'Horrible Histories' approach, so beloved by children in recent times?

In somewhat different mode, Eric has written a very useful and instructive introduction to – mostly English – selected popular literature. In *Novel Approaches: A Guide to the Popular Classic Novel* (2003), once again published by Third Age Press, he provides brief analytical notes on 35 novels, starting with *Robinson Crusoe*, written by Daniel Defoe in 1719, and ending with Iris Murdoch's *The Sandcastle* from 1957. Along the way, as might be expected, a number of Eric's favourite 19th century authors are featured, including well-chosen examples from the works of Charlotte and Emily Brontë, Jane Austen, Dickens, Thackeray, Trollope, George Eliot, Hardy, as well as other key authors from the 18th and 20th centuries. This book reveals, once again, the considerable breadth of Eric's reading, knowledge and interests, although, with characteristic generosity, he does acknowledge substantial help in its preparation from his great friend and literary expert, Brian Walsh.

Novel Approaches

a guide to the popular classic novel

Eric Midwinter

Of course, evidence of Eric's consummate skills as a communicator with the written word comes not only from his impressive list of published books but also from his innumerable articles and reviews in newspapers, journals, magazines and newsletters. His writings in all these different formats are very prolific and demonstrate, once again, the enormous range of subjects on which he has the expertise to shed new light, based on knowledge and a deep understanding of the relevant background issues. He is generous in his willingness to share these skills with others and has helped a number of his friends, including the author, in their tentative first efforts as writers.

Reflecting on his life as a writer, Eric has revealingly provided the following self-assessment:

> Moreover, turning to my 'general' writing, I never regarded myself really as a cricket historian or a theatre historian but as a social historian anxious to see how cricket or comedy was created by, fitted into, or reflected its social context. Except for one or two old age reports (and I think I could find a historical motif therein), all my books are history books.

> I am a Victorian *manqué*; my religious beliefs are Victorian, my political opinions are derived from 19th century thinkers; my sporting and theatre interests emanate from Victorian constructs (Lancashire Cricket Club, Manchester United FC, Gilbert and Sullivan, music hall), I read very little fiction dating from either before 1830 or after 1914 – and so on and so on. Much as I hate travel, I enjoy these constant journeys into the not so distant past.

Further to this theme of a strong Victorian legacy, the first time Eric became entirely conscious of it was about 1970 when he was interviewed for thirty minutes or so during a magazine programme on Radio Merseyside. After a period of talking about sport, music, theatre, politics, religion, and other topics, the interviewer remarked 'everything about you and what you do and what you believe in is Victorian in origin. You don't belong in the 20th century at all. You even walked into the studio wearing a black overcoat looking like a Victorian'. Eric was happy to acknowledge that he is 'Guilty as charged'. In an oblique reference to the general public's common perception of meetings of Alcoholics Anonymous, he confesses 'My name's Eric and I'm an historian'. If he had been given the option to be born in another era, Eric's preference would have been to live his life as an adult in the period 1870-1914, after the invention of the water closet but before the start of World War I.

On moving to work in London in 1975, Eric sought the opportunity to write in more general terms, but deploying the same basic approach as previously, that is, the historical use of the social environment to assess the themes under review. He was eager to play off life-long, non-work-related interests and began with comedy, seeking to judge comedians against their social and cultural background. On one occasion the *Observer* ran a series on 'Benign Obsessions', at a time when Eric happened to know the features editor, and he wrote an article for that newspaper on 'Wartime Radio' in which he described his own almost total recall of many of the signature tunes used for the programmes of that era.

Eric's great love of and amazing facility with words, and his excellent ability to recall music and songs of various types, is in marked contrast to his very limited visual acuity. He freely admits that he has little appreciation of the delights of natural scenery, architecture and works of art, and does not remember details such as the colours of the bedroom curtains or the dining room carpet at home, nor can he easily describe what cricket pictures currently adorn the walls of his study – for some reason he seems unable to carry such images in his mind. When visiting an art gallery, for example, he soon finds himself just reading the captions. Eric reckons that he learned more about Germany by reading the first twenty pages of Geoffrey Barraclough's book *The Origins of Modern Germany* than by spending eighteen months in the country during his National Service.

This weakness in his ability to enjoy and retain visual impressions, coupled with a strong disinclination to travel unnecessarily, unless it happens to be by rail, may partly explain why Eric has never been particularly keen on sight-seeing expeditions and holidays. He is also a non-driver and is not keen on travelling long distances by road. When he was working at the CPA the staff thought he was very generous in allowing others to attend and speak at overseas conferences rather than accept such invitations himself. It took some time for his colleagues to realize that Eric never travelled anywhere outside the British Isles if he could help it, and when he did have to travel he always preferred to go by rail, if possible, so that he could carry on reading and writing throughout the journey. Coincidentally, he also felt that many big conferences were a waste of time and that they just provided an opportunity for social 'jollies' for the delegates. Similar criticisms have also been levelled at scientific conferences from time to time, although it is hard to deny the occasional value of networking and meeting colleagues in similar fields of study.

An allied point about Eric's approach to written and verbal communication is that since about his late twenties he determined on a path that he believes has served him well in terms of economy of effort and productivity. He decided that he would make his speaking and writing style as close as possible and, although this might be regarded by some as evidence of laziness, it meant that lectures and talks were readily transmutable into written articles, and chapters of books and other essays have swiftly been transformed into lectures. Even his informal Savage Club lunchtime talks suffer the same fate and many of them have subsequently been published in one form or another, or were verbal adaptations of recently written pieces. Basically, he is very fond of words and likes to make good use of them.

Eric's highly developed skills as an orator and spoken word communicator have taken a number of forms over the years. These include formal lectures, teaching classes and seminars, informal talks in a variety of settings, after-dinner speeches, funeral orations, introductions to book launches and other special events, speeches at retirement and birthday parties, literary award ceremonies, entertainments in different settings, as well as numerous radio and television broadcasts. To this day he is in much demand as a speaker at U3A, Civic Society and other meetings, rugby and cricket club dinners, and at various Savage Club functions, where he never fails to edify, amuse and entertain his audiences.

Eric's varied talents as an entertainer started to be revealed whilst he was at school, appearing in school plays with contemporaries such as Philip Jenkinson, Robert Gillespie, Graham Armitage and Bob Greaves, all of whom actually went on the stage after leaving school, with the latter becoming a television newsreader. He developed this interest locally in Sale with the Montague Players during the period 1947-59, doing mostly concert party-style entertainments, and opportunities for this style of performance were continued and extended with the Midnight Howlers in Cambridge.

After graduation, from 1959 until the mid-1960s, Eric performed regularly in pantomimes and cabaret with the Sale Nomads, as well as writing much of the material, including six pantomimes, which were constantly recycled thereafter. In almost all of the places where he worked, Eric was involved with organizing and providing some form of local entertainment, with a succession of pantomimes, musicals, cabarets and revues, all of which provided further opportunities for Eric to display his comic and thespian talents as performer, writer and director.

This thread of involvement with entertainment was maintained during Eric's time in Liverpool (1968-75), then in London at the NCC (1975-80) and CPA (1980-92), as well as with the U3A and LRPC, including doing 'turns' at various peoples' retirement or leaving parties, and other special celebrations.

When reflecting on his long experience of speaking in public, Eric is ever mindful of the important influence of his father. He has written:

> I want to say here that little of this would have happened without the support of my father, who was very keen on the whole idea of me performing and writing, encouraging me particularly from the start when, as a 14/15 year old, I began to perform with the Montague Players. This is of some import because I do very fundamentally believe that it gave me the confidence to face a career in which public speaking has been an essential part – you could argue that I chose such a career because I enjoyed doing public speaking and that I made sure any jobs I had included such an element, but nonetheless 'Ack' was to the fore. When teaching I used to think – where else would a performer have a captive audience?

The biggest live audience that Eric ever addressed was at a packed Queen Elizabeth Hall on the South Bank. With overflow delegates watching on screens outside the main auditorium, this occurred during a conference on education in deprived areas, chaired by Shirley Williams. It was on this occasion that he came up with what he considers to be one of his best replies to an adversarial question from the floor, which emanated from a rather grumpy traditional headmaster who was giving Eric considerable stick by constantly calling him a 'revolutionary'. His response to this gentleman was 'Were the revolution to be successful and as you were being carried in the tumbril towards the guillotine, you would be able to say "it is a far, far better thing that I do than I have ever done".' He has also observed that, contrary to expectation, speakers generally tend to be safer from hostile questions when confronting a huge audience, whereas within a smaller group setting the participants might almost assassinate you if they are so minded.

Another classic example of an amusing and effective put-down comes from the Savage Club 150th Anniversary Founder's Dinner in 2007, at which Eric had been invited to speak. One of the members present called out something vaguely insulting before he had even had a chance to start speaking, to which he responded, after a suitable pause, 'I shall continue in spite of that premature ejaculation.'

As mentioned previously, Eric did quite a lot of speaking on educational matters around the country, some of it in tandem with his great friend John Rennie. He recalls affectionately that John often began by saying, in addition to remarking upon the difference between his North Manchester accent and Eric's South Manchester version, 'I'm going to tell a joke to put myself at ease.' It is certainly true that Eric often starts his talks and lectures with a well-chosen story or joke. This certainly helps to 'break the ice', thus enabling both speaker and audience to feel more at ease. On one occasion, John Rennie was all for remonstrating forcibly with someone in the audience who was heckling and being somewhat obnoxious towards Eric, and on being restrained from taking any physical action in retaliation remarked 'the only vice Cambridge taught you was tolerance.'

Eric takes the preparation of talks very seriously, giving close attention to details such as duration and timing, as well as construct and content. He often writes vocal directions, indicating pauses and emphasis, in his script, and he carries with him a portable lectern for his notes in case one is not available at the venue. Until a few years ago, he used to rehearse his talks whilst walking the dog, a regular habit that had developed over a period of 25-30 years.

Eric's friend Dave Walmsley, a fellow old boy who attended Sale Grammar School from 1958-65 and later returned as a member of staff, shared speaking duties with Eric on a number of occasions at Old Salians' dinners, including during the school's 50th anniversary celebrations. He has made some interesting and perceptive observations about Eric's approach to such presentations :

> I increasingly modelled my style on Eric's – having witnessed him speaking on a number of occasions from the floor. Eric left joke telling to others – his style was to weave an improbable narrative, interlaced with germs of real events, and crucially and heavily based on real life characters, known to his audience, invariably present at the dinners and invariably those who could take a joke and some mild ribbing at their own expense. Eric's humour was thus based like all great classical comedy writing on the comedy of character observation – and Eric added to this a rich and inventive language aimed at an intelligent listener – he had a great feel for the right word and the right phrase – and sometimes it was the choice of language that was the source of amusement. Great use of irony, pathos, bathos and the mild ridiculing of human weakness and foibles were all tools in his impressive armoury – and it is noteworthy that his speeches were often as good to read as to listen to. His speeches were delivered in a mock oratorical style, with pace and energy, a northern twang and with perfect natural timing – the sign of a true master of his art. And like any great performer – there were stage nerves and a nervous energy, which created momentum and life. He was a great observer, a great describer, a great animator.

As mentioned earlier, many of Eric's talks have subsequently appeared as written articles or chapters and vice-versa. As a result the talks often seem a bit literary and the writings tend to be rather colloquial in nature. Certainly, it would seem that none of his carefully researched material is ever wasted or squandered. When preparing lecture-type presentations, as opposed to those intended purely for entertainment purposes, Eric always tries to match the funniest parts with the more serious or significant sections, in order to make the effect more enduring.

During his time with the EPA in Liverpool, Eric did a lot of writing of articles for various journals and newspapers, as well as his books, and he also became involved with broadcasting, particularly on Radio Merseyside. Once or twice he appeared on programmes alongside a youthful Robert Kilroy-Silk, then a lecturer at Liverpool University, and they also both served for a short time on the same school governing body. Some years later, whilst he was at the CPA, Eric appeared on Kilroy-Silk's BBC One daytime chat show called 'Kilroy', which started in 1986 and was eventually taken off the air in 2004. He did the odd radio piece about the EPA project and also became education guru to and on the Granada TV programme 'This is Your Right', run by the Liberal MP Dr Michael Winstanley (later Lord Winstanley). Eric was also involved with one or two BBC Two specials on education, one with David Dimbleby and the other with Desmond Wilcox, the husband of Esther Rantzen, and appeared on the BBC series called 'The Education Programme', launched in 1969, which was produced by Roger Owen and included a programme about the Educational Priority Areas.

Eric tells an amusing tale from his time in Liverpool, which illustrates the aura of fame he acquired after one of his appearances on television.

I often used to lunch in the Liverpool post-graduate cafe where I would ask for bacon and egg and two rounds of bread, so that I could make it into a bacon and egg buttie. It being post-graduate, they cut the bread diagonally. I said to the very pleasant lady who ran it; 'with bread in triangles, you end up with the bacon stuck outside and the egg all over the shop. Either get a hen with a triangular bottom and a lob-sided pig, or leave the bread square'. Thereafter when she saw me join the queue, she would shout 'Bacon and egg and two rounds of square bread'. 'The Education Programme' went out on a Sunday afternoon – on Monday I rolled into the caff – and this lady hailed me excitedly, crying in impeccable scouse, 'I saw you on the telly yesterday afternoon; me mother was upstairs and I ran into the hall and shouted 'quick, Mother, come downstairs – the Square Bread Man's on telly.'

By their cuisine shalt thou know them.

There was a significant half hour film that Eric and his Liverpool EPA colleagues made for TV in 1970 – it was for 'This Week', the flagship Thames Television current affairs weekly programme – and it had the advantage of being in colour. The team used a copy of the film in conferences and presentations thereafter, but, unfortunately, more recent attempts to trace a copy of the film have failed. In Eric's opinion, this was probably the most important educational TV programme that he did.

Following his appearance on one or two Granada adult education shows, Eric eventually became presenter of a thirteen-episode programme called 'Chalkface', which had tidy viewing figures of 1.5 million and was moved to later in the afternoon as a result. As he recalls:

People who know you mention when they see you or hear you but, oddly, one of the only times I have been approached by a stranger was on a train when a young soldier returning to a troubled Northern Ireland told me that, after a patrol in Belfast, the lads would settle down and watch this programme. As Frankie Howerd would have said, 'I was amazed'.

This series was followed by a further thirteen episodes co-presented with the well-known educationalist Ted Wragg, who was later responsible for Eric's appointment as Visiting Professor at Exeter University. Eric presented a weekly feature on the theme 'What the papers say about education.' By the time of these television series Eric was in London at the NCC, but he used to do a regular weekly day in Manchester.

Since Eric's brief at NCC encompassed not only the specific interests of consumers of public services but also public relations, including such things as annual congresses, parliamentary lobbying, publishing, press and media, he inevitably became much involved with radio and some television coverage of events. This media involvement increased further when he also took on the chairmanship of the LRPC in 1977, leading to frequent visits to various London broadcasting studios.

On one occasion, it had been arranged for a colleague of Eric to talk about a consumer issue at the BBC. On arrival, she was parked in the restaurant and asked to wait there, but, because of some internal breakdown in communications, her location was confused and an anxious programme representative called the NCC office to say that she was nowhere to be found. As a result, a copy of the relevant press release was urgently put in Eric's hand and he had to do the live interview blind over the telephone, to the astonishment of his stranded colleague who was still sitting in the restaurant and listening to the programme whilst waiting to be called to the studio.

On another occasion Eric was booked to do a piece about a railway matter for a BBC evening programme and he sat waiting next to a rather taciturn young man with an Irish accent. Eric was taken and placed next to Sue Lawley, who seemed very nice but was not the interviewer he was expecting. When he mentioned something about his subject, she reacted swiftly and Eric was rapidly exchanged for the Irish lad, who was due to be interrogated as a representative of Sinn Fein. It is arguable which of the two men would have been more surprised to be faced with the other's set of questions.

Eric did quite a few items for the BBC Radio Four 'Today' programme. He knew Brian Redhead from Cambridge days and when Brian was a journalist, working as northern editor of the *Guardian*, Eric, still in Liverpool, took part in a couple of his 'A Word in Edgeway' programmes and a futher two when he moved south. When in London, after Eric had left NCC to join CPA, Eric received a phone call one Sunday evening asking, 'would you come in tomorrow morning' in order to talk about some consumer matter that was before parliament; he patiently explained that he was now doing 'older age' and asked the caller to change the data base then and now. 'Hang on a minute' he said – a minute or so later he came back on the line – 'could you come in tomorrow morning to talk about the United Nations Conference on ageing in Vienna?' Eric told him that, in reward for his sheer cheek, he would.

The previously mentioned Roger Owen provided Eric with further opportunities for television work. He took part in one of five programmes that Roger was producing for BBC2 on equality, his contribution being about education. Roger Owen also got Eric to devise and present the five programme series called '10 Million People' about old age, broadcast in 1983, which was perhaps the biggest and most significant media production with which he has ever been involved.

In addition to writing many articles about older age during his time at CPA, he also did a considerable number of radio broadcasts, being interviewed at various times by Mary Parkinson, Sarah Kennedy and Gloria Hunniford, amongst others. The main outlet, however, was the 'Jimmy Young Programme', on which he often appeared. Eric found these occasions very satisfactory, since the researchers for the programme were good and he considered Jimmy Young to be a top class interviewer, who was sympathetic in approach and always gave his interviewees a chance to put across their points. Eric received a very warm and friendly letter from Jimmy Young when he retired, so they had obviously struck up a good relationship when they worked together.

Eric has fond memories of meeting some interesting people in waiting rooms prior to appearing on radio or television programmes. Amongst these, in addition to the man from Sinn

Fein, are Clarence Wright (one of several Savage Club members who were in the original cast of ITMA), Jean Anderson, Geoffrey Holland (from 'Hi-Di-Hi') and Tommy Steele, with whom he had an interesting conversation about dieting and their shared love of bacon butties.

Apart from writing extensively about sport, Eric has also talked a lot about it to different audiences around the country. By his own reckoning, he has probably spoken at over a hundred rugby (including Sale RFC), football and cricket (including one for the MCC) club dinners. An old school friend, Brian Lee, who was at one time director of Bisham Abbey, the national sports centre, and manager (later chairman) of Wycombe Wanderers, booked Eric as speaker for a few dinners, including one where his fellow speakers were Malcolm MacDonald ('Super Mac'), the England centre forward and Ian St John ('The Saint'), the former Scotland and Liverpool player and TV football pundit. During his speech, he thanked the former for the meal of fishburger and french fries he had enjoyed in one of his restaurants earlier in the day, and returned a crepe bandage to the latter which had been put on his knee when playing soccer by a member of his ambulance brigade. This story illustrates, once again, Eric's brilliant ability to find humour in almost any set of circumstances and use it to entertain the particular audience he is addressing.

Eric's extensive knowledge and understanding of history and literature, and his deep love of words and language, coupled with passionate egalitarian beliefs and a highly developed sense of humour, have enabled him to inform, enlighten, entertain, and, sometimes, provoke his readers and audiences over many years. The range of subjects he has covered in his time is most impressive, as is the sheer volume of material that he has generated. There can be few, if any, other communicators who are equally at home writing or talking with authority about social history, social policy and administration, education, old age, transport, sport, theatre and entertainers. Without any doubt, Eric is a great communicator, who continues to be in great demand as a speaker and can be relied upon to stimulate and amuse almost any audience, whatever the nature and circumstances of his presentation.

Eric recruits a 'volunteer' during a convivial after-dinner speech

THE WORLDS OF ERIC MIDWINTER

THE WORLD OF NEIGHBOURS

Since moving from the north in 1975 Margaret and Eric, who have now been happily married for fifty years, have lived contentedly in Harpenden, Hertfordshire. They are delighted that their three children all live within easy reach. Both Matthew, with his wife Maureen and son Patrick, and Kate, with her two children Niamh and Sam, live nearby in Bedfordshire, while their other son Daniel lives not far away at Crystal Palace. Theirs is a loving and mutually supportive family group.

Eric is one of a close-knit group of neighbours in Harpenden. Three of these are David Rankin, Chris Marsden and Richard Thomas, each of whom has known Eric for over twenty years. They communicate with one another frequently, either face-to-face or by email and telephone, and are great pals. They are all very active in the Harpenden Society, which has about 1,000 members, and all are also active members of the Harpenden Green Belt Association.

David Rankin's perceptive comments about Eric offer some interesting insights into one aspect of Eric's character that has not hitherto been explored, apart from a brief passing remark by Harry Pepp that was quoted earlier, and in John Wade's engaging Foreword:

> Eric's brainpower may be awe-inspiring but there is one area where that brain does not stretch to helping

him much and that is dealing with mechanical matters. Though never ever unappreciative of the help he gets from neighbours, he watches with studied disinterest as a tap washer in his house is replaced or a new lawnmower assembled from the box in which it has just arrived. All he wants to know is that the tap works again and that the lawnmower will cut the grass. He has, incidentally, no interest in the fact that the lawnmower is sophisticated enough to cut grass to three different levels. The shortest level will do for Eric so that the grass will play but a bit part in his life.

His total lack of interest in mechanical processes also extends to material possessions, apart, of course, from books. Even a writing desk once used by Charles Dickens and up for auction failed to spark Eric's interest, his comment being that 'you could buy a lot of books for £800', which was what the writing desk eventually sold for.

Eric's obvious lack of interest and skill in technical and mechanical matters extends to some degree to other areas. He admits to having a strong dislike for gardening, despite (or may be because of) having to carry out the chore of cutting the grass from time to time. He has no interest in cars or their inner workings and does not drive, but can cook a bit. Erecting shelves at home, or putting together flat-pack items of furniture is certainly not his particular forté. Eric does regularly use a computer for writing and communications via e-mail, although he is not particularly adept at, or interested in, harnessing its full capabilities, such as, for example, manipulation of digital photographic images or sound and music files. For a man who generates so many written words on a daily basis, the easy-to-use word processing facility provided by today's computer software is clearly a great boon and one of the few examples of modern technology being fully embraced by Eric, unlike the mobile telephone.

David Rankin continues:

> Eric's inbred dislike of 'top down' directives from government and his desire to 'involve the people' in as much decision making as possible is evident in so many of the things that now involve him in Harpenden. Active consultation with residents and focused committee work have been his contribution, as has his unremitting support for me over the last four years of 'Issue Response', Harpenden's quick, easy, on-line survey initiative. This was my creation and I am still working on improving it, and Eric is helping me do that.

Harpenden's 'Issue Response' scheme is very much the sort of community-based initiative that is close to Eric's heart. David Rankin's testimony concludes:

> His vast experience in opinion seeking has been an invaluable contribution to making 'Issue Response' such a local success. His comments are to the point and always light of touch as in the following email to me: 'I was mind-blown by the brilliance of my previous email and fear I have not much more glitter to add to such a sparkling analysis'.

> Always gentle, always considerate.

Wendy Rankin, David's wife, has added her own affectionate comments to those of her husband. Amongst other distinctions, Wendy has starred as the principal boy in some of the pantomimes written and produced by Eric for, and performed by, his neighbours.

> He is one of the gentlest people I have met and he has an ability to communicate with all ages. I remember that a couple of years ago I took my eldest grandaughter to see Margaret, with whom I have been friends for years, when Emily was about two and a half and very shy, especially with men she didn't know. Eric greeted her in his gentle way and sat on the grass to enable her to speak 'eye to eye' with him. Put at her ease and with his quiet manner

she was soon chatting away with the few words she knew and with plenty of smiles and chuckles. It was a joy to see them both so at ease with each other.

He is quite a charmer too and always seems comfortable in the company of the ladies and will join in with their less than academic conversations. Eric is always funny and with many anecdotes, never pretentious and invariably welcoming. Whenever we bump into each other in the road we chat about many topics and he always becomes more animated when musical theatre is mentioned and there's often a song and a little dance performed by Eric to illustrate his knowledge of the shows.

My mother is ten years older than him and whenever she comes to stay he makes a point of coming to see her to chat about the old days; there is always great hilarity from both of them!

A true gentleman.

Perhaps Wendy Rankin would agree with Michael Young's earlier judicious assessment that Eric might appeal to women voters, should he ever choose to stand in an election?

Another of the close group of local friends is Chris Marsden, who has written:

I have known Eric as a neighbour, friend and sometime colleague for twenty years or more. As perhaps one of the world's greatest polymaths, the complete antithesis to the old adage 'jack of all trades and master of none', Eric has immense expertise in fields as varied as education, ageing, disability, transport, music hall and variety theatre, classic novels and above all cricket. The connecting factor in all these is probably his immense knowledge of and interest in social history, which is revealed in many of the books that he has written. His award winning recent book, *The Cricketer's Progress: Meadowland to Mumbai*, is just one example, where he combines his detailed knowledge of cricket history with deeply insightful social commentary.

Our first professional encounter was when he invited me to become a Board member of the Community Education Development Centre. I attended a number of meetings under his chairmanship, during which he always combined depth of knowledge, experience and wisdom with a wonderful sense of humour.

This joint work led to us realising our shared interests in education, community and broader social and economic issues, which in turn led to regular conversations which helped us both in our respective activities. It was perhaps written in the stars that, when I was asked to become Chairman of the Harpenden Society, the Town's civic society concerned with all aspects of its welfare, Eric agreed also to join the committee and take on the demanding editorship of the Newsletter. The Society was in danger of losing its way and its subsequent resurgence owes much to Eric's indefatigable support and brilliant articulation of what was needed. Not only has he transformed this paper with erudite journalistic flair, including deep and wide-ranging editorials on key aspects of creating a healthy community, he has led two working groups championing issues concerning local education provision and the creation of a 'wellness' centre, which combines many aspects of the community health and welfare needs, especially for older people.

As neighbour and friend he has been a constant source of entertainment and conversation stimulant as he has brought his many talents to bear on social gatherings. Perhaps his greatest achievement in this respect was to write a Millennium Pantomime for our regular neighbours' New Year Party, in which up to twelve participants took their turns as actors, chorus and audience. This was so successful and so much enjoyed that two further pantomimes were written and performed in subsequent years.

Further helpful comments have been received from Richard Thomas, who wrote:

I was struck on first acquaintance, and still am, by Eric's amazing breadth of interests and knowledge. Who else could write vivaciously about Lord Salisbury, music hall, Greek philosophy and longevity? With his great range of friendships, his curiosity about human behaviour and a good memory, he is an amusing conversationalist who is never at a loss for an anecdote to illustrate the point he is making. I remember once when walking down our road in the snow being surprised to see Eric outside his house dabbing at the snow with a broom. He explained that Margaret had asked him to clear the drive while she was out. It was a painful sight, as nobody will be surprised to hear that Eric is not at his best with a broom in his hands. I suggested that I swept the drive while he talked, which he did very entertainingly, and we both enjoyed ourselves.

Eric was one of the prime movers in the setting up in 2002 of an association to protect our local green belt. Anyone who 'googles' green belt' can find out its statutory purposes, but it was Eric who led us to realise that the concept lent itself to a completely modern interpretation – sustainability – and that it could be, and should be, used to balance a town's resources with the needs of the residents. Eric also came up with the completely original idea of a ready reckoner for town planners, which he described in a paper called 'Home Rule'. He pointed out that in a town with given characteristics it should be possible to find out what demands an extra thousand inhabitants would create on, for example, schools or different kinds of medical facilities, and that norms might be developed for wider use. Unfortunately our local planners decided that 'not invented here' was the right reaction to this very practical notion. Eric has also used his experience of local and central government to guide us on how we should campaign, and he deserves the thanks of our town for all we have achieved in the last ten years in defending something valued by our residents.

Eric's wide knowledge and his story telling are well known, but I am always conscious of his kindness. While many people's political views have bitter roots, Eric's seem to spring from a simpler desire for justice and fair play, and are all the more palatable. I think that his benevolent outlook must be the reason for his most surprising characteristic, which is that he does not talk down to people. We have all suffered from experts who treat us like idiots, but Eric has the knack of teaching us without making us wretchedly aware of our ignorance. Long may he flourish.

Richard added as a postscript to his comments:

No doubt others will be covering Eric's funny pantomimes for our neighbours, cleverly constructed so that complete amateurs can take part, and rehearse their parts without becoming aware of the whole thing. And his terrific work for our Civic Society, which has drawn on his deep beliefs of how a civil society should function and have its needs met.

As well as being Editor of the Harpenden Society News, referred to earlier by Chris Marsden, Eric is also co-convenor of two of the Society's Working Groups. One of these is the Health and Social Welfare Group, which, amongst other things, is concerned with encouraging and facilitating the refurbishment of the local hospital, and the other is the Education and Leisure Group. In addition to several other activities, for each year since 2013, the latter group, and in particular Eric's valued friend the energetic Ron Taylor, has organized an innovative and popular Primary Schools Arts Competition, for three age groups, each year's event being based on a selected theme of local significance. Importantly, this competition includes all the 'Creative Arts' within its scope, including music, drama,

Imagine

It is 2100. 86 years have passed. You will be a very old person, possibly a grandad or grandmother. Harpenden will have changed a lot. But in what way? Imagine how different life will be like then. Be like Dr Who and fast forward yourself to see what it is like in Harpenden in 2100.

'Forward to the future...Harpenden 2100'

Just think what Harpenden will be like?

ART/CRAFTS
Show us what the town will look like and your school too. How will people dress. Will digital techniques take over from traditional drawing and painting. What will we be eating & drinking?

WRITING
How will we be talking to each other? How will our language change? Will we use paper or all digital?

Just think of the changes that will take place?

DRAMA
Write/act a play for theatres of the future, or a programme for the latest smart phones; invent a new digital game

MUSIC
Compose/perform some music or a dance that you think will be popular.

PHOTOGRAPHY
Produce a film or shoot some photographs that portray Harpenden's future.

WRITE ABOUT IT...PAINT IT...MAKE A MODEL...TAKE A PHOTOGRAPH...MAKE A VIDEO...ACT IT...SING IT...DESIGN IT

and creative writing, as well as arts, crafts, IT and photography, so that children with many different interests and talents are able to take part. The subject for the inaugural competition 2013 was 'What do I like about Harpenden?', in 2014 it was 'Hail Harpendonia', and for 2015 children have been invited to turn their creative talents to the idea 'Forward to the future

THE WORLDS OF ERIC MIDWINTER

... Harpenden in 2100'. It is evident from these latest educational activities that Eric is still putting into practical effect some of the 'child-centred' and 'community orientated' ideas he started to develop many years earlier whilst working as a teacher and in the Liverpool Educational Priority Area, albeit in the somewhat different environment of Harpenden in Hertfordshire.

In addition to his significant involvement with the Harpenden Society and the Harpenden Green Belt Association, Eric has made major contributions to the U3A's activities in his home town, as referred to in an earlier chapter. As President of the Harpenden U3A, he wrote the following contribution in the group's newsletter headed 'Movement and Mime':

I have written in the newsletter before of how, when Harpenden U3A began in 1982, Thursday afternoon in the Trust Hall was already the weekly date. I was then working full-time as Director of the Centre for Policy on Ageing which acted as a committee meeting base and financial conduit for the U3A nationally, until such time as it became a registered charity in its own right and, later on, had its own office. I took the role of General Secretary of the national body but I was also working on persuading people to start U3As up and down the country. At this point there was barely a dozen U3As in the UK and, of course, we had no practical idea of what might work and what wouldn't. So, almost every Thursday, I arrived at the Trust Hall and tried out some new wheeze on my very willing and patient friends, the, I am happy to say, growing squad of trialists who cheerfully fell in with what must have seemed my crazy demands.

One Thursday we did movement and mime. We wrote our names and addresses in the air with flourishing fencing-type gesticulation. We were given (well, 'I gave them' would be more accurate) moods, such as happiness, misery, anger and so forth, and the individuals had to describe them facially and bodily. The rest had to guess what each was. After the personal exercises we turned to tableaux. I gave small groups a scene to assemble in still-life, like the old Victorian parlour game; Daniel in the Lions' Den or Oliver Twist asking for more. I recall a particular jolly Death of Nelson, with the dying admiral (a survivor of the horrors of being a Japanese POW building railway lines in Burma) appearing to enjoy his forthcoming demise immensely.

Another exercise – and this may have been on another occasion as I did this two or three times – was the months of the year. Small groups were detailed to January, February and so on and they had to mime the month, this time by action, not still-life, and, as with the tableaux, the others had to guess which month it was. I have a very acute memory of a group who marvellously contrived to mime dancing around a Maypole. I leave it to you bright readers of this U3A newsletter to determine which month it was ...

It is over thirty years ago and I was, of course, still in the Second Age of gainful employ, but I hope you will glean from such reminiscences what affectionate memories I have of your gallant predecessors.

Eric's involvement with the Harpenden Society is very much a continuation of his long-standing interest in civic affairs generally. As he has written to the author:

I have found the whole issue of the place of local government in respect of the individual and the state (is it part of the central mechanism or the defender of the citizen against central control?) not only interesting but at the heart of much of the work I have done professionally. Even now, in doing things with the Harpenden Society I find myself guided by an acute awareness of the collapse of local government over the last 35/40 years and the growth of central intervention under both Labour and Tory administrations. Having been brought up with and having closely studied the Victorian/ early 20th Century sense of a balanced equation of central and local involvement, I am distressed at the fact that the see-saw is now upended.

Eric much enjoys both solving and setting crossword puzzles, and has been regularly attempting the *Guardian* cryptic crossword since 1971. For many years, the Midwinters have sent their friends and relations a unique home-constructed 'Chrissy Chrossy' instead of a more conventional Christmas card, thus providing the lucky recipients with a challenging brain-teaser for the festive season. On one occasion, Eric and the author enjoyed a pleasant summer's day together watching the cricket at Lord's and solving a specially commissioned crossword on the theme of cricket, set for them by a fellow Savage Club member, the eminent musician and cruciverbalist, John Elliott, who is also known to some as 'Bombardone'.

One of Eric's acquaintances, whom he had met and been interviewed by at the Granada studios in Manchester, was the TV presenter, journalist and photographer Bob Smithies. Bob's *alter ego* was the fiendish *Guardian* crossword setter known as 'Bunthorne', who regularly provided puzzles for this newspaper from 1966 until his death in 2006. The name Bunthorne was taken from the leading character in Gilbert and Sullivan's light opera *Patience*. On one occasion, whilst he was working at the NCC in 1978, Eric had dropped him a line and was delighted when Bob sent him back the following cryptic crossword clue:

'NCC man resolves it: consumer credit row. I'd suggest you leave 'us' out!' (6,4,9)

Those who may like to work out the solution to this clue for themselves should not forget that Eric is a Doctor of Philosophy. As Eric has said, having a personalised crossword clue devised by such a famous setter is a considerable honour and it ranks as one of his proudest achievements.

The solution, in fact, provides a perfect finish to this wide-ranging review of the 'worlds' of Doctor Eric Midwinter.

Eric at home in his garden in 2014
Photo courtesy of Philippa Le Marquand,
Palm PR/Hertfordshire

WORLDLY THOUGHTS

This has been for the author an intriguing, occasionally complex, and always enjoyable journey through the various worlds in which Eric Midwinter has spent his long and highly eventful life. The wealth of written material available, in addition to the testimonies so generously offered by many of his friends and colleagues, has provided an enormous amount of evidence upon which to draw whilst attempting to build up a fair and accurate picture of the life of this multi-talented man, and at times it has been necessary to condense or discard some parts of this great mass of information in the interests of producing a reasonably concise and, hopefully, readable account. Fortunately, at every stage of the process, Eric has been on hand to explain and amplify the material available, respond to innumerable questions and requests for clarification, and, as far as possible, to correct factual errors that may inadvertently have been recorded.

There can be no doubt that Eric is an extremely talented and industrious person who has followed a somewhat unusual, but highly successful, career pathway. His strong academic potential was evident from early childhood days, heavily influenced as it was by his grandmother who encouraged him to read and write before he had even started at primary school. This supportive family background, coupled with his own natural ability, eventually led to Eric gaining a scholarship to the local grammar school, from which he never really looked back. The subsequent Open Exhibition to Cambridge, the first class honours degree in History, the DPhil and other qualifications, are all indicators of a high academic achiever, as well as of an extremely diligent and hard worker.

In some ways, it seems slightly surprising that Eric did not end up as a high-flying university academic, since he clearly had the ability – if not the inclination – to pursue such a career. In fact, he was interviewed for professorial appointments on three or four occasions, but he always seemed destined to end up as the brilliant 'maverick' second choice candidate. The fact that he had never held a full-time university position, and therefore had not worked his way up the academic ladder in the conventional way, probably counted against him in the minds of some members of the various appointments committees. This uncharacteristic lack of success when he sought professorial appointments demonstrates one possible drawback of the unusual horizontal trajectory of his career pathway that has been referred to throughout this account of Eric's life, during which he moved more or less sideways from one field to another. However, he did eventually achieve his rightful academic recognition when he was appointed as a Visiting Professor of Education at the University of Exeter.

In several of the different worlds that Eric has worked, particularly as a secondary school teacher, in teachers' training colleges, and as an educationalist and policy maker in educational priority areas, in each of which roles he excelled at a remarkably young age, he might well have stayed longer and reached the top of that particular tree. However, as has been described, new career opportunities repeatedly arose at critical moments, several of them linked to the many enterprises initiated by the great social entrepreneur Michael Young, who clearly saw in Eric the potential to succeed in a number of different and highly innovative roles. This means that he has built up what must be a unique portfolio of areas of expertise.

Given Eric's strong egalitarian political interests and beliefs, and his great skills as a communicator, he might also have carved out a completely different sort of career as a politician. However, the various jobs that he has undertaken have allowed him to be highly influential in a number of areas of social policy, without ever wielding quite the same power as a successful politician. Nonetheless, the numerous books, reports, articles and papers that Eric has written on topics such as education, consumer affairs, transport, and the concerns of older people, remain as a lasting testament to his many significant contributions in these fields, and these will always be available for future reference by students, teachers, politicians, social entrepreneurs and policy makers.

Emphasis has been laid throughout this journey on Eric's consummate ability as a communicator, both with the written word and orally. His many books, on such a wide range of subjects, provide clear evidence of the workings of a talented and versatile polymath, despite Eric's light-hearted claim in an interview for *Third Age Matters*, when challenged with this description of his achievements, that 'plastic is one of the few things that he does not know much about.' Many of the friends and colleagues who have provided testimonies about Eric have commented about one or more of his books, and several of them have picked out *Make 'em Laugh* as a particular favourite. This seems to have been seminal work amongst his prolific literary output, presaging as it did an important series of further books and articles about comedians and entertainers. Surely Eric's father, Ack, who was instrumental in introducing his young son to the pleasures of live entertainment, and enjoying them with him, would have been delighted to see the published fruits of their shared enthusiasm for the many characters who took to the stage or studio and kept generations of audiences, from all social backgrounds, amused over the years. It is particularly fitting that this book was dedicated to Ack.

Eric's great love of sport, especially football and cricket, can also be traced back in some ways to his father's influence during his early formative years at home in Sale in the 1930's and 40's. In addition to his continuing support of his favourite Lancastrian teams, he has further indulged this passion by writing books about sport, many of them to great critical acclaim. Eric's celebrated biography of W.G. Grace has been referred to enthusiastically by several of his friends and his books *Red Shirts and Roses* and *The Cricketer's Progress* have both won prestigious literary awards. *Quill on Willow: Cricket in Literature*, whilst not winning any prizes, is a unique contribution to sporting scholarship that is also widely appreciated.

A particular feature of Eric's writing, as alluded to several times previously, whether he is considering sport, comedians or any other topic, is his great skill in setting his subject in its proper social and historical context, which is invariably highly illuminating, and this is coupled with his ability to lighten the serious content with well-chosen touches of humour. This talent for humour is also a strong feature of Eric's approach to public speaking, whether in formal lectures and extended talks, after dinner speeches, or cabaret-style entertainment. Whatever the occasion, Eric puts on a proper performance, always seeking to entertain as well as to enlighten his audience.

One strong characteristic of Eric's illustrious career has been his ability to put together and motivate effective teams of colleagues to work closely together towards common objectives. His approach has always been to guide such teams with a light touch, working collaboratively and encouraging people to bring out their best qualities for the benefit of the whole enterprise. As many of his former colleagues have reported, working with Eric was always good fun, and the long periods of hard graft were often punctuated with opportunities to enjoy happy social occasions together. Eric's management approach has also been clearly evident in the way he has chaired various committees over the years, never bombastic or domineering, but relying on gentle persuasion and well-argued suggestions to get people working together constructively. The occasional parties, Christmas pantomimes and other entertainments that were organized, so fondly remembered by colleagues, were all part of this team-building process, since Eric was well aware that a happy team, working in a relaxed environment, was more likely to produce good results.

Eric's life after retirement from full-time employment might almost have been treated as another 'world', to stand alongside all the others described in the previous chapters. Apart from continuing to work part-time for various organisations in an advisory capacity for several years, Eric has produced a steady stream of new books since the mid-1990s and has given many talks all over the country. He has been particularly active within the Savage Club, amongst other things chairing the Benevolent Fund Committee with great skill and sensitivity, organizing Benevolent Fund awareness evenings every two years, giving talks at Club Lunches every year, and performing regularly as an after dinner entertainer.

It has been a great privilege and a pleasure to explore the many worlds of Eric Midwinter in this way, and it is hoped that his unusual journey from childhood in Sale in the 1930s and 40s, through National Service, university and several distinctly different types of employment will have been of interest to others, especially those who may previously have come across only one or two aspects of his multi-faceted career. Eric has achieved much during his long and productive life and he has received a number of well-deserved accolades and awards.

Perhaps the distinctions which have afforded him the greatest pride and pleasure are his Open Exhibition to Cambridge, the award of an Open University doctorate, the creation of a dance, *Midwinter's Jig*, in his honour, the devising of a cryptic crossword clue based on his name by the famous Guardian setter, Bunthorne, the award of his O.B.E., and being granted the title 'Founder Member Emeritus' of the U3A .

Eric would say that, aside from some of his favourite books, the practical and visible achievements he most relishes are the contributions he has made to improved relations between schools and parents and the shift towards a more positive view of older age, plus his major part in both the acceptance of the all-systems London Travel Card and the decision not to privatise but to tender London bus services, and, finally, as a crowning glory, his being one of the three founding fathers of U3A. Taken together, these achievements surely represent a unique combination of socially valuable outcomes for one person to have accomplished during his lifetime, from which generations of people have gained considerable benefit and will continue to do so for years to come.

What Eric's friends and colleagues will undoubtedly remember, in addition to his great knowledge and intellectual powers, and his ability to see everything in its historical context, is his kindness and consideration for others, his concern for humanity as a whole, and his great sense of humour. These qualities have shone through in each of the great variety of worlds in which Eric has moved and worked and, taken together, help to define a man of his times who has made tremendous contributions to the well-being of his fellow citizens in many different ways. Despite Eric's initial reticence about having a biographical study dedicated to his life, it should by now be abundantly clear that he is an eminently worthy subject for such attention. It is a gratifying story of hope, aspiration, hard work and achievement, coupled with enjoyment and many great friendships that, hopefully, will be an inspiration to others in the future. It has been a joy to know and to work with Eric over recent years, my only regret is that we did not meet much earlier.

BIBLIOGRAPHY
A. Books

1) MODERN HISTORY

Victorian Social Reform (1968)

Law and Order in Victorian Lancashire (1968)

Social Administration in Lancashire, 1830-60 (Based on D.Phil Thesis, 1969)

Old Liverpool (1971)

The Development of Social Welfare in Britain (1994)

Yesterdays: The Way We Were 1919-1939 (1998)

Yesterdays: Our Finest Hours 1939-1953 (2001)

Lord Salisbury (20 Prime Ministers of the 20th Century) (2007)

An Outline of Political Thought and Practice (2008)

Britain's Story: An Overview of British History (2012)

2) EDUCATION

Nineteenth Century Education (1970)

Projections (Ed. Midwinter, 1972)

Social Environment and the Urban School (1972)

Schools in Society: the Evolution of English Education (1972)

Priority Education: An Account of the Liverpool Project (1972)

Teaching in the Urban Community School (ed. Midwinter, 1972)

Patterns of Community Education (1972)

Pre-school Priorities (ed. Midwinter, 1974)

Education and the Community (1975)

Education for sale (Classroom close-ups) (1977, reprint 2012)

State Educator: The Life and Enduring Influence of WE Forster (1995)

The Billy Bunter Syndrome: Or Why Britain Failed to Create Relevant Secondary School System (1998)

Novel Approaches: A Guide to the Popular Classic Novel (2003)

3) OLDER AGE

Age is Opportunity: Education and Older People (1982)

Ten Million People (1983)

Mutual Aid Universities (ed. Midwinter, 1984, reprinted 2015)

The Wage of Retirement: the case for a new pensions policy (1985)

Future Imponderable: the issue of private domiciliary care (1985)

Caring for Cash: the issue of private domiciliary care (1986)

Redefining Old Age: a review of CPA's recent contributions to social policy (1987)

Polls Apart? Older Voters and the 1987 General Election (1987)

New Design for Old: function, style and older people (1988)

The Old Order: crime and elderly people (1990)

Creating Chances: arts by older people (1990)

Community Life: a code of practice for community care (1990)

Out of Focus: old age, the press and broadcasting (1991)

The British Gas Report on Attitudes to Ageing (1991)

Citizenship: from Ageism to Participation (Carnegie Inquiry into the Third Age, 1992)

Leisure: New Opportunities in the Third Age (Carnegie Inquiry into the Third Age, 1992)

The Rhubarb People: A Childhood Memoir of Manchester in the '30s (Lifelines, 1993)

Encore: Guide to Planning a Celebration of Your Life (Lifelines, 1993)

A Voyage of Discovery (Lifelines, 1993)

Thriving People: the growth and prospects of the U3A in the UK (1996)

Pensioned Off: Retirement and Income Examined (Rethinking Ageing) (1997)

'Age and Education' (in *The Social Policy of Old Age*, edited by Miriam Bernard and Judith Phillips, 1998)

'Towards a Balanced Society: a contextual commentary on the Debate of the Age' (in *Debate of the Age*, Age Concern England, 2000)

500 Beacons: The U3A Story (2004)

4) THEATRE AND ENTERTAINERS

Make 'em Laugh: Famous Comedians and their World (1979)

Best Remembered: A Hundred Stars of Yesteryear (2001)

As One Stage Door Closes: The Story of John Wade – Jobbing Conjuror (2002)

The People's Jesters: Twentieth Century British Comedians (2006)

I say, I Say, I Say: The Double Act Story (2009)

Best Remembered Two: Cinema and Radio (2013)

5) SPORT

WG Grace: His Life and Times (1981)

Fair Game: Myth and Reality in Sport (1986, reprint 2013)

The Lost Seasons: Cricket in Wartime (1987)

Red Roses Crest the Caps; Story of Lancashire Cricket Club (1989)

Brylcreem Summer: 1947 Cricket Season (1991)

The Illustrated History of County Cricket (1992)

First Knock; Cricket's Opening Pairs (1994)

Surrey CCC: 150 Years – A Celebration (Ed, 1995)

Darling Old Oval: Surrey Cricket at the Oval (1995)

From Meadowland to Multinational: a Review of Cricket's Social History (2000)

Quill on Willow: Cricket in Literature (2001)

Red Shirts and Roses: The Tale of Two Old Traffords (2006)

Parish to Planet: How Football Came to Rule the World (2007)

George Duckworth: Warrington's Ambassador at Large (2008)

The Cricketer's Progress: Meadowland to Mumbai (2010)

Cricket Lore: the guide (ed. Midwinter, 2014)

6) TRANSPORT

The Clandestine Railway (LRPC Report, 1986)

Get Staffed! (LRPC Report, 1991)

Inconvenience (LRPC Report, 1994)

Towards a Senior Euro Pass: The Final Report (1997)

B. NATIONAL DICTIONARY OF BIOGRAHY ENTRIES (2004)

CRICKET

Bobby Abel

Benjamin Aislabie

Lord Frederick Beauclerk

Bill Edrich

Thomas Walter Hayward

A. N. Hornby (cricket and rugby)

Jim Laker

Fred Lillywhite

Phil Mead

Maurice Tate

John Wisden

THEATRE AND OTHERS

Hylda Baker

Billy Bennett

Jimmy Clitheroe

Tony Hancock

Robertson Hare

Will Hay

Stanley Holloway

Jimmy James

Fred Karno

Stan Laurel

Dorothea Ramsay (social worker)

Ted Ray

Max Wall

Robb Wilton

Appendix 1: Midwinter's Jig

As was mentioned in the earlier description of the party held at Lord's Cricket Ground when Eric retired from the CPA in December, 1991, a special dance called *Midwinter's Jig* (or Midwinter's Contra) was enjoyed by all those present. This had been created and dedicated to Eric a year or two earlier by Peter Shea and was first performed at a local school barn dance, which Eric also attended. Attempts to track down further details of this dance were greatly facilitated by Laura Smyth, Librarian of the Vaughan Williams Memorial Library at the English Folk Dance and Song Society, Cecil Sharp House, and through her contact was made with country dance enthusiasts Ann and Derek Appling, Richard Thom and Chris Turner, and, eventually, with Chris Shea, Peter's son.

Chris Shea kindly sent the following details of the dance:

> I have Dad's box of dance cards. I looked through it and found 'Midwinter's Contra'. His instructions are as follows:
>
> Longways improper.
>
> A1. (Hands on Hips) Rigadoon step to partner.
>
> > Feet together R. together L.
> >
> > Hands claps, tog. R. together
>
> L. Two hand turn
>
> A.2 Repeat with contrary (Keep hold of hands)
>
> B.1 four slipsteps sideways and back with contrary
>
> > Half R. and L. beginning with contrary.
>
> B2. Along lines F&B
>
> > half turn partner.
>
> For music he has written '32 bar steady jigs' and 'Try *Silver Celebration*.'

Not being an expert on country dancing, the above 'shorthand' prescription did not mean much to the author, but the leader of the Malvern U3A Country Dancing Group, Pam Evans, has very kindly provided the following more detailed explanation of the steps.

MIDWINTER'S CONTRA (JIG): A LONGWAYS SET FOR ANY NUMBER OF COUPLES

In this dance, as in many longways sets, the dancers are grouped into 'mini' sets of two couples, numbered one and two, all the way down the set.

To illustrate the term 'Proper', if all the dancers face the top of the set (where the musicians usually are) the men would have their lady partners on their right. It follows that when the lady partners are on the left of the men, the situation is described as 'Improper'. In many cases of this type of dance, it is the first couples who are in the Improper position and the second couples are Proper.

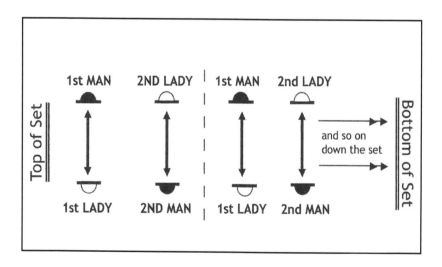

The term 'Contrary' (sometimes called 'Contras') refers to the dancers' neighbours and not to their partners.

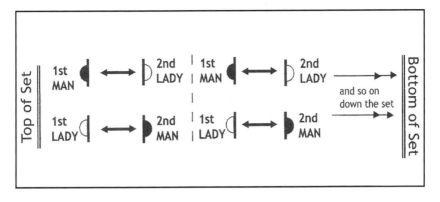

HALF RIGHT AND LEFT

In this dance, all couples give their right hand to their contrary and change places, the first couple moving down towards the bottom of the set, whilst the second couple move up towards the top. Then, all couples give their left hands across the set to their partners and change places. This movement is known as progression, preparatory to meeting a new couple, when the whole dance is repeated.

ALONG LINES F AND B

A simple figure where both sides of the set advance to meet each other- four steps forward, four steps back.

The 'half turn with partner' means that all the dancers simply change places to finish in the correct position, as at the start, since the earlier 'half right and half left' steps resulted in the couples ending on the 'wrong' sides of one another (i.e. Proper or Improper).

RIGADOON STEP

A rigadoon is a lively ancient type of dance. The 'Rigadoon step' mentioned in Peter Shea's notes refer to a kind of jumping step on the spot, of which there appear to be several different interpretations. According to Eric, in line with the 'Midwinter' theme, there was also a certain amount of foot stamping to keep everyone warm.

SILVER CELEBRATION

Silver Celebration is the name of a dance devised by Anne Clayton, with music composed by Joan Windsor. This is another longways set dance and the details of both steps and music were published in English Dance and Song, Volume XXVII, No. 4, August 1965. It is a lively tune and musicians will soon recognize an obvious reference to Mendelssohn's *Wedding March* in the final bars.

Reproduced courtesy of The English Folk Dance and Song Society

FOOTNOTE

When Eric wrote to Peter Shea to thank him for the dance, he replied that he had used it along with some medieval material on a course he did for folk dance callers from all over the world at Cecil Sharp House, ending his letter, 'so in hundreds of years time your name will be celebrated all over the world when the name of Thatcher is no more than a black footnote on the bottom of a forgotten page of history'. Eric was considerably cheered up by this notion.

ABOUT THE AUTHOR

Jeremy Hardie is a retired university academic who trained initially as a dentist, before becoming a microbiologist, specialising in the microbiology of the mouth. He worked for most of his career at The London Hospital Medical College Dental School in Whitechapel, now known as Bart's and The London School of Medicine and Dentistry, Queen Mary, University of London. Since retiring in 2000, he has moved from London, where he was born and educated, and now lives in Great Malvern, Worcestershire. Like Eric Midwinter, he is a member of the Savage Club in London, and of the MCC, and they share a keen interest in cricket. Before starting work on this book, Jeremy published in 2012 a well-received biography of the man who designed his house, entitled *Troyte Griffith: Malvern Architect and Elgar's Friend.*

INDEX

Murdoch, Richard 230

NOVEL APPROACHES:
a guide to the popular classic novel
180 pages £8.00   For KINDLE £3.80

35 novels that have stood the test of time embedded in historical and literary commentary.

BRITAIN'S STORY: an overview of British History
60 page booklet £3.50 Or for KINDLE £2.80

500 BEACONS : The U3A Story
[Out of print] but available for KINDLE £4.99

VOYAGE OF REDISCOVERY:
a guide to writing your life story
. . . a 'sea chart' to guide your reminiscence   **36 pages £4.50**

ENCORE: a guide to planning a celebration of your life
20 pages £2.00

THE RHUBARB PEOPLE:
Eric Midwinter's 'Voyage of Rediscovery'
**32 page booklet £4.50
or audio tape read by the author £5.00**

GETTING TO KNOW ME
. . . *a guide for carers to provide a useful profile of an older person to support positive experience* **24 pages £2.00**

Third Age Press *is an independent publishing company inspired by older people . . . recogizing that this period of life is a time of fulfilment & continuing development . . . a time of regeneration. Please visit our website to see our wide range of books & read & contribute to our blog.*

www.thirdagepress.co.uk